West Germans an(

Routledge Studies in Modern European History

1 Facing Fascism
The Conservative Party and the
European dictators 1935–1940
Nick Crowson

2 French Foreign and Defence
Policy, 1918–1940
The Decline and Fall of a
Great Power
Edited by Robert Boyce

3 Britain and the Problem of
International Disarmament
1919–1934
Carolyn Kitching

4 British Foreign Policy 1874–1914
The Role of India
Sneh Mahajan

5 Racial Theories in Fascist Italy
Aaron Gilette

6 Stormtroopers and Crisis in the
Nazi Movement
Activism, Ideology and Dissolution
Thomas D. Grant

7 Trials of Irish History
Genesis and Evolution of a
Reappraisal 1938–2000
Evi Gkotzaridis

8 From Slave Trade to Empire
European Colonisation of
Black Africa 1780s–1880s
Edited by Olivier Pétré-
Grenouilleau

9 The Russian Revolution of 1905
Centenary Perspectives
Edited by Anthony Heywood
and Jonathan D. Smele

10 Weimar Cities
The Challenge of Urban
Modernity in Germany
John Bingham

11 The Nazi Party and the German
Foreign Office
Hans-Adolf Jacobsen and
Arthur L. Smith, Jr.

12 The Politics of Culture in
Liberal Italy
From Unification to Fascism
Axel Körner

13 German Colonialism, Visual
Culture and Modern Memory
Edited by Volker M. Langbehn

14 German Colonialism and
National Identity
Edited by Michael Perraudin
and Jürgen Zimmerer

15 Landscapes of the Western Front
Materiality during the Great War
Ross J. Wilson

16 West Germans and the
Nazi Legacy
Caroline Sharples

West Germans and the Nazi Legacy

Caroline Sharples

Routledge
Taylor & Francis Group
NEW YORK AND LONDON

First published in paperback 2024

First published 2012
by Routledge
605 Third Avenue, New York, NY 10158

and by Routledge
4 Park Square, Milton Park, Abingdon, Oxon OX14 4RN

Routledge is an imprint of the Taylor & Francis Group, an informa business

© 2012, 2024 Taylor & Francis

The right of Caroline Sharples to be identified as author of this work has been asserted by her in accordance with sections 77 and 78 of the Copyright, Designs and Patents Act 1988.

All rights reserved. No part of this book may be reprinted or reproduced or utilised in any form or by any electronic, mechanical, or other means, now known or hereafter invented, including photocopying and recording, or in any information storage or retrieval system, without permission in writing from the publishers.

Trademark notice: Product or corporate names may be trademarks or registered trademarks and are used only for identification and explanation without intent to infringe.

Publisher's Note
The publisher has gone to great lengths to ensure the quality of this reprint but points out that some imperfections in the original copies may be apparent.

Library of Congress Cataloging-in-Publication Data
Sharples, Caroline, 1979–
  West Germans and the Nazi legacy / by Caroline Sharples.
    p. cm. — (Routledge studies in modern European history ; 16)
  Includes bibliographical references and index.
  1. War crime trials—Germany (West) 2. War crime trials—Social aspects—Germany (West) 3. Memory—Social—Germany (West) 4. National socialism—Social aspects. 5. Public opinion—Germany (West) 6. Germany (West)—Social conditions. I. Title.
  DD259.25.S53 2011
  943.087—dc23
                               2011032954

ISBN: 978-0-415-89240-7 (hbk)
ISBN: 978-1-03-292781-7 (pbk)
ISBN: 978-0-203-12910-4 (ebk)

DOI: 10.4324/9780203129104

Typeset in Sabon by IBT Global.

For Neil and for Martin

Contents

List of Figures		ix
Acknowledgements		xi
	Introduction	1
1	The Victors and the Vanquished	9
2	'The Murderers among Us'	30
3	Recalling Resistance	51
4	Eichmann: A Nation on Trial?	73
5	One of Us	92
6	Draw a Line?	112
	Conclusion	132
	Notes	139
	Bibliography	167
	Index	185

Figures

1.1	Map showing the concentration of Nazi war crimes trials in West Germany, 1946–1969.	24
1.2	Graph showing the number of war crimes trials in West Germany, 1946–1969.	25
1.3	Chart showing the results of war crimes trials in West Germany, 1946–1969.	25
2.1	Graph showing broad responses to the Ulm Einsatzkommando trial, 1958.	42
3.1	Graph showing attitudes to the Nazi past, based on awareness of the Sommer trial, 1958.	62
3.2	Graph showing attitudes to the Nazi past by political affiliation, 1958.	63
4.1	Graph showing West German public opinion on the Eichmann trial, 1961.	88

Acknowledgements

This book has been fashioned from the generous support of many individuals. I wish to express my gratitude, first of all, to the University of Southampton for the 2003 Archive Research Studentship and the Department of History's Research Support Awards Scheme for helping to fund this project. I also wish to thank all the archivists who have provided invaluable assistance over the course of my research within the University of Southampton Special Collections, the Wiener Library in London, the British Newspaper Library at Colindale and the National Archives at Kew. In Germany, special thanks must go to Erika Bartsch and Broder Schwensen, who provided a warm welcome at the Stadtarchiv Flensburg, and Reimer Witt and Elke Imberger who did likewise at the Landsarchiv Schleswig. Wolfgang Thiele of the Gemeinschaftsarchiv des Kreises Schleswig-Flensburg provided numerous items relating to the trial of Martin Fellenz and put me in touch with Dr. Hans-Jörg Herold, who, in turn, kindly shared his memories of observing that case as a student. Further assistance and material was supplied by Manfred Werth, President of the Landgericht Bayreuth, Thomas Janovsky, Chief Prosecutor in Bayreuth, Ulrich Duhr and Stefan Flesch of the Archiv der Evangelischen Kirche im Rheinland, Rainer Stahlschmidt of the Hauptstaatsarchiv Düsseldorf, Ulrich Seemüller of the Stadtarchiv Ulm, Andreas Heusler of the Stadtarchiv München and Norbert Grube of the Institut für Demoskopie Allensbach.

I am indebted to Mark Roseman, Tony Kushner, Nils Roemer, Mark Levene, Tobias Brinkmann and Mary Fulbrook for their constructive comments at various stages in this project, as well as seminar and conference audiences in Southampton, Winchester, Chester and Leicester. I would also like to take this opportunity to thank Laura Stearns and Stacy Noto at Routledge for overseeing the publication process with such enthusiasm.

Over the course of this project, I have been fortunate enough to benefit from some fantastic collegial support. Andrew Johnstone provided invaluable publication advice and, together with Caroline Dodds Pennock, Olaf Jensen, Zoe Knox and George Lewis, offered much merriment along the way. Tim Grady's continued friendship and helpful suggestions are similarly very much appreciated. Particular thanks must be extended to James

xii *Acknowledgements*

Campbell, who has been the most amazing friend, colleague and landlord anyone could wish for. Much of this book was written on his dining table and I am eternally grateful for his patient forbearance with this, as well his willingness to read and comment upon draft chapters.

Finally, I would like to thank my parents for all their love and support throughout my studies, as well as two further individuals without whose constant encouragement none of this would have been possible. In Neil Gregor I was fortunate to have a truly inspiring PhD supervisor. His unwavering faith has always succeeded in pushing me to new levels and his critical insights have undoubtedly helped to make this book what it is. Innumerable thanks are also owed to Martin, for living with this project for so long, always asking the right questions and accompanying me on my adventures abroad. This book is dedicated to them.

Introduction

In January 1967, Courtroom 270 on the second floor of the Munich Justizpalast became the focal point for a high-profile public protest against the murderous legacy of the Third Reich. Inside, three former members of the SS, Wilhelm Harster, Wilhelm Zoepf and Gertrud Slottke, stood before a packed court to face charges of complicity in the murder of more than 105,000 Dutch Jews deported to Sobibor and Auschwitz between 1940 and 1945. The highly charged trial received sensational coverage in the West German press, with *Die Zeit* heralding its significance as the first prosecution of three prominent 'desk murderers' in the history of Nazi war crimes trials.[1] Eventually convicted of aiding and abetting the Nazi genocide, the defendants received prison sentences ranging from five to fifteen years, a result greeted with shouts of 'string them up' from spectators in the public gallery and the attempted assault of Slottke by the crowds waiting outside the courthouse.[2]

On the face of it, these events in Munich were indicative of a country that had come to terms with its past; the public were actively engaging with a war crimes trial and clearly advocating that those guilty of atrocities should be brought to account in a suitably harsh manner. This form of response supports the findings of any number of opinion polls conducted during this period in which people would affirm very quickly their feeling that such trials were necessary and that it was important for any remaining perpetrators to be brought to account. Vocal criticisms of 'lenient' sentences found an echo at the conclusion of many other proceedings too, as this book will show.

The actual timing of these events is also significant. The late 1960s were a period in which the Holocaust seemed to be occupying an increasingly central position within public discourse on National Socialism; a wave of films and commemorative activities focussed on the persecution of the so-called 'racial enemies' of the Reich. Coupled with an outpouring of survivor testimony, this new focal point was a far cry from the emphasis on non-Jewish German victimhood which had characterised the immediate postwar years.[3] It was the coming of age of a new generation blessed with the grace of a 'late birth' which left them personally unencumbered by the past

2 West Germans and the Nazi Legacy

and more prepared to challenge the silence of their elders. The year after the Harster trial would, famously, be marked by the student protest movement, a key element of which was the shadow of the Nazi past and the current assault on parliamentary democracy posed by Chancellor Kiesinger's emergency laws.[4] As a result, this episode in Munich can be seen as fitting into conventional historical narratives of the 1960s as an era of widespread critical confrontation with the crimes of the Third Reich.

However, it should be noted that much of the interest surrounding this specific case stemmed from the plight of the Dutch Jews under consideration or, rather, the involvement of the defendants in the deportation of one Dutch Jew in particular: Anne Frank. This then was not a trial dealing with anonymous figures in unfamiliar places as could, perhaps, be argued for many other war crimes proceedings. The trial in Munich captured the public imagination because the name of this victim already held great currency. Since the publication of her diary in 1955, the story of Anne Frank had been turned into both a stage play and a Hollywood film. Her book had become a bestseller in West Germany (and, indeed, around the globe) and was increasingly being used within schools as a valuable educational resource. Many West German schools ran field trips to Frankfurt—her place of birth—and to the site of the Bergen-Belsen concentration camp in Lower Saxony where Anne and her sister Margot died.[5] Furthermore, the link with Anne Frank was deliberately cultivated throughout the Harster trial. Anne's diary was submitted as evidence for the prosecution; her father, Otto, was co-plaintiff and personally questioned the defendants when they took to the stand, and the jostling crowds waiting outside the court waved placards emblazoned with her image.

The responses generated by this case, then, are more complicated than they might first appear. It was not necessarily the fate of the Dutch Jews *en masse* that was inciting public outcry, but that of one individual young girl. This raises the question of whether the enormity of the Holocaust was being recognised by these spectators. It could be argued that it is relatively easy to generate public interest and outcry when a trial involves a famous, emotive figure such as Anne Frank—but what about those cases where the victims remain nameless statistics? What about those trials without any sensational courtroom exchanges between a survivor and his former tormentors? The 'Anne Frank' trial was one of many being conducted across the Federal Republic during this period and it would certainly be fair to say that few of them were able to generate similar levels of interest, reporting or attendance. Indeed, given the sheer number of war crimes hearings that had taken place in West Germany by this point, it could be argued that a media presence such as that surrounding the prosecution of Harster *et al.* could only have been conditioned by atypical circumstances. How far can we really take the scenes in Munich as an accurate reflection of popular West German responses to the past?

Much has been written on the subject of German history and memory since 1945. West Germany, given the limits of its denazification process and the continued presence of former Nazis within public life long after the end of the war, has proved a particularly constant source of interest and debate. Scholars have variously explored the physical legacy or cultural representation of the Third Reich, as well as the rituals and commemorative activities that have characterised post-war responses to Nazism.[6] There have been examinations of government policy, as well as case studies of civic culture and the process of *Vergangenheitsbewältigung* ('overcoming the past') within individual West German cities.[7] There is also a growing canon of literature specifically on war crime trials: their organisation, implementation and legacy. We now have a very good insight into both Allied and West German policies on the investigation of war crimes, the legal definition of genocide and questions of both perpetrator motivation and post-war apologia, and there is an emerging interest too in the relationship between judicial process, history and memory, Donald Bloxham's critically acclaimed *Genocide on Trial* being a key example.[8]

Most scholars have also now moved away from the traditional depiction of the post-war era which simplistically cast the 1950s and 1960s as periods of 'silence' and 'engagement', respectively. Indeed, there is now a consensus that both decades were much more complicated, each filled with a range of voices that were competing to make themselves heard, whether from survivors' groups, determined prosecutors, crusading journalists and inquiring students, or from former prisoners of war, expellees, veterans' organisations and the war widowed.[9] Each of these groups had very different experiences of Nazism and the Second World War and would thus have very different opinions regarding what, if anything, should be recalled from the recent past. Silences, evasions, distortions and mythologies persisted into the 1960s, and by the end of the decade there remained an ongoing tension between the perceived need to ameliorate foreign opinion by being seen to face up to the crimes of the Third Reich and the far more popular desire to draw a final line under the whole National Socialist epoch. The evolution of memory culture within the Federal Republic was thus complicated and protracted.

Yet for all this existing literature, some important questions still remain. Firstly, in charting historical memory, there is a necessary distinction to be made between public and private spheres of remembrance. There were several famous moments of public reference to the past during the post-war era, ranging from Konrad Adenauer's diplomatic overtures to Israel in the 1950s (and the related Bundestag debates over the payment of reparations to former victims of Nazi persecution) to Willy Brandt's symbolic kneeling before the Warsaw Ghetto Memorial during an official visit to Poland in 1970, the first such visit to be undertaken by a serving West German chancellor. Such scenes fostered a useful image of a nation facing up to its

4 West Germans and the Nazi Legacy

demons and rehabilitating itself on the international stage, but how far did the rest of the population share these attitudes to the past?

Determining how ordinary people felt about these events is, admittedly, fraught with difficulty. Wolfgang Benz has already pointed out how, after the Second World War, it was considered taboo in West Germany to articulate Neo-Nazi or anti-Semitic viewpoints in public; anyone wishing to express such ideas was confined to daubing anonymous graffiti on walls or conducting cautious conversations among like-minded individuals within the privacy of their own home if they did not want to run the risk of prosecution.[10] Echoes of the old ideology continued to be heard, however, as evidenced by the regular news reports in both the German and Anglo-Jewish press on the desecration of Jewish cemeteries, and the various legal actions taken against those caught bemoaning the number of Jews who had managed to escape the 'Final Solution'.[11] Claudia Koonz has also described overhearing a conversation around a Bavarian *Stammtisch* where the regulars reminisced about the 'good old days' when 'the riffraff got what was coming to them'.[12] Needless to say, these are examples of the some of the most extreme, reactionary forces present within West German society and should not be taken as typical of the population as a whole. Nonetheless, they underscore the fact that there can be a significant gulf between state-sponsored memory of the past and personal recollections.

Secondly, although the prosecution of Nazi war criminals is a key issue within the history of *Vergangenheitsbewältigung*, the impact of these cases upon the popular West German consciousness has generally been assumed rather than studied in any critical depth. This may partly stem from the tendency of the literature on war crimes proceedings to concentrate on the largest and most high-profile cases. Works on the International Military Tribunal at Nuremberg continue to abound, as do studies of Eichmann, an interest no doubt fuelled by the fact that the case marked the first to be heard in Israel, as well as the sensational manner of the defendant's capture, kidnapped from his Argentinean hideout by Mossad agents.[13] Interest in the 1963–5 Frankfurt Auschwitz trial is also flourishing thanks to important recent contributions by Devin Pendas and Rebecca Wittmann.[14] Collectively, these hearings involved some of the most notorious participants behind the extermination process, figures against whom the remainder of the West German population could arguably continue to impose some level of distance and thereby avoid making a connection between the trial and questions regarding their own level of complicity with the Nazi regime. The blame for the Holocaust and other atrocities could thus still be placed on a radical, sadistic few.

What happened, though, when a war crimes trial involved neither a particularly infamous perpetrator nor an easily recognisable victim? Did the same angry pro-trial sentiments emerge? Did people still take an interest in the case when the international media was not camped out on their doorstep? Above all, how did people react when the defendant was a well-

Introduction 5

respected figure from their own community, someone that could not be quite so easily rendered distinct from themselves?

This book sets out to explore these issues. In the process, it bridges a gap within the current historiography between localised memory studies and analyses of war crimes trials. By fusing these approaches to consider the impact of smaller, localised prosecutions, it can start to uncover the attitudes of ordinary people at the grass roots level of West German society. That war crimes trials can offer a valuable way into exploring processes of *Vergangenheitsbewältigung* has already been illustrated by the Harster case. Often commanding a vast degree of public attention, they can evoke a highly emotional response from observers and are often bound up in a prosecutor or politician's larger didactic aim of raising awareness about the lessons of the past. Indeed, throughout the 1960s, many people appeared to share the belief that such legal proceedings could play a crucial role in teaching others about the dangers of intolerance. Several towns and cities across West Germany marked the opening of a war crimes case in their vicinity by staging exhibitions on the Nazi era or by conducting research projects into the fate of their own local Jewish population between 1933 and 1945. These were public events specifically designed to foster a wider discussion of the crimes being presented to the court. Several schools across the Federal Republic organised trips to their local court so that pupils might have the opportunity to observe the trials firsthand. Such journeys played out against a background of ongoing educational debates over the best method for informing the next generation about the Nazi past and the belief, popular in the early 1960s in particular, that young people were still quite ignorant of this 'darkest chapter' in German history.[15] War crimes trials, then, had an ability to resonate far beyond the immediate confines of the courtroom walls and make themselves felt within the wider spheres of popular culture and local commemorative activities.

Locality too assumed a special importance after 1945. Celia Applegate and Alon Confino have both written at length on the issue of *Heimat*—the nostalgic construction of an idyllic local community in which past cultural achievements were celebrated and traditional modes of life carefully preserved.[16] The ideal had its origins in the rapid process of social change and industrial upheaval that followed Unification in 1871, offering the population 'a bridge between a past and a present that looked uniquely dissimilar'.[17] Following the Second World War, *Heimat* was revived as a way of rediscovering the 'other' Germany, distinct from the Holocaust, a Germany in which some sense of pride could still be taken. By pointing to evidence of longstanding healthy customs, people could depict Nazism as an aberration, a destructive but temporary phenomenon that had little to do with the nation itself. Similarly, by concentrating firmly on those localised traditions, Nazism could be portrayed as an alien force imposed from the outside, separate from the local community. As Alon Confino has argued, 'German history became meaningful as the scale of observation grew smaller. Subsumed within the locality, the nation was . . . portrayed as an innocent victim of the war and of Hitler'.[18] Playing host to a war crimes trial disrupted this comfortable mythology and had the potential to shatter a town's carefully constructed narrative of the recent past.

This book thus moves away from the much-discussed diplomatic overtures of leading politicians, state-sponsored memorials and other official events and instead offers a series of regional case studies of the impact of Nazi war crime trials. Reactions to these proceedings are gauged through a variety of sources, from local, national and international newspaper reports and editorials, to a series of opinion poll surveys conducted across the Federal Republic. None of this material is without its limitations, of course. Public opinion data can be skewed by the problems of leading questions, unrepresentative samples and people's reluctance to share their real thoughts on an issue (particularly when dealing with something as sensitive as the crimes of the Third Reich). Newspapers too cannot be accepted as reliable indicators of public opinion on their own although, as scholars have accepted, they can be a useful source for presenting and interpreting the attitudes of the wider population.[19] However, by examining a *combination* of this material we can start to identify some common concerns. Most importantly, this book also draws upon previously ignored primary source material in the form of private letters sent by members of the West German population to local prosecutors or even the defendants themselves. Collectively, this material enables us to gain new insights into the impact of war crimes proceedings.

The first chapter sets the scene by examining West German responses to the International Military Tribunal at Nuremberg. It emphasises how the case facilitated a popular rhetoric which assigned all the blame for the atrocities on the Nazi leadership and underlines the popular media representation of the accused as 'demonic' individuals, enabling the perpetrators of the Third Reich to be rendered distinct from the ordinary population. Questions of any wider guilt or complicity were conveniently sidestepped and an emphasis was instead placed upon the notion of 'victors' justice', the idea that such trials were only taking place because Germany had lost the war. Chapter 1 then proceeds to illustrate how such responses affected the treatment of suspected war criminals during the 1950s, once the Federal Republic had gained its sovereignty and thus the right to deal with such figures as it thought fit. The early part of the decade was characterised by a rising acquittal rate, a popular clamouring for a general amnesty for convicted personnel and a rapid decline in war crimes prosecutions. For many West Germans, the focus was upon looking towards a brighter future, rather than dwelling on a painful past.

Chapter 2 then details how a new wave of war crimes proceedings was eventually set in motion by the 1958 Ulm Einsatzkommando trial, which dealt with the mass shooting of Jews and Communists along the Lithuanian border in the summer of 1941. Arguably, with the pressing needs for post-war reconstruction now sated, this trial took place in a very different climate than its predecessors, enabling people to reflect upon the proceedings—and the National Socialist past as a whole—in a more critical fashion. This trial has been identified by several historians as an important turning point in the process of *Vergangenheitsbewältigung*, although to date there has been little critical analysis undertaken to justify some of these claims. As the largest trial to take place before a West German court up to that time, the Ulm proceeding certainly put pressure on the Ministry of Justice to take more concerted action in rooting out any remaining suspects. Yet despite emotive editorials in the press, the case ultimately failed to sustain the interest of the general public.

The same cannot be said for the prosecution of former Buchenwald guard, Martin Sommer, which forms the subject of Chapter 3. Taking place around the same time as the Ulm hearings, this case generated huge excitement among journalists and spectators alike. In part, this may be explicable to the peculiarly sadistic nature of his crimes, but the fact that he operated within one of the earliest Nazi concentration camps also served to recall the persecution of trade unionists and political opponents and thus gave credence to an ongoing post-war emphasis on German victimhood. The Sommer trial thus offers a window into the role of non-Jewish survivors' groups in forging West German memory cultures and the mythologies that surrounded the extent of resistance to Nazism. This chapter also explores how the town of Bayreuth, which provided the location for the Sommer trial, had its own peculiarly close relationship with the old regime to overcome, Wagner's birthplace having been a much-publicised cultural quarter for the Third Reich.

By the start of the 1960s, the war crimes issue had thus been revived in West German public discourse. At the beginning of that decade, the rest of the western world also became increasingly aware of the peculiar fate of the Jews under National Socialism, largely as a result of the 1961 Eichmann trial in Jerusalem. This case, which has been well documented over the years, is routinely cited by historians as one of the major impulses behind the emergence of a more critical West German engagement with the recent past. However, there remains very little examination of just how the events in Jerusalem were received back in the Federal Republic. Chapter 4 redresses this balance and underlines how responses to Eichmann were much more complicated than conventionally surmised. While the Holocaust did begin to gain greater currency in the popular imagination, political scandals and concerns for how the case might affect the Federal Republic's own reputation overshadowed much of the discussion of this trial.

Arguably, many of the perpetrators under discussion here could be dismissed as unusual figures, being either peculiarly zealous and callous individuals who shocked their own comrades with their actions or high-ranking bureaucrats known to be at the heart of the Nazi 'system', neither type seeming to have much in common with the 'ordinary' West German population. Chapter 5, by contrast, moves away from figures such as Sommer and Eichmann, whose notoriety enabled people to put some distance between themselves and the defendants, to consider the impact of a trial where the accused was actually a prominent and well-respected member of the local community. Offering a case study of the 1962 prosecution in Flensburg of Martin Fellenz, a former police officer involved in the so-called 'Resettlement' of Polish Jews during the war, it emphasises the level of support the defendant continued to receive after his arrest and the series of similar scandals that led some contemporary critics to regard the northern state of Schleswig-Holstein as a veritable haven for former Nazis.

Following the series of localised, individual case studies, the final chapter steps back to consider some of the broader features of West German memory culture during the 1960s. It draws upon the Treblinka and Sachsenhausen trials conducted across North Rhine Westphalia as well as the effects of the 1963–5 Frankfurt Auschwitz trial in the neighbouring state of Hesse. It emphasises the way in which such proceedings could influence wider cultural and educational activities and contrasts high profile moments of 'engagement' with revived debates over the very necessity of continued war crimes trials.

Taken as a whole, this book focuses on responses to the prospect of continuing investigations, the reception afforded to those found to be implicated in the crimes of the regime and the effects that courtroom proceedings could generate within a local community. Besides re-examining some of the most well-known trials of this period, it also provides the first detailed analysis of some of the less prominent proceedings then underway in the Federal Republic. It draws upon case studies dealing with different modes of criminal behaviour, from the deliberately sadistic actions of individual concentration camp guards to the level of knowledge held by police officers overseeing the 'resettlement' of Polish Jews. It also compares responses afforded to trials conducted in different regions of the Federal Republic, areas with contrasting political, social and religious constituencies who often had their own peculiarly close relationship with the former Nazi regime to contend with. Ultimately, it underscores the complex and imperfect nature of West German patterns of remembrance after 1945.

1 The Victors and the Vanquished

In October 1943, the Allies signed the Moscow Declaration, announcing their intention to punish anyone guilty of atrocities, massacres and executions at the end of the Second World War. While this move came in the wake of growing reports of extreme violence being committed in Nazi-occupied Europe, nothing could have prepared them for the horrifying sights that greeted troops liberating the concentration camps in early 1945. Mounds of corpses and thousands of skeletal survivors appalled observers, who immediately asked how such crimes could be possible in a modern, cultured and civilised nation state. In the immediate post-war period, there was a fervent Allied desire to acquaint the German population with the murderous reality of National Socialism and the issue of bringing those responsible for both the war and the Holocaust to account gained a new urgency. It was not until the London Charter of 8 August 1945, though, that the establishment of an International Military Tribunal (IMT) was formally decided upon as the best means for achieving this.[1]

Conducted in Nuremberg, a city long associated with Nazi Party rallies, as well as the notorious 1935 race laws, the tribunal was intended to be a symbolic affair. Twenty-one surviving members of the Nazi leadership faced counts of conspiracy, crimes against peace, war crimes and crimes against humanity.[2] The proceedings, which lasted for almost a year, have long been heralded as setting a precedent for international law. The pedagogic ambitions harboured by the Allies were laid bare in the opening address by Chief Prosecutor Robert Jackson when he stated, 'The wrongs which we seek to condemn and punish have been so calculated, so malignant and so devastating that civilisation cannot tolerate their being ignored because it cannot survive their being repeated'.[3] This sense of 'never again' was reiterated in the wider Allied programmes of re-education and denazification between 1945–9. However, the extent to which any of this succeeded in fostering a critical engagement with the crimes of the Third Reich among the general German population is debatable. For many Germans struggling to come to terms with total defeat in 1945, it would be very difficult to get past the fact that the impetus for such measures was coming from the victors of the recent war.

10 West Germans and the Nazi Legacy

In the immediate aftermath of the conflict, the Allies embarked upon a series of measures to shock the German public into confronting the grim nature of the Nazi regime. Those living near concentration camp sites were forced to tour the facilities and, in some cases, even help bury the dead. Elsewhere, there were cases of the German population being marched to watch newsreel footage from the liberation which the Allies hoped would inspire reflection and some acceptance of collective responsibility.[4] The extent to which these 'lessons' sank in, though, is unclear. Writing about West German campaigns during the 1950s to secure the release of thousands of German prisoners of war still being held in Soviet captivity, Robert Moeller draws upon various posters and images produced by the SPD which depict the soldiers behind barbed wire, in stripped uniforms and with shaven heads.[5] The connotations of such images suggest that the iconic imagery of the concentration camps had, indeed, seeped into the West German consciousness and thus it could be argued the Allies' re-education activities had some effect. However, rather than inspiring a critical engagement with the Holocaust itself, it became a means to perpetuate a narrative of German suffering. The appropriation of this recognisable symbol of persecution to recall the plight of interned soldiers, many of whom had been charged by the Russians of having committed war crimes themselves, is indicative of the way in which the distinctive experiences of 'ordinary' Germans and the victims of racial persecution were blurred after the war.

The effects of the International Military Tribunal at Nuremberg upon the German population are similarly worthy of closer attention. The legacy of the IMT is multifaceted. Its sheer size, international constitution and use of then novel technology in the form of simultaneous translation all gave it a unique and remarkable character. It has consequently enjoyed much scholarly and public interest, inspiring films and television miniseries. Courtroom 600 itself within the Nuremberg Palace of Justice has become a popular tourist attraction, receiving 13,138 visitors in 2005 alone, and a permanent memorial and exhibition have now been created at the site.[6] These factors, together with the trial's obvious significance for the development of international criminal law, particularly the concept of 'crimes against humanity', have lent themselves to a very celebratory representation of the proceedings. Michael Marrus, for example, emphasises its historical importance as the first comprehensive documentation of the Holocaust for a non-Jewish audience.[7]

Other scholars, though, have been rather more circumspect in detailing the resonance of the IMT. One of the key criticisms that has been levelled at the Nuremberg tribunal concerns the way in which the Holocaust was depicted as just one in a series of Nazi transgressions. Furthermore, when discussing the Nazi genocide, the various camps tended to be grouped together in quite an uncomplicated manner. There was an emphasis, for example, on the scenes in the western camps such as Dachau, Buchenwald and Bergen-Belsen, locations that British and American troops had become all too familiar with, while the significance of the Operation Reinhard camps in the east was not fully grasped.[8] The identity of the Holocaust victims themselves was similarly obscured. The USSR placed an emphasis on Soviet 'victims of fascism' while the West preferred to speak in quite universal terms, reluctant to elevate the suffering of any one victim group over another. Such issues give weight to Erich Haberer's conclusion that the IMT 'minimised the Holocaust, marginalised the victims and misrepresented the complexity of the continent-wide implementation of the Nazi genocidal policies'.[9]

A slightly more positive assessment of the IMT's role in the formation of Holocaust memory is offered by Tony Kushner, who points to its significance in giving currency to the figure of six million murdered Jews as well as making people more aware of the Nazis' killing methods. However, he adds that 'in Britain and the United States, the public soon tired of the meticulous attention to detail in the trials and there was relief when they finally finished nearly a year later'.[10] The sheer length of the proceedings and its primary basis upon the submission of official documents generated by the perpetrators themselves created a rather sterile atmosphere. Such a format, together with frequent debates within the court over procedural matters or the accurate translation of a particular phrase, was not necessarily conducive to sustaining the interest of the lay public. Donald Bloxham, describing the principal feature of the IMT as one of 'tedium', comments on how even those directly involved in the proceedings failed to 'summon up enthusiasm for the central event in their lives'; he cites the example of Justice Biddle and reporter Rebecca West, who were much more wrapped up in their own brief relationship.[11]

Traditionally, historians have likewise depicted the German people as having little interest in the case, fuelling the conventional image of the immediate post-war era as one of collective silence or evasion with regards to the recent past. More recently, Christoph Burchard has emphasised how emerging Cold War tensions meant that the IMT engendered differing responses in the East and West of the country. He argues that while East Germans embraced the message to deal with Nazi perpetrators, their Western counterparts remained suspicious and pessimistic about the precedent set at Nuremberg; it was only with reunification in 1990, Burchard claims, that the legacy of the IMT was finally reappraised and Germany began to truly accept the concept of international law.[12]

An analysis of contemporary German responses to the IMT, however, shows that reactions were far too complex to be easily dichotomised along East-West lines, or even in terms of Left-Right political cultures. By exploring the complicated responses to Nuremberg, we can trace the early tensions associated with *Vergangenheitsbewältigung*, the beginnings of generational conflict over the Nazi past and the difficult relationship between the victors and the vanquished in the immediate post-war period.

In order for the Allies' educational objectives to be achieved, it was clearly necessary to ensure that details of the IMT were relayed to as wide an audience as possible. In December 1945, just one month into the proceedings, the Chief of the U.S. Information Control Division, Brigadier General Robert A. McClure, boasted that twelve million Germans living within the American occupation zone had access to such information through the media.[13] Summaries of the tribunal's progress were included in the weekly newsreels while the *New York Times*, surveying a sample of eleven newspapers licensed within the U.S. zone, found that 19 percent of their columns were devoted to the IMT.[14] More recently, Akiba Cohen's analysis of trial coverage within three of the leading Western newspapers at the time, *Frankfurter Rundschau*, *Süddeutsche Zeitung* and *Die Welt* has agreed that the IMT attracted great attention, with just under a third of reports making the front page.[15]

However, despite all of the Allies' best intentions, popular responses to the IMT seemed relatively muted. Throughout the trial, external observers within the international media and foreign consulates maintained a close eye on German behaviour. An examination of these sources suggests that the IMT failed to attract widespread or sustained public interest. Indeed, there seems to be some disparity between McClure's account of the scale of press and radio coverage and the reality of daily German contact with the trial. Reporting for the *New York Times*, Raymond Daniell argued that any reports on the IMT within the licensed German press had been published for political reasons rather than any genuine interest in or moral commitment to the prosecution of Nazi war criminals. In addition, when discussing the printing of indictments at the start of proceedings, he commented:

> It was interesting to watch the Germans skip that part of the paper. As far as reader interest was concerned, the space might have been used to better advantage for almost anything else. . . . In Frankfurt, it is very noticeable that in restaurants newspaper readers fold their papers so that they can ignore the unpleasant reminders from Nuremberg. The trials are rarely discussed in conversation.[16]

Similarly, just days into the case in November 1945, Pulitzer Prize–winning journalist Anne O'Hare McCormick noted 'it's too bad more Germans are not present at the trial and that it is not extensively reported in German or, better, fully broadcast so that the people most concerned should know the inevitable details of the plot they supported'—a comment which clearly contradicts McClure's assessment of media coverage.[17] Raising concerns over just how much of a lasting impact the trial could thus hope to achieve, McCormick added:

> Nobody seems to care what happens to Göring and Streicher. The Nuremberg trial is more remote from Nuremberg than it is from New York. Certainly it is more scantily reported in Germany than in the

United States. . . . While the accused represent Germany, Germans as a whole appear curiously uninterested in them.[18]

It is all very well decrying the apparent public apathy to the Nuremberg proceedings, but it is necessary to consider just what sort of a response could ever have been expected from a population suddenly having to contend with the collapse of a political regime, total defeat, foreign occupation and division. O'Hare McCormick's conclusion that the IMT was enjoying a greater resonance in the United States than in Germany may well be accurate, but her article failed to recognise the legitimate reasons for this disparity. The Americans, for example, did not have to deal with the economic woes or pressing needs for reconstruction that the Germans were now facing. Indeed, when Daniell referred to the idea that many people would have preferred the newspapers to deal with other issues, coverage of food and fuel supplies and the means to trace missing relatives were among his suggestions for topics that currently held the utmost importance for the population.[19] Understandably, the struggle for day to day subsistence in the aftermath of the war took precedence over events in a Nuremberg courtroom. The trauma of these recent experiences, meanwhile, meant that it was 'easier' to treat 1945 as something of a 'Zero Hour' and concentrate on the prospect of a brighter future ahead. The United States was unencumbered by any sense of personal guilt or responsibility for the Third Reich and the Holocaust, perhaps making it psychologically far easier for the audience there to devour details of the IMT as they could treat it as something of a macabre curio. For foreign observers, the terrible revelations emerging from Courtroom 600 could be dissipated with the reassuring thought that this was a 'German problem' and not one that they themselves necessarily had to think very deeply about. This was a period, after all, when many commentators, desperately trying to comprehend how such atrocities could have ever occurred, were speaking of the need to 're-civilise' the Germans in the wake of their apparent descent into medieval-style barbarism.[20] On a more basic level, of course, McCormick's claim that the press coverage was higher in the United States than in Germany may also have something to do with the fact that U.S. publications were not as hampered by a lack of paper or ink as their heavily rationed European counterparts.

It must also be stressed that any apparent lack of public interest in the IMT was far from confined to Germany. In Britain too it seems that the tribunal was unable to sustain public attention. Interest peaked at a few key moments, such as the screening of the atrocity films, the testimony of Hermann Göring and the final sentencing of the accused. However, the trauma of the Holocaust was such that even the *Jewish Chronicle* adopted a restrained style of coverage, preferring to generate many more columns on the struggle over Palestine as a means of looking to the future rather than dwelling on a painful past.[21]

Nevertheless, the fundamental notion that there was little, if any, German engagement with the IMT is flawed. The local *Nürnberger Nachricten* attacked the foreign accusations of German disinterest—typified by McCormick—and stressed that while ordinary people may not rush out to mob the accused, they were reflecting on the proceedings and desired to learn about the recent past.[22] The Office of Military Government, United States (OMGUS) was also monitoring public opinion very carefully, conducting eight separate surveys over the course of the trial. In contrast to the assessments of various Allied journalists, it concluded that interest levels were, in actual fact, very high. For instance, 78 percent of those surveyed in the American occupation zone in January 1946 claimed to have been following the course of events closely in the press, and other surveys conducted by OMGUS during this period would certainly suggest at least some degree of general knowledge about the IMT. Initial studies carried out during the opening weeks of the tribunal found that 65 percent claimed to have learned something from the IMT (a figure that in subsequent surveys rose to 87 percent).[23] For the majority of such respondents, this 'something new' involved details of the Nazi concentration camps. On the one hand, such responses could indicate that the prosecutors were achieving some of their educational ambitions after all. On the other hand, though, it is unclear from the opinion poll data whether such reactions constituted genuine engagement with the trial or whether these protestations of previous ignorance were simply a quick and easy way to reiterate a sense of distance between the crimes of the Third Reich and the ordinary population. Bloxham likewise counters claims of a wholesale disinterest in the IMT by pointing to the 'reasonable audiences' that attended the screenings of the documentary *Nürnberg und seine Lehren* in 1949, while noting the way in which many people walked out when the film proceeded to the concentration camp footage, almost mimicked Schacht's courtroom attempts to dissociate himself from any responsibility for these scenes.[24]

There has also been a tendency among some historians to summarise German responses to the IMT as dominated by charges of 'victors' justice'.[25] Over the course of the OMGUS surveys, however, an average of 80 percent of those questioned stated a belief that the accused would receive a fair trial, with 70 percent feeling that all of the defendants were guilty. Among the others, Rudolf Hess was the defendant most often singled out as innocent of the charges, presumably as a result of ongoing questions over his sanity. Opinion was divided, though, over whether the guilty would all receive the same punishment, 37 percent believing they would (with the death penalty deemed the most likely result) and 46 percent saying that sentences would vary among the defendants.[26] This figure would again suggest that at least some sectors of the population were following the events in Nuremberg in sufficient depth to demonstrate an awareness of the different responsibilities and levels of involvement in the Nazi regime of the accused.

At the same time, and underlining the responses Bloxham described within West German cinemas, there were noticeable attempts by members of the 'ordinary' population to distance themselves from the Nuremberg accused. It is important to note that such efforts were facilitated by press reports which frequently described defendants—at both the IMT and other hearings—as 'devils', 'monsters' or 'beasts'. This dramatic but dehumanising rhetoric would become a longstanding trope of Allied and West German media coverage of war crimes trials and enable their audience everywhere to subscribe to the comforting notion that those responsible for the genocide were inherently 'abnormal' specimens.[27] Investigations conducted in December 1945 by the American Control Division revealed efforts to put all the blame for recent events on the figures at the highest level of the Nazi state, as well as to relativise Nazi crimes by pointing to the effects of Allied bombing campaigns. The survey, conducted partly by U.S. uniformed personnel and partly by German civilians employed by the ICD, explored responses in forty different towns and villages. One third of those questioned opposed the blanket indictment of Nazi organisations such as the SA 'for the obvious reason', the *New York Times* noted, 'that almost every family in Germany has relatives in them'. By contrast, Jackson's opening speech, in which he distinguished carefully between the Nazis and the wider population, was received favourably.[28] However, even OMGUS was forced to concede that interest in the IMT began to decline as the year went by. By March 1946, the number of people admitting to regularly following the press coverage of the trial had fallen to 67 percent, and less than half of these had read the reports in their entirety.[29]

Given all of these factors, it seems that a more accurate description of German responses to the IMT would be one of *selective* interest, one which was very much bound up in people's own experiences of National Socialism, war and defeat. This manifested itself in a critique of the Nuremberg defendants who had 'lost the war'. The *Toronto Daily Star*, for example, relayed the results of an opinion poll suggesting that 'average Germans seemed interested in seeing Nazi leaders wiped out only because they blame them for their present misfortune—not for moral reasons, but chiefly because they were on the losing side'.[30] The *Milwaukee Journal*, while noting popular concerns about the failure to include a German judge in the tribunal, pointed to a general support for the IMT, noting that 'most Germans hope that the trial will "prove" that the regime misled the population and bear all the blame for recent events'.[31]

Such sentiments would persist throughout the case. Almost a year on and days before the pronouncement of the verdict in 1946, *The Times* reported that the principal response of the German population to the IMT was one of boredom and scepticism. 'Some way behind comes a certain satisfaction that the men who led Germany into her present mess are going to suffer for it', the newspaper noted.[32] *The Times* concluded that the length of the proceedings was largely responsible for the malaise, suggesting that with the passage of time, the population was becoming less concerned about their former leadership and more embittered with the Allied occupation. There were increasing critiques of the Allies' own wartime behaviour, with references to the bombing of Dresden and the reprisals enacted by the Red Army during the final throes of the conflict, both of which served to offer further evidence of German victimhood. Frustration at the protracted nature of the IMT was also evident as journalists took to the streets to gauge opinion. Typical of the comments that they encountered was the following argument: 'I would have liked to see them all shot the minute they were captured but why take eighteen months over it?'[33] Other notable themes included concern over the addition of Wehrmacht personnel alongside Party and SS figures—a factor which challenged longstanding notions of the honourable German soldier and the necessity of doing one's duty—as well as the impact such proceedings could have upon foreign opinions of the German people.[34]

Reflecting at the end of the proceedings, the American prosecutor, Robert M.W. Kempner, offered a positive assessment of the level of German engagement with the IMT. He emphasised that thousands of letters expressing an opinion on the proceedings had been sent to members of the tribunal from all four occupation zones and argued that the IMT's extensive reliance on official German documents had impressed observers, commenting that 'the Germans are a document-minded people'.[35] He also described how the trial had been able to make itself felt beyond the Nuremberg courtroom, noting references to the case by law professors at Heidelberg University in their teaching as well as discussion groups set up between university and local *Gymnasium* students. The younger generation, it seemed, were already taking a very keen interest in these issues.

For Kempner, there were several distinct phases in the population's attitude to the IMT. Initially, he noted, there was much interest amid the expectation of summary executions. The length of the trial, however, as already noted, dissipated this interest and even went so far as to provoke the belief among some that the trial was just a figment of Allied propaganda. In his mind, public interest only really revived when the defendants began to testify and the tribunal discussed the criminality of various Nazi organisations. 'The volume of letters rose', and he noted that '75 percent contained views favourable to the trial. Some were messages of congratulations or made proposals for further investigations against the defendants or against a witness who tried to cover up the activities of defendants'.[36] Other communications, though, reiterated ongoing concerns over the legitimacy of the court and the problem of retrospective legislation; yet others sent unsigned messages which drew upon Nazi rhetoric to denounce the whole affair. Amid his obvious pride and satisfaction in the course of the IMT, Kempner did admit that 'there remain large bodies of Germans on whom the trials have had no effect whatsoever, who have withdrawn into themselves and ignored every development in public life since defeat'.[37]

Rather like the pattern of responses to the trial by the British population, there were several key moments in the IMT which generated a greater degree of public interest. One such incident was the testimony of Hermann Göring, whose stance in the witness box revived some respect for the former World War One fighter ace and subsequent Luftwaffe chief.[38] Another was the announcement of the verdict in October 1946. Reporting on the increased security measures to be put in place for the tribunal's pronouncement, the *New York Times* commented upon new levels of local engagement, reporting 'it was noted that every head turned and every neck was craned toward the huge gray building as trolley cars passed this point, indicating the acute awareness in Nuremberg that the long trial was nearing its end'.[39] No doubt there is some degree of journalistic licence here with the idea that *everyone* was gazing up at the Palace of Justice, but nonetheless, the verdict, when it finally came down, produced much press coverage and condemnation from both sides of the political spectrum.

Having considered the evidence against the accused, the tribunal found the majority of defendants guilty of at least one of the charges that had been levelled against them; six were found guilty on all four charges.[40] Twelve were sentenced to death and seven men faced prison sentences ranging from ten years to life. Three of the Nuremberg accused, former head of the radio division in the propaganda ministry Hans Fritzsche, former ambassador Franz von Papen and former Minister of Economics Hjalmar Schacht were acquitted, and it was these latter results which attracted the biggest public outcry. Put very simply, the political Left attacked the resultant sentences as being too soft, while the remnants of the extreme Right, unsurprisingly, denounced the entire IMT process as deeply flawed and unjust. In the Soviet zone, and particularly amid the heightened political atmosphere in Berlin, the results of the IMT were greeted with public demonstrations organised by the Socialist Unity Party. Banners and placards were waved demanding the death sentence for all of the defendants and the British News Service reported that Berlin factories were planning a ten minute strike in response to the verdict.[41] These public rallies in Eastern Germany can be seen as typical of the hard-line stance that the German Democratic Republic would subsequently take on former Nazi personnel. However, the *New York Times* reported that the socialist protests were actually a relatively muted affair, attracting around 1500 East Germans. 'Only a few people followed the poster bearers', the newspaper concluded.[42]

The SPD, meanwhile, demanded the immediate retrial of Fritzsche, Schacht and von Papen; the *Manchester Guardian*'s Berlin correspondent commented that this was one of the few issues that the Social Democrats and the Communists seemed able to agree upon at this time.[43] It was argued that these three men did, in fact, bear much guilt towards the German people, with references to the misleading nature of Nazi propaganda (Fritzsche) and the manner in which Hitler had been helped into power in the first place through conservative intrigue (von Papen). The latter argument

18 *West Germans and the Nazi Legacy*

accentuated the concept of National Socialism as having come from 'elsewhere' and while the political machinations of the early 1930s cannot be denied, the emphasis on von Papen's guilt nonetheless helped to downplay the level of popular consensus behind the Nazi regime and the electoral success that the NSDAP had been able to enjoy after September 1930. By contrast, the execution of von Ribbentrop was seen as thoroughly deserved on the grounds that he 'was a bad foreign minister', again underscoring the notion that the primary reason these men needed to be punished was for leading Germany into a disastrous war and consequently causing suffering to the German people.[44] Rebecca West likewise recorded an encounter with a local Nuremberg woman who was particularly eager to hear whether Sauckel had been sentenced yet:

> 'I shall not sleep happy till I have heard that that scoundrel pays for his crimes', the woman proclaimed, 'Never will we undo the harm he did by bringing these wretched foreign labourers into our Germany. I had a nice house, *a home* . . . and what did this Sauckel do but send two thousand foreign workers to the factories in the district, two thousand wretches, cannibals, scum of the earth Russians, Balks, Balts, Slavs, Slavs I tell you. What did they do when our armies were defeated but break loose? For three days they kept carnival, they looted and they ate and drank of our goods.'[45]

The conditions that these forced workers had been kept in, however, went unacknowledged.

The attention afforded to the three exonerated individuals was not confined to left-wing political activists. Newspapers licensed by the British and Americans in the Western parts of the country also suggested that the three were 'guilty in the eyes of the German people'. The *Tagesspiegel*, for example, remarked upon how 'justified and logical the Soviet dissent against the three acquittals and the sparing of Hess's life' was, and the chief editor of a Hannover newspaper resigned his position as chair of a denazification panel upon learning of Fritzsche's acquittal.[46] British observers concluded that the general comment emanating from the West German population was 'it is just one of those cases of common sense versus the law'.[47] Nor was criticism of the IMT confined to the treatment of these three particular defendants. Younger Germans singled out the sentencing of former Hitler Youth leader Baldur von Schirach to twenty years imprisonment as being too lenient, arguing that he 'was a fanatic who merited the full death sentence'.[48] The fact that the tribunal had also ruled that the SA and military High Command could not be considered criminal organisations was similarly rued by the SPD-affiliated editor of the Berlin *Telegraf.*[49] However, while the acquittal of Fritzsche, Schacht and von Papen certainly raised a few eyebrows, it did have the additional effect of encouraging others to view the IMT in a more positive light. While noting that 'surprise at the acquittals is in fact

expressed by most Germans one meets', *The Times* pointed out that 'some
. . . (whether they regret the acquittals or accept them) are prepared to see
them as an indication that the tribunal was not after all, as most Germans
thought, merely a façade for an act of vengeance and that an attempt was
made to mete out justice and distinguish between degrees of guilt'.[50]

Not all protests witnessed in the aftermath of the tribunal, though, shared
this belief that the court had not gone far enough in its treatment of the Nazi
leadership. In November 1946, the *New York Times* noted the appearance
of Nazi-style propaganda posters in Frankfurt am Main which glorified the
defendants and demanded death sentences for Jews and democrats instead.[51]
Given that the Nuremberg executions had been carried out twenty-four days
earlier, these reactionary protests held little more than a symbolic purpose
and it is therefore interesting that they came on 9 November, a day of recurring significance in modern German history, marking the date not only of the
declaration of the Weimar Republic in 1918 but also Hitler's failed Munich
Putsch of 1923 and, of course, *Kristallnacht* in 1938. Staging protests on
this particular day provided an opportunity to recall alternative memories
of the recent past, and the singling out of Jews and democrats for reprisals
fitted into the legend of the November Criminals and the 'stab in the back'
that had circulated since the end of the First World War. In Stuttgart too,
posters had appeared declaring 'Nuremberg: not justice but murder' and 'on
October 16 1946 twelve Germans are being murdered by our enemies. Germans wake up'—the latter reminiscent of the old Nazi election posters that
had enjoined the country to arise from its slumber. A cemetery in Hersfeld,
meanwhile, saw a wreath adorned with swastikas and iron crosses promising to avenge the 'martyrs of Nuremberg', and in Angersbach a Nazi flag
was found flying from a First World War memorial.[52]

In the midst of these reactions, there remained particular interest in the
fate of Göring. A number of Germans experienced some satisfaction in the
fact he had succeeded in thwarting the hangman; others persisted in bizarre
rumours that he was not actually dead but being held by the western Allies
in the new fight against the USSR.[53] The *New York Times* commented:

> All other aspects of the trial and executions were completely overshadowed as thousands of Germans chuckled over the trick he had played
> on the occupying powers and once more thought of him as a hero.
> Göring's dramatic gesture in death appeared to have helped these Germans to forget his crimes, the millions of deaths in the concentration
> camps and in the war caused by the Nazi regime and the lessons of the
> ten month trial. The event that was to have been a weapon in the hands
> of democracy suddenly became one in the hands of unrepentant German nationalism.[54]

The extent to which any of these sentiments was indicative of the German population as a whole is, of course, highly questionable. References to German nationalism in the Allied press were perhaps influenced by a tendency to cling to hostile impressions of the German enemy. At the same time, though, the idea that *some* people expressed pride in Göring or condemned the tribunal as 'the work of the Jews' does underscore the impossibility of older sentiments dying out overnight. The process of re-education and 'coming to terms' with the recent past would take time.

Observers in the *New York Times*, however, clung to the conclusion that such responses were confined to a lunatic fringe. To support this claim, the newspaper pointed to the results of a 1946 opinion poll conducted in Berlin in which 76.11 percent of those questioned said they found the sentences too lenient and only 1.42 percent, by contrast, thought they were too harsh.[55]

Surveys in the British zone yielded similar sentiments. The Information Services Control Branch concluded that the population generally fell into one of two categories: those who rejected the entire tribunal as illegal and unjustified and those who accepted the necessity of the IMT but disagreed with its results; 'hardly anyone seems to be wholly satisfied'.[56] A poll of 3935 people in December 1946 as to whether they would like a summary of the IMT produced by a 'reliable' German source resulted in 37.2 percent saying they never wanted to hear another word about Nuremberg. British sources reflected that this statistic 'is not as high as might have been expected'.[57]

In Hannover, there was dissatisfaction 'in all classes of society' that von Papen was let off. In Schleswig-Holstein, opinion seemed to find the sentences 'inevitable' and there was little open comment against the verdicts, apart from that delivered on Jödl. In Düsseldorf, there were again expressions of shock that military leaders had been sentenced to death. Many workers also 'regretted' Göring's inclusion on the execution list 'because he was thought to have had pluck, courage and a heart for the common people.'[58] The people of North Rhine Westphalia also continued to debate the legality (and morality) of the trial. A doctor was recorded as saying 'there has never been such a thing before as that the victor should sit in judgment and condemn the government of the beaten enemy. That is plain murder. We cannot sink any lower than that'. Former soldiers themselves, however, expressed agreement with the IMT results.[59]

In the Ruhr, there was particular interest in the fate of von Papen and some feeling that the trial should have been held before a German court. 'Many young Germans think that those condemned may become martyrs and feel that they all should have been quietly liquidated'. In Hamburg, there was some argument that 'those in other countries, including Allied countries, responsible for starting the war should have been brought to trial', an opinion that was expressed 'particularly strongly amongst the victims of bombing and among refugees'. Across the British zone, there was also much surprise that Raeder was given a life prison sentence while Dönitz received just ten years.[60]

Statements from Hamburg senators, meanwhile, showed a new political leadership keen to distinguish their anti-Nazi credentials. Bürgermeister

Rudolf Petersen (CDU) declared, 'I have formed the impression that the trial was conducted with the greatest thoroughness and objectivity. I am thankful that the trial is now ended and a source of political danger thereby removed'. Senator Friedrich Dettmann (KPD), Head of the Hamburg Health Administration, expressed the ubiquitous surprise at the three exonerated individuals, arguing 'none of the accused should have been acquitted because each of them had knowledge of the terrible crimes committed in Germany against German nationals'. The Head of the Hamburg City Administration, Senator Heinrich Landahl (SPD), however, accentuated the guilt that Schacht, von Papen and Fritzsche bore for German suffering, noting that 'the verdict is founded without doubt on the assumption that an international tribunal adjudicates only from the aspect of crime on an international scale. The vital aspect of the case can only be judged from the German standpoint'.[61] In the end, the British were forced to conclude that 'although the verdicts have reawakened interest in the trials, they have done little to deepen understanding of their significance'.[62]

For the British, there was an added concern for the effect that the IMT results would have on their standing as an occupying force. In the aftermath of the executions, the German News Service put out the story that Alfred Jödl and Joachim von Ribbentrop had taken sixteen and fourteen minutes to die, respectively. The decision to hang, rather than shoot, the military figures of Jödl, Keitel and Raeder had already been perceived as an added indignity by many Germans. The news that at least two of the condemned men suffered a slow death prompted further criticisms, and the popular claim that these figures had, in fact, been strangled. It was an allegation that revived memories of how the Nazis had reintroduced hanging in the summer of 1944 as a deliberately humiliating manner of executing those suspected of involvement in the failed July bomb plot against Hitler; rather than quickly breaking the condemned's neck, the alleged conspirators were subjected to a combination of piano wire and meat hooks which ensured an agonising death would be induced by strangulation. Consequently, in 1946, there were popular allegations that the Allies were also behaving inhumanely. 'British prestige', noted observers within North Rhine Westphalia, 'is suffering considerable damage'.[63] Reluctant to deny the allegations for fear of only inflaming the situation, M.L.G. Balfour of the Information Services Control Branch argued this, however, was merely further evidence of the Germans' reluctance to face up to the criminality of the Third Reich, saying 'this strikes me as a typical misunderstanding fostered because the public want to misunderstand'.[64]

Interestingly, popular impressions of the IMT experienced further revision in the period after the tribunal's conclusion. Jürgen Wilke has compared the OMGUS polling conducted during the trial itself to subsequent polls carried out in the early 1950s. The results showed that, in the space of just four years, the popular approval rating for the IMT had declined sharply from 80 percent to just 59 percent. Similarly, by 1950, 30 percent of those questioned now believed that the trial had been unfair.⁶⁵ How can we account for this shift in public attitudes? For Christoph Burchard, the answer lies within renewed debates over *ex post facto* law and the legitimacy of the Allied military tribunals and, by extension, Control Council Law 10, which would provide the basis for continued war crimes trials, together with a changing political climate in which the needs of the emerging Cold War conflict would take precedence over any western efforts to pursue Nazi perpetrators.⁶⁶ Moreover, the simple fact that the end of the IMT did not bring about the immediate end of war crimes or denazification proceedings, as some may have hoped, could also be seen as fostering a sense of disillusionment among the German people.

In 1947, reports from the British occupation zone underscored the extent to which German attention was firmly focussed on the continuing food and fuel shortages and how news of anti-Jewish demonstrations in England was greeted with 'a certain amount of "Schadenfreude" and "I told you so" attitude'. Observers commented:

> The mood of the German people can be described as "querulous". They do not seem to realise that there has been a major war and that someone has to pay for it. They talk glibly of international law and accuse the Allies of turning Germany into a vast concentration camp. . . . The catchword of the day is "Poor Germany".⁶⁷

In 1948, a particularly critical retort to continuing Allied war crimes proceedings was printed in the weekly newspaper *Die Zeit*. Amid claims that witness statements had been coerced and manipulated and that innocent people had been detained for months on end, the conservative editor-in-chief, Richard Tüngel, stated:

> We do not want to be accused once again of merely watching like cowards when we believe that the law is being violated. We accuse. We, who have always hated Hitler and his 'Third Reich', we, who have demanded that the guilty of the Nazi system should be severely punished, we now find ourselves compelled to stand up and ensure that justice is done in Nuremberg. Six German lawyers have been arrested. Under the American legal system that is permissible—in Germany this happened only in the special courts of the 'Third Reich'.⁶⁸

For Tüngel, though, it was not necessarily about a rejection of the IMT and everything it stood for *per se*, but more about the rejection of the methods allegedly being employed by the Americans. Furthermore, his protests were not simply out of concern for the fate of German defendants or witnesses, but also a fear over the impact that such issues could have on the wider population's attitude to the trials. Towards the end of his article, for example, Tüngel stressed that such criticisms were not confined to German circles, but shared by experienced legal personnel in the United States:

> The American lawyer Carroll told the Frankfurt correspondent of the *New York Herald Tribune* that the Nuremberg trials of war criminals were a 'tragic mockery of American justice'. We hope that the motion he will file with the Supreme Court of the United States to declare these trials invalid will at least lead to the review of the prosecution's method by a high-ranking, unbiased agency so that the German people can develop confidence in the Nuremberg trials.[69]

A sense of apathy or indifference to the wider Allied programmes of denazification and re-education during the immediate post-war period has also been well documented by historians. Denazification in particular was regarded by many Germans as a wholly unfair process and one which seemed to single out the 'little man' for harsh treatment. However, as Barbara Marshall has argued, even here popular responses can be seen as rather more complicated than conventional narratives would suggest. There were elements of the population who criticised the denazification programme for not going far enough in its treatment of suspected individuals.[70]

The IMT was followed by a series of other war crimes proceedings conducted by the Allies within their respective occupation zones of the newly divided Germany. There was some debate as to whether there should be a second international tribunal but these ideas never came to fruition.[71] In the months after the IMT, various representatives of the Nazi regime, including members of the German judiciary, the medical profession, industrialists and various concentration camp personnel, were brought to account by the Americans in twelve cases which became known as the Subsequent Nuremberg Trials. However, the emerging Cold War tensions between the former Allies soon took precedent over continuing prosecutions of Nazi war criminals; there was a new ideological enemy to contend with instead. The Allies also had to consider public opinion within their own countries. In Britain, for example, there was some incomprehension as to why the government continued to waste valuable time and resources on suspected war criminals when important reconstruction work still needed to be carried out at home.[72] Britain thus lost its zeal for prosecution quite quickly. Re-education and denazification programmes were similarly wound up in the other western occupation zones.

Increasingly responsibility for Nazi war criminals was being handed over to the Germans themselves to deal with. From late 1945, Allied Control Council Law 10 granted permission to restored courts in the western zones to try Nazi perpetrators, although they could only deal with those crimes committed against German nationals inside Germany itself.[73] Pre-war concentration camp murders, *Kristallnacht* brutalities and the 'euthanasia' scheme all fell within this remit and, while such acts did serve as some reminder as to the racial nature of Nazi propaganda and persecution, they also provided another means of cementing notions of German victimhood, elevating their suffering above that of other ethnic groups during the Second World War. The nature of these early war crimes trials in Western Germany consequently created only a partial understanding of Nazi criminality and fuelled confusion over the precise nature of the Nazi concentration camp system. It was not until the 1960s that war crimes trials would really begin to explore mass extermination crimes (see Figures 1.1 through 1.3).

Once the Federal Republic of Germany gained sovereignty in 1949, it could deal with suspected war criminals however it considered fit. The early part of the 1950s witnessed a steady decline in the number of war crimes

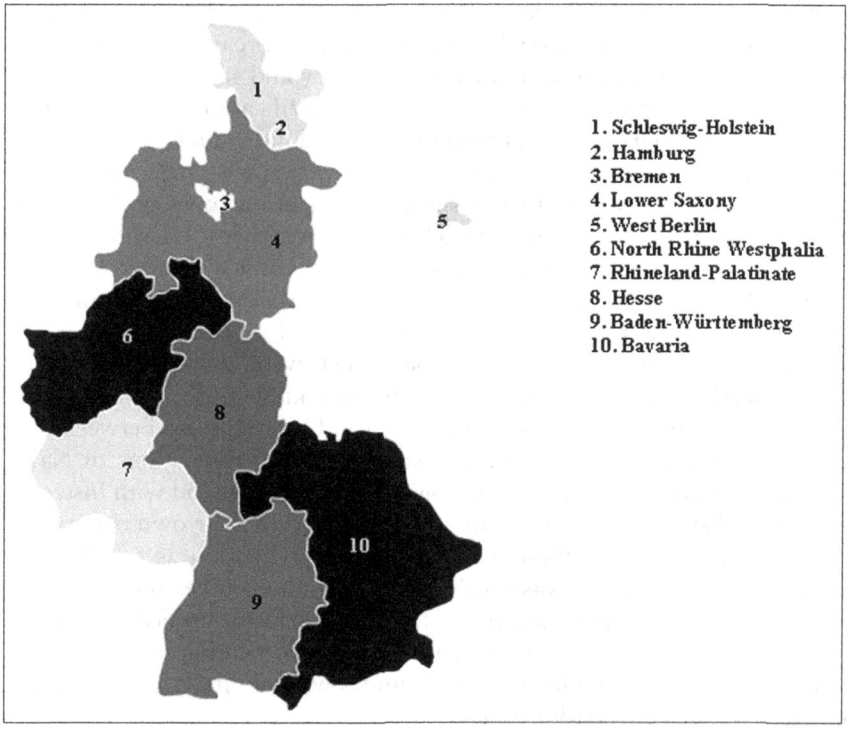

Figure 1.1 Map showing the concentration of Nazi war crimes trials* in West Germany, 1946–1969.
* Trials recorded relate only to homicidal cases (NS-Tötungsverbrechen) committed during the war.
Source: Data based upon trial records reproduced in Christiaan F. Rüter & Dick W. de Mildt eds., 'German Trial Judgments concerning National Socialist Homicidal Crimes, Vols I–XLVI', Nazi Crimes on Trial, http://www1.jur.uva.nl/junsv/.

The Victors and the Vanquished 25

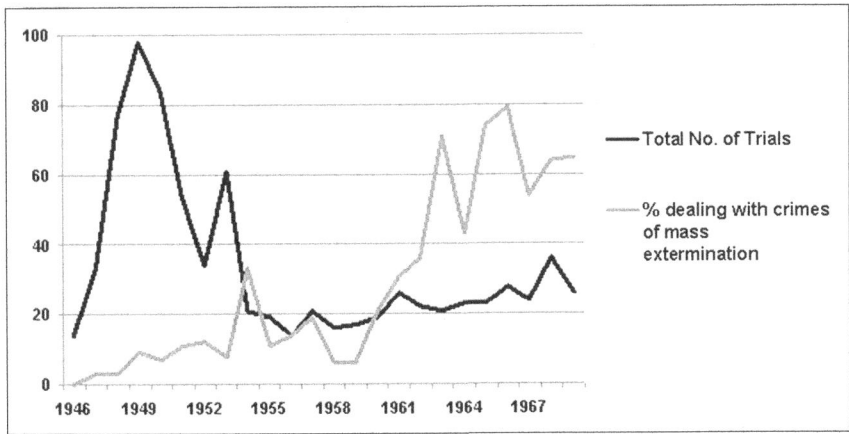

Figure 1.2 Graph showing the number of war crimes trials in West Germany, 1946–1969.
Source: Data based upon trial records reproduced in Christiaan F. Rüter & Dick W. de Mildt eds., 'German Trial Judgments concerning National Socialist Homicidal Crimes, Vols I–XLVI', Nazi Crimes on Trial, http://www1.jur.uva.nl/junsv/.

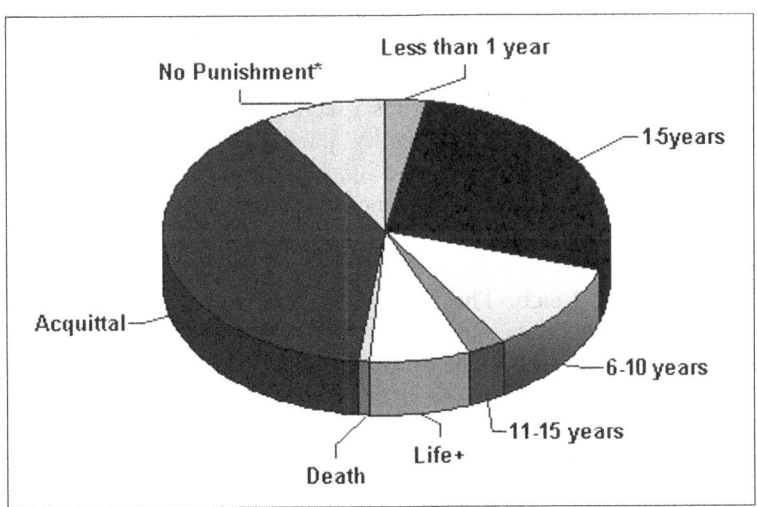

Figure 1.3 Chart showing the results of war crimes trials in West Germany, 1946–1969.
+ This category includes those defendants who received a life sentence, plus additional years in prison (i.e., life plus fifteen years).
* This category includes those defendants whose proceedings were suspended or quashed, those who died before the end of the trial and those whose crimes fell under §47 of the German Military Penal Code (i.e., following superior orders).

cases being heard compared with the number instigated by the Allies. Furthermore, the trials that were being carried out increasingly resulted in acquittals. Hermann Langbein records that between 8 May 1945 and 15 March 1961, a total of 12,715 people were charged with war crimes before West German courts. However, only 42 percent of these defendants were ever actually found guilty, and most of these sentences had been handed down by 1948.[74] By 1950, then, a sense of trial fatigue seemed to have set in and the early part of the decade saw only isolated trials taking place, usually the result of external impulses or chance discoveries of Nazi criminals, often by their former victims. Between 1947 and 1950, the Allies had rendered 5,006 convictions, of which 794 had resulted in the death penalty. While life imprisonment replaced capital punishment as the maximum penalty afforded under West German law, the conviction rate nonetheless declined sharply once the FRG came into being. In 1950, there was a total of 809 convictions for war crimes. In 1953, this figure fell to 123 and, by 1954, to just 44.[75] The *Justiz und Verbrechen* series, compiled by scholars in the Netherlands, similarly records the decline in war crimes trials conducted in West Germany from 68 in 1950 to just 17 by 1957. The trials that were conducted during this period tended to be relatively small affairs. Just 8 percent of the cases involved five or more defendants at any one time, and only 7 percent of the trials held between 1950 and 1957 resulted in a life prison sentence for at least one of the accused.[76] Those that did receive such punishments tended to be the last 'big names' of the Third Reich, including Ilse Koch, who stood trial in 1951. The preponderance of cases—38 percent—ended in the acquittal of all concerned.[77]

As early as the 1950s, there was thus a section of the West German population who claimed all the 'really guilty' parties had been dealt with and that trials should therefore be wound up. Such sentiments, together with dwindling judicial action and a tendency to favour leniency or amnesties over harsh punishment, would all seem to support conventional historical narratives of the 1950s as a decade of little popular engagement with the legacy of the Third Reich. The fact remains, though, that whatever the result of these proceedings, such trials *were* carried out throughout this period and, while a decline in the total number of prosecutions is, perhaps, only to be expected as one moves further away from the end of the Second World War, there remained at least some effort to bring any remaining suspects before a court. The trials themselves also continued to encompass a wide range of criminal activity, from mass shootings to isolated acts of murder through to the human experiments that were conducted in the concentration camps, ensuring that there was some form of public discussion of these atrocities taking place in the 1950s.

These trials of the 1950s, though, have been largely ignored by historiography. The principal exception concerns Alaric Searle's recent research into the prosecution of the former Wehrmacht generals between 1948 and 1960, the public responses to which he roots firmly in the rearmament

The Victors and the Vanquished 27

debates of the 1950s and the history of West Germany's 'coming to terms' with its military past.[78] Indeed, Searle himself takes issue with the assumption, implicit within so much of the existing secondary literature, that the declining number of war crimes trials during the 1950s equates to a lack of interest in confronting the past during this period. On the contrary, Searle argues that public opinion was much less responsive to the number of trials, but rather more influenced by the 'spectacular' cases. Given that the proceedings during the latter part of the decade no longer had to compete with numerous other trials for column space within the West German press, they were, he argues, actually more likely to become major media events and enjoy a wider resonance among the West German people as a result. Searle's own studies, for example, highlight the manner in which the prosecutions of Hasso von Manteuffel and Theodor Tolsdorff were able to capture the public imagination, commanding much press attention and even inspiring satirical newspaper cartoons.[79]

However, perhaps the most important factor in these cases was the nature of the accused. The IMT had already demonstrated that the treatment of former Wehrmacht personnel held a special point of interest for many Germans and this showed little sign of dissipating in the 1950s. An opinion survey conducted in September 1952, for example, saw a majority of people (over 60 percent) arguing that Kesselring and Dönitz had been unfairly imprisoned.[80] In part, this can be explained by longstanding traditions of the honourable German soldier, the emphasis on doing one's duty and following orders without question and an attempt to characterise the Second World War as a conventional military conflict rather than an example of genocide. This was evident at the start of the decade through the campaigns to release the last German prisoners of war from Russian captivity, as well as the ongoing efforts of former Waffen-SS members to carve out a respectable legacy for themselves by stressing their credentials as a purely military unit distinct from the general SS. Veterans' reunions and protests over revocations of pensions were indicative of this approach to the recent past.[81]

This inclination to believe in the fundamental integrity of the Wehrmacht was not confined to the German population. The British were similarly reluctant to countenance the military's involvement in the crimes of the Third Reich. While members of the High Command had been included in the IMT, further Allied attempts to prosecute German generals after 1945 made little headway.[82] Given this background, is it really surprising that the prosecution of German generals was able to spark public interest during the 1950s?

Furthermore, given that most German families would have had a relative involved in the fighting, the resonance of this particular set of trials may owe something to the fact that 'ordinary' people could relate more easily to the issues under discussion. The extent to which other types of war crimes trials during this period were able to enjoy similar levels of public interest and media 'spectacle' thus remains rather questionable. In other words, is it not more accurate to depict the 1950s as a period when people took an interest in those cases that had greater personal relevance? Searle's connection between the generals' trials and wider rearmament debates are more convincing. The Korean War had underlined the importance of being able to draw upon additional military might in the fight against Communism and by 1955 West Germany had been rehabilitated on the international stage to the extent that it was allowed to join NATO as an important Cold War ally. These events revived questions over German militarism and nationalism and thus examples of Wehrmacht transgressions during the Second World War had a particular resonance for those wary of renewing German military strength just ten years after that devastating conflict.

The globalisation of the Cold War after Korea, though, also provided an opportunity for others within West Germany to once again try to put the Nazi era firmly behind them. There was much political pressure, especially from the Right, to link rearmament and West German support for the United States to a general rehabilitation of German soldiers, and the issue of a general amnesty for former Nazis gained momentum.[83]

A desire to move on from the war years and focus instead upon the blossoming economic miracle is understandable. Historians such as Frei have argued that the maintenance of former Nazis within institutions such as the civil service eased the transition to democracy and aided the country's rapid road to economic recovery. However, the persistence of these figures would prove a highly contentious issue for East-West German relations for decades to come. The GDR would routinely name and shame ex-Nazis occupying positions of responsibility in the Federal Republic, including members of Adenauer's own cabinet, throughout this period, most famously with the publication of the so-called *Brown Book* in 1965.[84]

The issue in the 1950s, though, was not merely about preventing new investigations into suspected war criminals. Calls for a general amnesty included those already sentenced by the Allies; rather than seeking to uncover more murderers and to follow up Allied initiatives with a concerted war crimes prosecution programme of their own, the West German emphasis was upon undoing previous results and pardoning the guilty. Norbert Frei has shown how, during this period, many convicted war criminals were able to enjoy sympathy and solidarity from their compatriots. Candlelit vigils were staged outside their prisons and a 1952 campaign by the Frankfurt-based *Abendpost* resulted in over 200 offers from members of the public to swap places with prisoners on Christmas Eve so the latter might spend time with their families. Frei also recounts the case of two prisoners who escaped from Werl and were able to elude the authorities through the support of members of the public; the fishmonger who denounced their temporary hideout in Aurich, on the other hand, was labelled a 'traitor' and had his house targeted by an angry mob.[85]

By the 1950s, even the term 'war criminal' had become contested. There was a growing preference to use the term 'Nazi criminal' instead, the distinction between the two helping to impose a sense of distance between the atrocities and the majority of the population while, again, also trying to safeguard the reputation of the armed services during the conflict. The term *Kriegsverurteilten* ('war condemned') was also favoured when speaking of those already sentenced for their crimes, a phrase distinct from *Kriegsschuldig* ('war guilty').[86] Conducting an opinion poll survey in 1952, it is telling that Elizabeth Noelle-Neumann was inviting people to comment on the *sogenannten* ('so-called') war criminals sentenced at Nuremberg.[87]

Not surprisingly, given all of these factors, many historians have been tempted to label this immediate post-war period as one of silence or even 'collective amnesia' with regards to the recent past. However, as the responses outlined above indicate, this was far from being a straightforward era of silence. There was a discussion of the past, albeit a very onesided one which gave precedence to German suffering and mythologised the extent of resistance against the Third Reich.

It is important to remember too that there were also elements of the population during this period who were seeking to address Nazi crimes and encourage wider reflection on the past. This sector of society was comprised most notably of survivors, liberal members of the press, prosecutors and some school teachers. In 1959, for example, a group of Karlsruhe students mounted their own assault on the prevailing silence by targeting the number of ex-Nazis who had retained positions of authority in the Federal Republic. An exhibition entitled *Ungesühnte Nazijustiz* toured Karlsruhe, West Berlin and Tübingen, detailing 100 cases where people had fallen foul of the National Socialist concept of justice and listing the current whereabouts of 206 judges and prosecutors who had worked in the former People's Courts— many of whom were still employed in the West German judiciary. One of the organisers behind the exhibition was himself the son of a former Nazi judge, suggesting that generational conflict was already apparent long before the much-heralded student protest movement of 1968.[88]

The late 1940s and early 1950s were thus characterised by multifaceted responses to the recent past. Any initial expectations that the execution of the Nazi leadership at Nuremberg would enable West Germans to make a complete break with the National Socialist era were soon frustrated as, indeed, were any hopes that the new Cold War climate would divert all the attention away from German transgressions. Pressure to confront the crimes of the Third Reich continued to be mounted from both within and outside of the Federal Republic. West German society was already witnessing a tension between a desire to forget and a compulsion to remember, and this would only accelerate at the turn of the decade as the Federal Republic, bowing to the inescapable scale of the Holocaust, ushered in a brand new era of war crimes trials.

2 'The Murderers among Us'

Themes of retribution, guilt and atonement for Nazi atrocities were articulated within popular culture as early as 1946, with the release of the very first post-war German film, Wolfgang Staudte's *Die Mörder sind unter uns* (The Murderers Are Among Us). First screened just two weeks after the conclusion of the IMT at Nuremberg, the film told the tale of former surgeon Dr. Mertens who returns to a ruined Berlin after the war, traumatised by his experiences on the Eastern Front. Suffering from depression and unable to rebuild his shattered life, Mertens proceeds to track down his former commander, Captain Brückner, who was responsible for the massacre of over a hundred Polish civilians on Christmas Eve, 1942. The protagonist's aim is simple: to kill the man responsible for his continued nightmares. At the last minute, however, he is interrupted by Susanne, a former concentration camp prisoner who persuades him that the pursuit of justice before the courts is the better means of overcoming the horrors of the recent past.

Audience reactions to *Die Mörder sind unter uns* were generally uncritical. Many people clung to the sense of German victimhood encapsulated by these characters and, given the film's timing, could all too easily identify with the rubble-strewn urban landscape it depicted. The more challenging questions of complicity in crimes against humanity, personified by both Brückner and Mertens, were shoved aside.[1] Just over a decade later, though, Staudte's rhetoric of 'the murderers among us' gained a new salience. In the film, the character Brückner had successfully carved out a new career for himself as a businessman, recycling military helmets into pots and pans. By the late 1950s, it was becoming increasingly clear that the ability of war criminals to slip quietly back into civilian life had not been confined to the realms of fiction.

In the spring of 1956, the head of the refugee camp in the southwest town of Ulm, one 'Herr Fischer', decided to reapply for his pre-war position in the German civil service. His petition was noted by a small piece in the local newspaper, whereby one reader chanced to recognise this figure as the former SS-*Oberführer* Bernhard Fischer-Schweder, one-time police director of Memel and the head of an Einsatzkommando unit responsible for the mass shooting of Lithuanian Jews and Communists during the summer of 1941. Fischer-Schweder was quickly arrested and subsequent investigations launched by the public prosecutor, Dr. Erwin Schüle, unearthed nine more members of his wartime unit. They had all been living innocuously in post-war West Germany as lawyers, salesman, policemen or, in one case, as an optician.[2] The resulting four month trial that began in April 1958 was one of the biggest prosecutions of former Nazi personnel to take place under West German jurisdiction and has been regarded by many historians as marking the definitive turning point in popular attitudes to the Nazi past, following the silences and evasions that had characterised the earlier part of the decade.[3] In reality, though, the results of the trial were mixed and despite sudden public discussion about how many other mass murderers remained undetected within West German society, the case ultimately failed to sustain the interest of the general population.

On the face of it, the Ulm Einsatzkommando trial was not an unusual event for 1950s West Germany. In 1958 alone, fifteen other trials were held across the Federal Republic, although, continuing the earlier pattern of West German war crimes trials, the majority concluded with the acquittal of all concerned.[4] The Ulm trial did, however, constitute one of the largest prosecutions of former Nazi personnel to take place under the jurisdiction of the Federal Republic at that time, placing as it did ten former Einsatzkommando members in the dock. It was certainly the largest case to be heard in 1958.

THE BACKGROUND TO THE
ULM EINSATZKOMMANDO TRIAL

Comprising four main groups labelled A, B, C and D, and subdivided in turn into a plethora of smaller commando units, the Einsatzgruppen were mobile killing units that followed the Wehrmacht into the Soviet Union from June 1941 and liquidated Jews and Communists rounded up in eastern towns and villages. The mass shootings carried out by these units were a clear indicator that the Nazi regime was moving towards the physical destruction of those deemed 'enemies of the Reich', a pattern that would lead to the construction of the extermination camps in Eastern Europe.

The Tilsit Einsatzkommando, which became the subject of the 1958 Ulm proceedings, was established at the start of the German invasion of the Soviet Union and was attached to Einsatzgruppe A. The head of the Staatspolizeistelle (Stapo) in the East Prussian city of Tilsit—and later one of the chief defendants at Ulm—SS-*Sturmbannführer* Hans-Joachim Böhme had long been involved in the plans for Operation Barbarossa and subsequent border area operations. The Stapo had been authorised to extend its jurisdiction beyond the Reich and was commissioned with the promulgation of executive measures against the civilian population in the border districts. Böhme was effectively granted permission by the Reich Main Security

Office (RSHA) to set up his own mobile killing unit, which then crossed over into Lithuania just after the Wehrmacht had launched its attack.[5]

In addition to the 54 year old Bernhard Fischer-Schweder and 49 year old Hans-Joachim Böhme, the men who appeared in the dock in Ulm included Werner Schmidt-Hammer (51), Werner Hersmann (54), Hans Willms Harms (66), Franz Behrendt (46) and Lithuanian national Pranas Lukys (58), along with Edwin Sakuth, Gerhard Carsten and Werner Kreuzmann, all aged 49. Together, they were charged with participating in a series of massacres along the Lithuanian border during the summer and autumn of 1941. These included the murder of 201 Jews in Gargzdai on 24 June 1941 just two days after the start of the Nazi attack on the Soviet Union, 214 people in Kretinga on 25 June and a further 111 people on 27 June in Palanga. The statistics recorded in the indictment illustrate the speed of the Einsatzgruppen's movement through the Eastern European countryside and their unrelenting determination to 'cleanse' the area of imagined ideological enemies.[6]

The role of the Einsatzgruppen in the evolution of the 'Final Solution' had been made known to the world as early as 1947 when twenty-four former personnel appeared before the U.S. tribunal at Nuremberg to answer charges of war crimes, crimes against humanity and membership of a criminal organisation. Over the course of approximately eight months, the court documented extensively the structure of the Einsatzgruppen, their place within the Nazi extermination programme and the scale of the atrocities perpetrated in the Baltic States. Fourteen of the accused were sentenced to death for their crimes, although ten later succeeded in having this penalty commuted to periods of imprisonment.[7] Ironically, these men had been released by the time of the Ulm trial.

However, it was the events in Ulm, a decade after the Nuremberg Einsatzgruppen case, which created the bigger impact upon the West German people. Several West German newspapers heralded the 1958 case as constituting an important learning curve for the population, informing them for the first time about the extent of Nazi criminality and the development of the Holocaust. The *Hannoversche Presse* was typical, declaring that the Ulm trial had provided a 'startling insight' into the crimes committed in the east, thereby ignoring the findings of the earlier Nuremberg case.[8]

A number of reasons could be put forward to explain why it was the Ulm case that produced the greater resonance. Firstly, the very structure of the two trials may have affected how members of the public viewed them. The Nuremberg Einsatzgruppen trial was one in a whole series of war crimes hearings staged in close proximity to one another in a relatively short space of time, the cumulative effect of which arguably produced a strong sense of trial fatigue among the West German population. This earlier case also dealt with representatives from all four of the Einsatzgruppen, as well as their various subdivisions: Einsatzkommandos, Sonderkommandos and the Vorkommando Moskau. A chart was drawn up, in accordance with details furnished by the chief defendant Otto Ohlendorf, to help remind the court

'The Murderers among Us' 33

of the chain of command within this complex hierarchy, although matters were further complicated as some defendants, such as *Brigadeführer* Otto Rasch, moved between Einsatzgruppen during the war. The Ulm trial, by contrast, was concerned with the activities of just a single unit and, while the prosecution was keen to outline the extent of the Nazi machinery for mass murder, this narrower focus may have made it easier for lay observers to follow the course of the proceedings and come to a better understanding of the crimes under discussion.

Secondly, the Ulm case may have produced a greater popular resonance owing to the type of men who were appearing in the dock. The Nuremberg trial involved defendants drawn predominantly from the upper echelons of the Einsatzgruppen hierarchy, thus facilitating early post-war mythologies that placed the blame for Nazi crimes firmly on those at the top.[9] The ten men tried at Ulm, however, included only four who had held an SS rank; the remainder included a commissar with the Gestapo, a Lithuanian national and various police personnel. While the defence continued to place responsibility on superior officers through an emphasis on 'orders from above', the realisation that seemingly 'ordinary' men were involved in such crimes had a significant impact upon observers and raised questions about the number of other former murderers who remained undetected among the West German population.

Thirdly, the real value of the Ulm trial rested in the fact that it was a West German court now speaking about these crimes. The prosecution of Einsatzkommando personnel could no longer be dismissed as victors' justice; the Ulm court possessed greater legitimacy in the eyes of 'ordinary' Germans, leaving little doubt that such crimes really had happened and now merited judicial action. The Coburg-based *Neue Presse* underscored this argument, ruefully noting at the time:

> When most of us were first acquainted with the terrible atrocities that were for years committed in concentration camps in the middle of Germany . . . they seemed incredible to us. Unfortunately, it was enemy soldiers and offices that had to show us the crimes which were committed by our government in our name. Today, no one can say anymore: "I don't believe all that!" Today the executioners and murders . . . are judged before German courts. German judges attempt to judge crimes of a satanic regime with the standards of democracy.[10]

Finally, it is striking that the Ulm trial was taking place in a very different atmosphere to the Nuremberg proceedings against Ohlendorf *et al*. The intervening years between the collapse of the Third Reich and the opening of the Ulm trial had given the West German people time to dwell on their own war losses, lick their wounds and rebuild their shattered lives. The rubble from the bombed-out cities had been cleared away, homes had been rebuilt and the last of the refugee camps had been closed—as exemplified by Fischer-Schweder's attempt to re-enter society. The Federal Republic was starting to reap the benefits of the 'economic miracle' and the West German people themselves appeared to be in better physical shape, not least now the food shortages that had characterised the late 1940s had been alleviated.[11] Put simply, the immediate post-war period had come to an end. The worst effects of the conflict were over, the pressing needs for reconstruction had been sated and greater temporal distance from the events in question helped to create a climate in which it became 'easier' to reflect on the suffering that the National Socialist regime had wreaked upon other peoples. In this climate, the rhetoric of the 'murderers among us' and the desire to attend to the question of the remaining Nazi criminals gradually became more attractive.

Over the years, the Ulm trial has remained a common point of reference among historians attempting to trace changing West German attitudes to the Nazi past. For some, Ulm's importance rests in the very nature of the crimes being dealt with by the court. While the various Allied proceedings had treated the Holocaust as just one of many criminal acts perpetrated by the Nazis, while also placing a greater emphasis on the western concentration camps liberated by Britain and the United States, Ulm shifted the spotlight to those crimes committed in Eastern Europe and exposed some glaring gaps within war crimes prosecutions to date. Adalbert Rückerl argues:

> The wide-ranging and meticulous investigations set in motion by his [Fischer-Schweder's] arrest and culminating in the 'Ulm Operational Unit Trial' revealed beyond doubt that many of the gravest Nazi crimes, most notably those perpetrated in the East, had not yet been punished at all.[12]

Hermann Langbein, meanwhile, underscores the educational impact of the Ulm case, emphasising how the prosecution's excellent documentation of the crimes meant that the court not only dealt with individual episodes, but also set out the whole organisational system and bureaucratic nature of the killings.[13] Jean-Paul Bier argues that the Ulm trial constituted a 'moral blow' for the West German people as it revealed how Nazi genocide could no longer be portrayed in terms of individual crimes, the actions of a radical few, but had to be seen within the wider framework of a large-scale machinery specifically designed to commit systematic mass murder.[14] Having described a series of war crimes trials that were conducted in West Germany after 1945, Ulrich Brochhagen likewise concludes that it was the Ulm trial 'above all' that succeeded in stirring up popular emotions in the Federal Republic.[15]

Ultimately, the real importance of the Ulm trial lay in the fact that it gave rise to a new judicial impetus. The unmasking of ten former members of the Einsatzkommando Tilsit at the end of the 1950s highlighted the need

'The Murderers among Us' 35

for stronger action in bringing more war criminals to account and consequently fostered a brand new series of war crimes proceedings. These new prosecutions, in turn, 'made a major contribution to the public and historical knowledge of the Nazi camps'.[16] Gorzkowska and Zakowska argue that the Ulm trial constituted a 'watershed' in the history of West Germany's prosecution of Nazi crimes, with the trial highlighting how the actions of the defendants were not an aberration, but part of a general policy of extermination that would be practised across Nazi-occupied Europe.[17] However, despite all this praise that has been heaped upon the Ulm trial, there has, to date, been little attempt to analyse the impact of this case in detail. Closer investigation suggests that the resonance of the Ulm proceedings was not quite so straightforward.

MEDIA INTEREST IN THE ULM TRIAL

The Ulm trial certainly provoked a large degree of excitement within the West German media. Although the first day of the trial received relatively little coverage, the rest of the proceedings were reported faithfully in the national press, with most publications granting the case at least one substantial paragraph.[18] There was a keen awareness that this was not the only such trial to be taking place, with regular references being made to the prosecution of the former Buchenwald guard Martin Sommer then underway in Bayreuth. Witness testimonies were reproduced extensively, describing the actions of the Einsatzkommando in all their gory detail, and the use of emotive language was common. Although the Einsatzkommando had initially limited itself to the mass shooting of adult male Jews and Communists (it was not until a month after the invasion of the Soviet Union that the elderly, women and children were termed 'useless eaters' and also rendered a target for the Einsatzgruppen), tales of female victims being forced to watch as their children were murdered in front of them quickly became a trope of West German media reporting on the Ulm case. The *Stuttgarter Nachrichten* was clearly outraged as it stressed how the victims of the Einsatzkommando Tilsit had consisted of 'men, *women and children*—one must say it twice—men, *women and children*'.[19]

However, despite the sensationalist nature of the trial coverage, the case did not become front page news until the final sentences were handed down four months later in August 1958. The court's rejection of the life sentences envisaged by the prosecution in favour of prison terms ranging from just three to fifteen years created a scandal, with a number of damning editorials produced on the subject. The *Bild-Zeitung am Abend* was typical, noting that three of the Ulm defendants had been able to go straight home after the trial as the court took into account the length of time served in custody while awaiting trial: 'They now sit again anywhere in West Germany at a desk and boast about their deeds'.[20]

Indeed, it proved to be the defendants, rather than their victims, who commanded the majority of media attention. Initial press reports struggled to get past the unnerving discrepancy between the details of the violent atrocities perpetrated by the Einsatzkommando Tilsit and the apparent 'normality' of the men who now stood before the Ulm court. At the start of the proceedings, the *Frankfurter Rundschau* remarked how the accused seemed to be 'more or less harmless-looking men' drawn from the ranks of the educated middle classes.[21] Similarly, the *Süddeutsche Zeitung*, comparing the charges listed in the indictment to the sight of the grey-haired or balding middle-aged defendants, declared 'their faces do not fit their crimes'.[22] It was a cry similar to that which would be expounded at the start of the 1961 Adolf Eichmann trial in Jerusalem, popularised by Hannah Arendt, of the 'banality of evil'.

Many newspapers nonetheless sought to reinforce the notion that these figures were somehow distinct from the rest of the West German and, indeed, human population. Terms such as 'bestial' or 'devils' were regularly employed to characterise the accused and some publications resorted to animal imagery to dehumanise the defendants; *Die Welt* likened the physique of chief defendant Bernhard Fischer-Schweder to that of a gorilla.[23] Such descriptions can be traced back to the media handling of the Allied war crimes proceedings which had branded concentration camp figures such as Josef Kramer and Ilse Koch as the 'Beast of Belsen' and 'Bitch of Buchenwald', respectively. There was thus a continuity in the language assigned to describe Nazi war crimes as the demonic discourse that had circulated within popular representations of Nazi war criminals since the end of the Second World War made itself felt within the West German coverage of the Ulm trial, accompanied by a continuing sense of shock, dismay and incredulity when the defendants appearing in the dock were shown to resemble the 'ordinary men' described by later historians.

Finding 'monstrous' aspects of the Ulm defendants' physical appearance mostly lacking, however, many West German newspapers resorted to highlighting the peculiarly calm and detached demeanour of the accused in the face of horrific witness testimony, thereby presenting them as devoid of basic human feelings—and again, by implication, as having little in common with 'ordinary' people. There was also an effort to contrast the wartime behaviour of concentration camp and Einsatzkommando killers with that of the honourable and courageous German soldier fighting valiantly for his country. The *Neue Presse* drew upon this theme as it took issue with the various excuses set forth by the Ulm defendants in an effort to explain their participation in Nazi crimes:

> They speak entirely of their so-called duty. They had to follow orders—as far as they had not given the orders for the mass shootings themselves. In these cases, they follow their old language: of inferior human material and potential enemies, [and that] the 'extermination' was their

'The Murderers among Us' 37

duty to the Fatherland. . . . They pretend to be soldiers. It has long been clear that these men were no soldiers but common murderers.[24]

Nonetheless, there were some elements within the West German media who did recognise the need to initiate a more critical engagement with the recent past. A series of passionate editorials strenuously denounced Nazi crimes and hailed the Ulm proceedings as a welcome educational process. Some questioned the number of war criminals or collaborators who remained in public life, attacking the judiciary's prosecution record to date. The *Stuttgarter Nachrichten* commented, 'We have seen all too often that our German lawyers are all too cautious in their treatment of the crimes of the Third Reich' and concluded that such failings, together with the leniency of the Ulm sentences, 'increase our red-faced shame and have destroyed much of the confidence that the Federal Republic has been trying to cultivate in the world'.[25]

An analysis of the press coverage relating to the 1958 Ulm Einsatzkommando trial thus reveals two main responses running through the reports. On the one hand, there remained attempts to distinguish between the brutal figures now sitting in the dock and the rest of the West German population. On the other hand, there was also a clear determination within many publications to condemn the atrocities described during the Ulm trial and to be seen as actively engaging with the problematic legacy of the Nazi regime. There was a growing awareness that little had been done to tackle this subject in the thirteen intervening years since the end of the war and, in particular, in the nine years since the foundation of the Federal Republic itself. The majority of the West German population were still held to be ignorant of the details surrounding the Nazi genocide, while many former participants in the crimes remained undetected and unpunished. The Ulm trial was thus presented as providing an urgent wake-up call, forcing the population into a confrontation with what the *Düsseldorfer Nachrichten*— amongst other publications—termed 'the darkest chapter of our history'.[26] That such a confrontation was, indeed, now occurring among the ordinary population was seemingly taken for granted.

PUBLIC RESPONSES TO THE ULM TRIAL

It would be easy to take the moralising rhetoric expounded by the press as evidence of the sentiments shared by the wider West German population and to see, in quite an uncomplicated manner, the Ulm trial as marking an important shift in public attitudes to the Nazi past. While the sheer scale of press reports published on the Ulm case would suggest that the proceedings were indeed regarded as an important event across the Federal Republic, it remains questionable as to how far such media interest translated into personal interest for the proverbial 'man on the street'. At the end of the proceedings, the *Jewish Chronicle*, while pleased at the judicial condemnation of the crimes, reflected that 'unfortunately there are other voices in Germany than that of the President of the court at Ulm'.[27] The British Consulate General in nearby Stuttgart, Robert G. Dundas, stressed the need to view public opinion against a background of a 'strong latent guilt complex' and a continuing fervent desire to assign all the blame for the crimes on 'National Socialism in general, and Hitler in particular'.[28] Officials at the British Embassy in Bonn likewise conceded:

> It is difficult to gauge the effect of these and other trials of Nazi criminals on ordinary Germans. The fact that the trials are carried out by German courts in a fair and impartial manner undoubtedly gives the verdicts more validity in German eyes than those of the Allied war crimes trials. From this, one would be inclined to deduce that, coming thirteen years after the end of the war, and even longer after the commission of the crimes themselves, and resulting from German prosecutions under German law . . . these trials would draw attention to the horror and enormity of the crimes to which, under Hitler, Germans lent themselves and would impress the German mind—and to some extent they must have this effect. But the reaction of most Germans seems, as far as one can judge, to be one of personal dissociation, as much as to say: 'whoever committed such crimes, it was not I, nor the Germans I knew and was brought up with'. This superficial facility for self-exculpation may not, however, reflect all that goes on in their minds and there is evidence that the younger generation are very critical of the behaviour of the Nazi Party and in many cases eager to see justice done.[29]

One of the most interesting insights into popular West German responses to the Ulm Einsatzkommando trial comes in the form of a special opinion survey conducted by the local newspaper, the *Schwäbische Donau-Zeitung*, in the immediate aftermath of the proceedings in September 1958. The newspaper polled local people of all ages and from all walks of life on how they had viewed the case and how they now regarded the final sentencing that had been passed down upon the ten former members of the Tilsit Einsatzkommando. Introducing the intentions behind the survey, the paper declared:

> The language of the Ulm court has caused a sensation in the whole German public. Most newspapers carry the sentence on the first page of their Saturday editions. This trial, once again, was the topic of conversation at the weekend for politically-interested citizens. We have attempted to explore through a poll, propagated by ourselves, the opinion of the men on the street. . . . We established, with satisfaction, that nearly all of our compatriots answered very candidly on both

questions: 'Do you think the Ulm trial is necessary and important?' and 'Do you think the sentence is just?' A considerable number of those questioned had followed the trial closely, admittedly predominantly through newspaper reports.[30]

The use of opinion poll data as an historical source is not without its problems. In this particular instance, the size of the survey conducted by the *Schwäbische Donau-Zeitung* was relatively small, with just thirty-eight responses printed in the newspaper. Four of these actually came from former victims of National Socialism, people who had been persecuted by the regime as political opponents or as Jews and who thus had a very personal reason for wishing to engage with Nazi war crimes trials. The language employed by the newspaper when conducting its survey may also have guided responses. Having set out to determine whether locals felt the trial was 'necessary' and 'important', it is telling that many interviewees drew upon exactly the same words when giving their replies. The extent to which they genuinely believed in the need for the trial, or were merely giving what they perceived to be the 'correct' answer, is unclear.

Nevertheless, this survey does shed some valuable light on the trial's impact within the local community and the subsequent reporting of the results in the local newspaper made it part of an even wider public discourse. The *Schwäbische Donau-Zeitung* admitted that it had granted its interviewees anonymity, enabling them to speak quite candidly. The fact that the newspaper felt obliged to make this promise in the first place, though, implies that there was still a widespread reluctance among the West German population to talk about the Nazi era, or at least give vent to their personal feelings on this issue within the public sphere. With the newspaper's guarantee of 'complete discretion', the residents of Ulm may have been more willing to speak unguarded, secure in the knowledge that no one could turn around and criticise them for their comments. The newspaper did confess to omitting those comments which were fiercely critical of the Einsatzkommando trial, but stressed such statements were rare and hardly representative of opinions held by the rest of the local community.[31]

An examination of the results gleaned by the *Schwäbische Donau-Zeitung* suggests three key categories of responses. Firstly, there were those who clearly recognised the need to address the past and the necessity of continuing to prosecute any remaining war criminals. Such persons showed themselves to have been following the Ulm trial fairly closely, often drawing upon the language of demonism running through the press coverage as they referred to the defendants as 'monsters' or 'devils'. These people could usually volunteer extra information about the particulars of the Einsatzkommando case, including the ability to name at least one of the defendants, relay elements of witness testimony or offer a critique of the final sentencing in view of what had been disclosed during the course of the trial. A 58 year old dentist questioned by the newspaper proved typical in this respect:

40 *West Germans and the Nazi Legacy*

> The trial had to take place. . . . Regarding the sentence, I am of the opinion that the main criminals are coming away too well with fifteen years imprisonment. That the defendant Lukys, for example, has only been given seven years imprisonment had disappointed me somewhat.[32]

Many of these people also appeared to have a degree of emotional investment in the trial. A 31 year old office worker displayed signs of having reflected soberly, with some empathy, upon the fate of the victims of the Third Reich:

> The necessity of these trials stands without doubt. What the accused did to women and children one can only begin to estimate correctly if one has a family himself. I therefore find the sentences very mild. I had expected 'life' for the main accused.[33]

This statement echoes that issued previously by the *Stuttgarter Nachrichten*, imbued with a sense of shock that women and children could have been subjected to such atrocities. Yet while the killing of women and children held a certain emotive power for the media and members of the public, the fate of Jewish men was once again allowed to pass without comment.

Secondly, the *Schwäbische Donau-Zeitung* encountered a group of people who readily agreed with the need for continued war crimes trials, but did not appear to have taken the same level of interest in the Ulm hearings as those falling into the first category. These people, having swiftly confirmed their support for such proceedings, were unable to provide any further details on the case recently conducted upon their own doorstep. A 24 year old clerical worker stated simply that 'such trials have to be carried out; one cannot simply let them fall under the table. I regard the sentence as just'.[34]

Such respondents appeared to accept whatever was happening around them, automatically agreeing with the assumption implicit within the *Schwäbische Donau-Zeitung*'s questions and readily concurring with the custodial results of the Ulm proceedings, without actually questioning whether the prison terms handed down by the court really did fit the crimes concerned. A 33 year old head teacher told the newspaper that 'the proceedings were carried out objectively, the sentence is just'—a comment that made an implicit contrast between this trial and the earlier war crimes proceedings conducted by the Allies, apparently drawing some level of comfort from the fact that at least it was the West German authorities who were now dealing with these matters.[35]

Finally, the *Schwäbische Donau-Zeitung* also uncovered a minority of people who remained opposed to the prospect of continuing war crimes trials so long after the commission of the atrocities in question. A 66 year old widow was among those questioning the wisdom of such proceedings:

'The Murderers among Us' 41

It is difficult to reconstruct the situation of that time after so many years. I have seen a series of such trials in the post-war years, for example in Penzberg and Munich. Many witnesses are too old and not many of them are wholly sensible. Also, the levels of punishment allow dispute. There are too many political prisoners who have received life and have much less human life on their conscience. They perceive their unjust sentence and ask: 'Why have we received life?' I am of the opinion that the people in command of the state at that time have been dealt with, for the orders all came from above. Insubordination at that time meant risking one's own life.[36]

Despite her assertion that all the really guilty people had now been dealt with, this woman proved unusual, as someone who had apparently gone out of her way to observe a number of different war crimes proceedings, exercising some interest in the legacy of the Nazi past. As her response indicates, though, there remained a desire, at least among some sections of the local Ulm population, to continue to place the blame for the crimes of the Third Reich firmly upon the shoulders of the Nazi leadership rather than admit any notions of wider guilt and responsibility.

Those opposing further war crimes trials also sought to relativise the crimes committed by the National Socialist regime and accentuate German suffering. A tourist from West Berlin was typical:

I think that a line should now finally be made under these things—and not only among us. I think the sentence was just as a deterrent—provided that each murder really did happen. In addition, I am of the opinion that we should be careful with such sentences as long as the Russians, who after their invasion in the East administered and treated us in a bestial manner, and each American who exterminated innocent lives in Hiroshima and Dresden are not similarly punished before a court.[37]

The proportion of the survey participants who fell into each of these three main categories is illustrated in the graph below. The data gleaned by the *Schwäbische Donau-Zeitung* suggests that responses cut across generational divides, particularly with regards to the sentencing of the accused. Older people born towards the end of the nineteenth century (and who thus had experience of political traditions other than Nazism) were just as likely to proclaim that the Ulm defendants 'deserve much harsher punishment', while not all members of the younger generation seemed especially inclined to explore the recent past. The *Schwäbische Donau-Zeitung* noted:

The attitude of the younger people questioned, many of whom were not in the position to express a particular view [of the trial] was remarkable—they maintained that trial did not interest them, or had no more mental images of the era of the Second World War.[38]

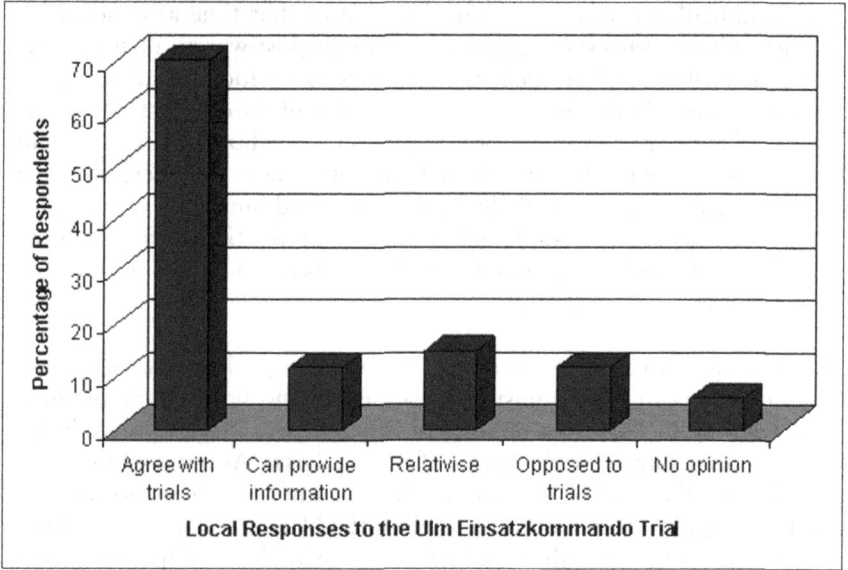

Figure 2.1 Graph showing broad responses to the Ulm Einsatzkommando trial, 1958.

Data sourced from 'Sühne für tausendfachen Mord' im Urteil des Volkes', *Schwäbische Donau-Zeitung*, September 1, 1958.

It was a conclusion backed up in a comment made by a 20 year old student who contrasted the revelations emerging from the Ulm courtroom with a lack of available historical information for those born towards the end of the Nazi regime:

> I knew the events of the war and Nazi era only from stories and dark childhood memories—I don't permit any judgement on whether such trials are necessary. I think the sentence is very mild compared with the usual punishments for murderers.[39]

These findings create a rather more complicated impression of West German responses than the assessments offered at the time by staff at the British Embassy in Bonn which declared 'the younger generation are very critical of the behaviour of the Nazi Party and in many cases eager to see justice done'.[40]

The gender of those surveyed by the *Schwäbische Donau-Zeitung* did not appear to be an issue either when discussing the merits of war crimes trials. However, while some people viewed the Ulm trial as shattering some of the silences surrounding the Nazi past, others—and especially the female interviewees—seized the opportunity to reflect upon their own war losses, giving their personal suffering precedence over the revelations then emerging from the Ulm courtroom concerning the fate of unknown Jews in the Baltic States. A 45 year old housewife confessed:

> I have not followed this trial with full attention so as not to be reminded again of the sorrowful time of expulsion from the homeland in the East. Is there any atonement at all in this world for the terrors that happened on all sides of the war?[41]

Another woman pointed out how 'many old people have lost their house, home and children and today have to live sparsely in a rented place' and contrasted the brutal behaviour of the Ulm defendants with the fate of her 'innocent' son who was killed on the battlefield aged just 21.[42] The ideal of the honourable fallen German soldier thus came to the fore once again. Indeed, it is worth noting that wider events during the summer of 1958 perhaps facilitated such thinking. The British Consulate in Stuttgart recorded that, shortly after the Ulm case, the Federal Republic's newly formed army began practice manoeuvres that were watched by 'thousands' of people. There were also reunions at this time for former members of both the Stalheim (the group of ex-servicemen who had played a prominent role in the politics of the 1920s and were subsumed into the SA following Hitler's rise to power in 1933) and the Desert Foxes, who had been part of Field Marshall Rommel's *Afrika Korps* during the Second World War.[43] These reunions provided an interesting juxtaposition with the war crimes proceedings in Ulm and can be seen as occasions which further emphasised the glory of the German soldier, while depicting him as having nothing to do with the crimes committed in Eastern Europe. It is not, perhaps, therefore surprising that some of the residents of Ulm continued to stress a distinction between the Wehrmacht and the Einsatzgruppen.

Further evasions and distortions emerged among the residents of Ulm when it came to discussing the nature of the accused themselves, with much debate as to how they could have brought themselves to commit acts of mass murder. Participants in the opinion survey frequently drew upon the demonic characterisations of the defendants that had been popularised in the West German press, suggesting that there was a fundamental flaw within the defendants' personalities that prompted them to lend themselves to the crimes of the Third Reich. Other respondents touched upon the sort of apologia normally utilised by the defence counsels during war crimes trials, emphasising the unusual circumstances and pressures of the war situation, the power of Nazi ideology and, of course, the need to follow orders for fear of serious reprisals. A 36 year old man argued:

> According to the criminal law, it is correct to recognise complicity in murder and not murder. In my view, however, the punishments of fifteen, ten, four and three years imprisonment are too short. The desire to murder

had to exist in the accused. . . . Under other circumstances no human in such a position would organise or participate in drinking with the victims' money after executing such atrocities. The trial clearly showed that ice cold and calculating people sat in the dock, whose repentant closing words stood in strange contrast to their behaviour during the proceedings, appearing exclusively to demand the leniency of the court.[44]

Even those local citizens, therefore, who did recognise the need for continued war crimes trials and who had been paying close attention to the course of these particular hearings, were not immune from imposing a sense of distance between those on trial and the wider West German population. A 39 year old mechanic elaborated further on this theme, stressing how the real guilt lay with the Nazi leadership and seemingly taking some comfort from the fact that, as illustrated with the defendant Lukys, Lithuanians had also participated in the commission of crimes—a factor that would help counter the idea that the Holocaust had been a peculiarly German crime:

> I found the whole trial extremely problematic. The accused, in my opinion, could not be put on a stage with common murderers. The particularly guilty are Hitler and Himmler, as the comments in the sentencing made clear. What happened at that time, sixteen or seventeen years ago, is horrible and can and must not be glossed over. But even after so long a time, it is difficult to go back to that time. It further appears that the Lithuanians joined in with all these murders with enthusiasm.[45]

Similarly, a 50 year old housewife insisted:

> One has to consider that it was the war at the time of these crimes and a general chaos prevailed. Standards were lost. Nevertheless, these crimes have to be judged.[46]

A 21 year old student also stressed the effect of the prevailing moral climate when trying to account for the crimes of the Einsatzkommando Tilsit and pointed to a long history of violence against the Jews. These comments can be seen as an attempt to show how such anti-Semitism was far from unique to Nazism or, indeed, to Germany itself:

> The accused were stuck in the middle of this whole spirit and perhaps felt the way in which they behaved was nothing criminal. With the Jewish persecutions in the Middle Ages, one also believed they were providing a service to God. Nevertheless, the accused are responsible for their crimes, the scale of the punishment measures is therefore, in my opinion, just.[47]

The impact of Nazi propaganda and ideology on the defendants' ability to reconcile themselves to committing such crimes was stressed by a 39 year old secretary:

'The Murderers among Us' 45

The State's demands at the time were placed above one's own conscience and individual human lives. The fanatical belief in the German master race was already manifest at the time in flesh and blood for the wide majority of the people so, to the accused, there was nothing at all illegal with the whole scope of their behaviour. We always hold that people at that time did not just act according to orders or in deadly obedience, but simply went along with it.[48]

A 32 year old housewife also began by declaring her support for continued war crimes trials, before again stressing the effects of the war situation and displaying her concern for the impact the Ulm trial could have on the reputation of the Federal Republic before the rest of the world. Suddenly going against her opening statement, the woman argued that the very continuance of Nazi war crimes trials, staged so long after the end of the war, would become a cause for ridicule from other nations:

> This trial was necessary, even important, and I can only regret that we Germans always cite the weakness before all the world of our 'dirtying of the nest'. . . . These shootings certainly resulted from the compulsion of the war situation and therefore do not have to be convicted as a criminal offence. A war is always terrible and events in it usually remain hanging over the defeated. For this reason, I think that the sentence is unjust. After so many years have slipped away, one may not sentence the accused to life imprisonment. Our friends at home and abroad will laugh.[49]

The results of the opinion survey conducted by the *Schwäbische Donau-Zeitung* thus underline the extent to which earlier post-war interpretations of National Socialism—interpretations that focussed extensively on German war losses while imposing a sense of distance between the perpetrators of the Nazi genocide and the "ordinary" population and stressing the climate of fear, terror and ideological fanaticism that rendered such crimes possible—continued to circulate freely amongst the West German population in the late 1950s. At the same time, though, there were members of the local community who were prepared to engage more critically with the legacy of the recent past. A 24 year old student noted that 'in the course of the trials there are, indeed, often loud voices that one should not always tear open the old wounds anew, but I don't think this view is representative'.[50] Similarly, a 40 year old farmer noted:

> This trial was certainly necessary, otherwise one doesn't know if there is still a justice. Crimes of such a scale may not be limited and if some think it could be harmful to the German reputation if these disgraceful deeds were dug up after seventeen years, then I cannot agree with this point of view. Even the honest and factual treatment of the

shooting of the Jews before the court has to show the world that we want to engage with the dark chapter of our past. I personally think that people who deny the necessity of these trials are suspect, that they want to cheapen the crimes committed or at least gloss over them. I think the sentence is just.[51]

In addition, there was some awareness among the citizens of Ulm of the need to accept a wider level of responsibility for the crimes of the Third Reich, rather than placing the onus solely on those at the highest levels of the regime. One of those questioned by the *Schwäbische Donau-Zeitung* happened to be the wife of one of the jurors on the Ulm case. Unsurprisingly, this woman had paid a great deal of attention to the proceedings and was able to speak at some length about them. Her statement rejected firmly any notion of using the peculiar climate of the Second World War as a means for attempting to justify the behaviour of the accused:

We were all complicit in every year of the events and should all do compensation for the past and do away with hate and bitterness, otherwise there is no new and better future for us. One cannot compare the atrocities of that time with the events of war.[52]

The Ulm Einsatzkommando trial did, therefore, evoke a wide spectrum of opinion. The British Consulate General in Stuttgart noted that while 'most intelligent' people agreed on the continuing need for war crimes trials in order to confront the Nazi past, some of the more 'pusillanimous' simply preferred to close their eyes to the whole affair and refused to read anything that was written about it in the press.[53] In the main, though, the Ulm trial did at least succeed in getting some of the West German population thinking about the crimes of the Third Reich again. The British Embassy in Bonn reported that 'these cases have aroused a revulsion in many German minds, which have tended to forget the post-war Allied tribunals or to regret these as prejudiced, and a suspicion that other criminals of this type may still be at large in Germany'.[54] Indeed, it was this latter suspicion that would help ensure the Ulm trial's lasting effect within West Germany.

THE LEGACY OF THE ULM TRIAL

One of the gravest concerns to be voiced in West Germany in relation to the Ulm trial surrounded the fact that men like chief defendant Bernhard Fischer-Schweder had managed to remain undetected for so long in the Federal Republic, and even enjoy prominent and well-respected positions in the community.[55] Such concerns fuelled the popular concept of 'the murderers among us' and Dick de Mildt argues that it is in this connection that the real impact of the 1958 Einsatzkommando trial can be seen, for, 'at one

'The Murderers among Us' 47

stroke, the Ulm trial painfully brought to light the poor quality of Germany's dealing with its past crimes, particularly with regard to their prosecution'.[56] Likewise, Peter Steinbach sees the Ulm case as helping to create the impression that many other Nazi criminals were still living securely among the West German population and convincing politicians and civilians alike of the need for an urgent, systematic examination of all Nazi crimes in order to take remedial action.[57]

One of the more concrete results of the 1958 Ulm Einsatzkommando trial thus saw the establishment of the *Zentrale Stelle der Landesjustizverwaltungen zur Aufklärung nationalsozialistischer Verbrechen* (Central Agency for the Prosecution of Nazi Crimes) in nearby Ludwigsburg on 1 December 1958. It was headed by Dr. Erwin Schüle, the chief prosecutor in the Ulm case. The creation of the Ludwigsburg Zentralstelle was the subject of some disquiet within West Germany, with many questioning the logic of implementing what was widely seen as another denazification process. The *Trierischer Volksfreund* addressed these concerns and took issue with those members of the population who continued to hope that a rapid end could be brought to war crimes trials:

> One at once objected that a systematic investigation of accusations of our past crimes would produce an endless unrest among the population. But one can only draw a line under the past if one can say, with some confidence, that all, or at least the predominant part, of the concentration camp criminals are punished.[58]

The creation of the Ludwigsburg Zentralstelle was of vital importance in sparking a whole new series of investigations and arrests and launching more co-ordinated and active research into Nazi crimes that paved the way for the trials which would dominate much of the 1960s. Adalbert Rückerl, himself a former head of this organisation, argues that its very structure produced an almost complete reversal of the former procedure adopted in the prosecution of Nazi crimes. Investigations were no longer only set in motion from chance information about a suspect; instead 'certain pointers to a crime still liable to prosecution triggered preliminary proceedings against a person or persons unknown or not yet traced'.[59] By the end of 1964, six years after its foundation, the Agency had conducted a total of 701 enquiries.[60]

In addition to these legal developments, the trial's resonance continued to be felt for some time within local commemorative culture. The revelations that had emerged about the fate of the Jews in Eastern Europe generated a significant degree of interest in the history of Ulm's own Jewish community. The town had been a centre of Jewish life since the Middle Ages and, most famously, was the birthplace of the Jewish scientist Albert Einstein. One of the most interesting examples of the legacy of the Ulm trial can subsequently be seen in the form of a special book entitled *Documents*

Relative to the Persecution of the Jewish Citizens of Ulm/Danube which was compiled in 1959. Tracing the history of the Jews in Ulm from the Middle Ages through to the end of the Second World War, the book noted the prominent role that many of them had been able to play within the local government during the nineteenth century and how eighteen Jewish residents of the town had been among those killed in action during the First World War. The volume also listed all Jews resident in Ulm in January 1933, detailing their full names, dates of birth, addresses and professions. In this way, the book restored some sense of individuality to the otherwise anonymous statistics of Holocaust victims. Finally, it proceeded to list the date and destination of each Jewish inhabitant during the deportations of 1941–3.[61]

Altogether, this book served to create a rather rose-tinted image of local Jewish/non-Jewish relations prior to Hitler's rise to power. There remained silences over the identities of the perpetrators who had subsequently committed the crimes against the Jews, as well as over the rise of National Socialism in the first place. Nazism was presented as something of an alien movement, a force imposed from the outside which had little to do with the inhabitants of Ulm themselves. Having spent several pages citing examples of local Jews, including Einstein, the book stated:

> Just a few of the aforementioned examples show how very assimilated the Jewish population was within our town. The biggest part by far was middle class and had suffered under the difficult economic burdens of the post-war years just as badly as the non-Jewish citizens. Numerous Jewish personalities had established their place in the intellectual and cultural, as well as scientific, life of our town. They were just as connected with their home town as every other non-Jewish citizen. If the Jewish population was already being attacked during the beginnings of the National Socialist 'movement', one could nevertheless say that for Ulm all these attacks had only a slight influence on the majority of the [local] population. But others very quickly aligned themselves with Hitler's growing power.[62]

Copies of the book were presented to every student leaving school in the area, although the Christian-Jewish journal *Common Ground* did point out that it might have been better to issue the volume at the start of the school year when it could have been followed up with a classroom discussion of the Third Reich and the Holocaust, rather than at the end of term.[63] It is, indeed, questionable as to how many youngsters, excited at the prospect of leaving their schooldays behind them, would have been prepared to engage with such a book at this stage in their lives. Despite these limitations, though, there was hope that the book would prove an important aid in fostering further understanding about the Nazi past. Penning the introduction to the work, the mayor of Ulm stated:

'The Murderers among Us' 49

The history of every nation has its bright side and its shadows. Perhaps the deepest shadows are to be found in that chapter of German history which recounts the persecution of the Jews in the years 1933 to 1945. What was done then by a criminal regime cannot be compensated. More and more opinions are voiced that one should not stir up the past, that one should turn one's back on the injustice and horror. But the voice that warns against forgetfulness of this heavy guilt, no less than of the misery, tears and blood of the victims, should not go unheard. By this carefully produced documentation concerning its own boundaries, Ulm desires to contribute to the illumination of the past, to confess the wrong it has committed and to warn future generations so that such events cannot happen again.[64]

The language employed by the mayor in this opening section is revealing in itself, referring as it does to a 'criminal regime'. In contrast to wide attempts to continue placing the blame on a radical few, this book offers an implicit acceptance of a wider level of guilt and responsibility for Nazi crimes as it condemns an entire political system.

Further reflection on the crimes of the Third Reich came with an epilogue produced by the volume's editor, Heinz Keil, which stated:

With the end of the war in 1945, we were faced with a tragic reckoning. 332 out of the 530 Jews of Ulm had successfully emigrated. The remainder who could not emigrate were, for the most part, murdered in the concentration camps. This shows how a people can vote for a system of government which abuses people and civil rights and produces terror and horrors. The youth who did not live through this time should address this theme coolly and soberly.

This documentation should therefore help connect with the facts and heavy sorrow that rests behind the fate of all those persecuted. . . . The persecution of the Jews in Ulm has to be seen in connection with the whole of the National Socialist measures against the Jewish population. Only then can an accurate picture of these events be created.

This documentation should also make clear how necessary it is to fight against the remnants—and new forms—of anti-Semitism. . . . Only with the greatest love for the truth and the most rigorous struggle against anti-Semitism can one hope to overcome the past.[65]

* * * * * * * *

The example of the 1958 Ulm Einsatzkommando trial therefore illustrates how earlier post-war myths centring upon German experiences of the Third Reich and a general reluctance to address the recent past did not disappear overnight. Many people still needed some convincing of the necessity for continued war crimes trials so long after the end of the war, and there remained a tendency to render the Nazi perpetrators distinct from the rest of the population. At the same time, though, a counter memory was starting to gain momentum. There were people prepared to ask more awkward questions, to delve deeper into their own town's recent activities and to start to address that "darkest chapter" of German history more critically.

The impact of the Ulm Einsatzkommando trial may have been exaggerated by historians over the years and there is a need, as this chapter has demonstrated, to go beyond a purely celebratory depiction of the Ulm trial and to start taking into account the presence of evasions, silences and distortions that persisted during this period. Nevertheless, the Ulm case played an important role in promoting a more critical West German engagement with the Nazi past as it disseminated more information about the crimes committed in Eastern Europe. Perhaps its greatest achievement, though, rested in the establishment of the Ludwigsburg Zentralstelle, staffed by a body of West German men and women determined to bring remaining war criminals to justice. Although it provoked some initial discomfort from members of the 'ordinary' population, this agency ensured that the Ulm trial would not remain a flash in the pan, an isolated judicial event which would be quickly forgotten, but instead marked the starting point for a brand new series of West German war crimes proceedings staged all across the Federal Republic of Germany, offering continuous opportunities for education and confrontation with the Nazi past throughout the 1960s.

3 Recalling Resistance

While the Ulm Einsatzkommando proceedings bequeathed an important legal legacy for the investigation of Nazi atrocities, it is fair to say that the trial itself was overshadowed at the time by another war crimes hearing taking place concurrently in Bayreuth. The prosecution of 42 year old former SS-*Hauptscharführer* Martin Sommer generated worldwide interest as he received a life prison sentence for twenty-five specimen counts of murder perpetrated in Buchenwald concentration camp between 1937 and 1943. The gruesome details of his acts of torture, combined with the peculiarly unruffled demeanour of his loyal, and much younger, wife, transformed this case into something of a thrilling soap opera, enabling it to capture the public imagination and arouse indignation among members of the local community. While the Ulm public gallery remained relatively empty, crowds were routinely jostling for space inside the Bayreuth Landgericht.

In part, the contrasting receptions afforded to these trials can be explained by the manner in which these proceedings were conducted, with the Ulm hearings dominated by debate on complex legal issues and the submission of documents, while the Sommer case placed a greater emphasis on the use of survivor testimony, restoring a human face to the victims of the Third Reich and imbuing the courthouse with an emotionally charged atmosphere. 'Here', concluded the *Schwäbische Donau-Zeitung*, 'one scented sensations; here it smelt of blood'.[1]

Moreover, while Ulm concerned itself with the mass shootings of Jews and Poles in Eastern Europe—actions perpetrated against unknown victims in unfamiliar, faraway places whose names held little currency within the popular West German consciousness—the Bayreuth proceedings dealt with crimes committed much closer to home, and largely against German political prisoners. Rather than challenging pre-existing patterns of remembrance, the trial thus became a medium for recalling acts of resistance against the Nazi regime, and an opportunity to persist with an emphasis on German suffering under Hitler.

The trial of Martin Sommer in Bayreuth during the summer of 1958 is conspicuously absent from existing historical works on the war crimes issue, referred to only fleetingly alongside some of the other trials occurring in that same year. Hermann Langbein is typical, noting that it was the resonance of the revelations emerging from Bayreuth over Sommer's 'sadistic madness', together with the 'strong echo' of the Ulm trial, that helped give rise to a new, more co-ordinated phase in the activities of the West German judiciary.[2] The nearest we get to an historical account of the trial's impact upon the wider West German consciousness comes courtesy of a former employee of the Bayreuth Landgericht, Helmut Paulus, who highlights the global media interest attached to the trial and how the court had received around 280 letters from members of the public expressing their views on the defendant. Paulus also acknowledges how spectators within the courtroom frequently heckled the accused amid horrific descriptions by the witnesses of his actions in Buchenwald. The overall focus of this work, though, remains on the bare facts of the case, with Paulus describing at length the protracted process of bringing Sommer before a judge and reproducing the indictment and key witness statements against the defendant.[3]

However, not only does the prosecution of Martin Sommer provide another fascinating case study into the potential resonance of a Nazi war crimes trial, it also demonstrates the efforts of an individual town to deal with its own compromised past after 1945. Bayreuth, situated within Northern Franconia, had experienced a peculiarly close association with National Socialism and during the seven Reichstag elections that were staged between 1924 and 1933, the region consistently provided the Nazis with some of their highest voting figures. In May 1928, for example, the NSDAP received just over 8 percent of the regional vote—the highest figure for any electoral district at the time.[4]

During the 1930s, Bayreuth, as the home of composer Richard Wagner, became a cultural centre of the Nazi regime. The nationalist sentiments embodied in Wagner's music suited National Socialist ideology and the summer operatic festivals that had been staged in the town every July since 1876 were quickly appropriated for propaganda purposes. Hitler himself was in annual attendance up until the outbreak of war in 1939. During the conflict, the event also became the destination for many injured members of the German armed forces, admission to the festival granted as a reward for their bravery and service from a Führer anxious to inflict his musical tastes on those around them.[5]

While Wagner's compositions were employed on-stage to illustrate Nazi ideology, the town itself displayed its unswerving support for the regime. Shops that had previously sold operatic souvenirs during the summer months now offered Nazi trinkets and literature, replacing busts of Wagner with those of Adolf Hitler. Houses along the route to the *Festspielhaus* were bedecked with swastikas and, as the war took its toll on the available manpower, uniformed members of the SS assumed an increasingly prominent role in the concerts, sounding the horns that traditionally summoned festival-goers to the performances and even participating in the chorus.[6]

This peculiarly close relationship with the Nazi leadership would have an interesting bearing on Bayreuth's handling of the Sommer case.

THE LIFE AND CAREER OF MARTIN SOMMER

Walter Gerhard Martin Sommer was born on 8 February 1915 in Schkölen, a village in Thuringia just over forty kilometres away from Buchenwald, where he would make his name.[7] He was the son of a farmer who instilled a strong sense of discipline in him from an early age. In 1931, the 16 year old Sommer joined the NSDAP and then, following Hitler's appointment as German Chancellor in 1933, became part of the SS. During his trial, Sommer claimed that his motivation for joining these organisations had come only from a desire to pursue a military career, rather than any deeply held political or ideological concerns. He insisted, 'I have received the book *Mein Kampf* on several occasions, but I can say today that I have never read it'.[8]

Rather than fulfilling his professed ambition to be a soldier, Sommer spent the 1930s employed as a guard in a series of concentration camps before moving to Buchenwald in the summer of 1937. On 1 September 1942, having impressed his superiors with his enthusiastic activities as the overseer of the cell block, he was promoted to the rank of SS-*Hauptscharführer*.

Sommer's fortunes, though, changed quickly. In the spring of 1943, as the regime increasingly drew upon any remaining young men to participate in the fighting, Sommer was transferred to an SS-Panzer regiment in France, but his separation from Buchenwald would not last long. Earlier in the year, the SS hierarchy had launched investigations into camp commandant Karl Koch amid a large corruption scandal. Koch was accused of enriching himself from the confiscated property of camp prisoners and diverting potentially valuable items away from the war effort. Sommer was also implicated. Arrested and returned to Buchenwald, Sommer found himself imprisoned in his own cell block. Koch was sentenced to death by an SS court and shot in April 1945. Sommer, though, managed to avoid court proceedings and in March 1945 was posted to an ill-fated military unit near Eisenach. As the Second World War drew to an end, he was seriously wounded in a tank battle, losing his right thumb and leg, badly fracturing his left arm, and suffering severe injuries to his abdomen from grenade splinters. The *Bayreuther Tagblatt* later referred to him as 'a human wreck'.[9]

The nature of Sommer's activities in Buchenwald was made known to the Allies while the Third Reich was still crumbling. His name featured prominently in *The Buchenwald Report*, a collection of interviews with camp survivors conducted by the U.S. Psychological Warfare Division, just days after their liberation on 11 April 1945. Lengthy descriptions of Sommer's preferred methods of torture and the obvious pleasure he derived from terrorising prisoners portrayed him as one of the very worst Nazi war criminals. Survivor Kurt Leeser recorded one of his peculiar characteristics:

Sommer was accustomed to summoning his victims to his room in the evening where he 'did them in'. He laid the corpses under his bed, upon which he immediately fell asleep, sleeping the sleep of the just, well satisfied with his successful day's work.[10]

Leeser affirmed that 'Martin Sommer' was 'a name that for years spread terror and horror in Buchenwald'. Fritz Männchen, another former Buchenwald prisoner, depicted him as a 'beast in human form'.[11] The same description also appeared in one of the earliest books to be published by a concentration camp survivor, Eugen Kogon's 1946 work, *Der SS-Staat*.[12]

Despite the infamy of his crimes, efforts to bring Sommer to account were fraught with difficulty. Like many former Nazis, he tried to conceal his true identity after the war by destroying his service book but was discovered by one of his former victims while recuperating at the Ilmenau Infirmary, an army hospital in Thüringia. Consequently reported to the U.S. authorities, Sommer was interned and housed in a series of different hospitals and infirmaries before eventually coming to the state-run hospital in Bayreuth on 15 February 1950. Efforts to try him at the start of the decade, though, failed as, in a move typical of Katharina von Kellenbach's description of the 'many legal quirks and evasive strategies that have characterised West German post-war proceedings', medical experts quickly concurred with Sommer's claims that the extent of his war wounds rendered him incapable of withstanding either the proposed trial or any lengthy time in custody.[13] From 1955, Sommer was ostensibly allowed to live as a free man within the Bayreuth hospital, where conditions seemed far from uncomfortable. Over the next three years, Sommer was able to marry his nurse and father a child before renewed legal action, as a result of his visibly improving health, interrupted his peaceful existence.[14] Sommer was subsequently brought to stand trial in Bayreuth between 11 June and 4 July 1958.

THE IMPACT OF THE SOMMER TRIAL

Media interest in the Sommer case was immense. Journalists and photographers from numerous West German newspapers and magazines, together with an impressive array of foreign correspondents, flocked to Bayreuth to report on every step of the events. The leading broadsheets, such as the *Frankfurter Allgemeine Zeitung*, generally carried at least one substantial paragraph on each courtroom session, while the local *Bayreuther Tagblatt* filled whole pages with each day of the trial.[15] The principal points of interest for the West German press concerned Sommer's excessive behaviour within Buchenwald, his personal life and the lengthy delay in bringing his case to court, together with wider debates over the extent of the 'murderers among us', and the educational imperative perceived to be bound up in such war crimes proceedings.

The character of the defendant dominated the trial proceedings and found a sensational echo within the watching media. Sommer was shown as falling clearly into the category of the 'excess perpetrator', an extremist who willingly stepped outside the boundaries of his own 'job description' to humiliate, torment and murder the prisoners who passed through the Buchenwald cell block. He arbitrarily constructed the 'Black Bunker' within the cell block, described by one witness as 'the worst place in Buchenwald'.[16] He also administered lethal injections to the inmates, a task usually reserved for the camp's doctors, particularly given the regime's preference for maintaining the illusion of a 'routine' medical examination for as long as possible when leading prisoners to their deaths.

Witness testimonies presented Sommer as a zealous, ambitious young man anxious for promotion through the ranks of the SS. He specialised in delivering blows that would cause the maximum injury to his victims, and reaped cigarette bonuses from his superiors for hanging prisoners from the trees that surrounded the camp. Sommer took visible delight in his 'work' and boasted of his achievements to anyone who would listen. Survivor Paul Grünewald told the court of an incident in the camp mortuary, where Sommer pointed out the body of a Polish worker who had been accused of having a relationship with a German woman, proudly saying, 'That is my work from this morning'.[17]

The West German media was quick to pick up on these images of Martin Sommer. Headlines screamed the news of the latest atrocities to be recounted in the courtroom, frequently incorporating lurid statements from the witnesses or the defendant himself. Vivid newspaper descriptions of Sommer's personality and physical appearance completed the picture being created by the witnesses of the defendant as a chilling, evil monster. On several occasions, the West German press made reference to Sommer's 'crude' or 'primitive' nature, while repeated comments about his 'cold staring eyes' added to the image of a man devoid of any basic human feeling.[18] Sommer was variously labelled 'the Beast of Buchenwald', 'the Devil in human form' and the 'Hangman of Buchenwald'.[19] Witness testimonies were relayed practically verbatim in all their gory detail, prompting observers within the British Embassy in Bonn to record how 'no attempt has been made to spare the public any of the horrors'.[20]

The notion of Sommer as an excess perpetrator, though, jarred with his wretched appearance before the Bayreuth court. To the uninitiated, Sommer was, to all intents and purposes, just a frail, harmless invalid who had to be transported to and from the proceedings by ambulance and required a doctor on constant standby. Several newspapers thus printed photographs of the defendant as a formidable uniformed figure from his Third Reich days alongside their trial reports.[21] The extent to which readers were able to connect these two sides of the accused is unclear.

The cumulative effect of these representations of Martin Sommer also enabled his former SS colleagues to distance themselves from the accused.

Ex-Nazis who testified during his trial unsurprisingly insisted that Sommer had always remained aloof, while former Waffen-SS General Kurt 'Panzer' Meyer seized the moment to declare, as part of an ongoing post-war campaign to try and restore the reputation of Waffen-SS members, that his organisation had nothing to do with such crimes. During a veterans' reunion which coincided with the end of the Sommer trial in July 1958, Meyer again defended their service:

> Just because of a few concentration camp transgressions committed by a tiny bunch of criminals, the many thousands of brave front soldiers of the Waffen-SS suffer constant defamation and the honour of the fallen is dragged through the mud.[22]

Much was also made of Sommer's involvement in the Koch corruption scandal, implying that he must have been one of the very worst criminals if even the SS had begun to investigate him. From there, it would have been but a short step to portraying his wartime arrest as evidence for the regime's disapproval of his activities in Buchenwald, which would then be understood as the result of individual initiative, thereby drawing the circle of perpetrators as small as possible.

The second major theme which came to dominate press coverage of the Sommer trial concerned the defendant's family life. His wife Barbara consistently accompanied him to and from the court and sat calmly behind him during the hearings. Her strong show of loyalty to her husband, and her detached demeanour as emotionally charged witnesses recalled their most painful experiences at his hands, attracted a vast degree of criticism. The tabloid press were particularly vocal, scrutinising the Sommers' marriage and constantly posing the question as to how this woman could have brought herself to marry such a monster. The popular magazine *Der Stern* was typical, leading with an article entitled 'Married to the Devil'.[23]

In part, the scandal surrounding Barbara Sommer may rest in the idea that she had broken one of the unofficial taboos of the Federal Republic in her refusal to embrace a public rejection of National Socialism. Rather than being repelled by allegations over Sommer's past, she had in 1956—six years after the initial attempt to prosecute him had failed—knowingly married a man associated with concentration camp crimes, and had then proceeded to coolly 'stand by her man'. Perhaps even more alarming for trial observers was her insistence throughout the proceedings that her husband was a wonderful man who doted on both herself and their baby daughter. Recognising that Sommer could be a loving family man as well as a notorious concentration camp killer undermined all efforts to dehumanise and segregate him from the rest of the population—raising awkward questions as to how many more seemingly gentle, insignificant figures now living freely in the Federal Republic had also participated in barbaric crimes during the Third Reich.[24]

Public criticism of Mrs. Sommer reached such levels that the Bayreuth hospital where she still worked as a nurse was deluged with letters from all over the country calling for her immediate dismissal. Although too young to be implicated in the crimes of the Third Reich herself, the weight of public pressure over her relationship with the former 'Hangman of Buchenwald' proved sufficient for the hospital administration to bow to popular demand and curtail her employment. That, in turn, provoked much media discussion, to the extent that by the end of the trial, Mrs. Sommer had practically overtaken the accused in terms of public interest. The *Frankfurter Rundschau* summed up this episode as being 'a clear example of how we very frequently respond to awkward things: either not at all or wrongly'.[25] The *Rhein-Zeitung* similarly condemned the treatment of the defendant's wife:

> In the time of the Third Reich, many thousands of people lost their position and their freedom just because they were related to those being politically persecuted or judged by the regime. Barbara Sommer was, as her superiors have to agree, a conscientious and self-sacrificing nurse whose patients had not objected to her care after the trial.... She is too young to have known the time of the Third Reich. Countless women were plunged into such a conflict after the war. They have responded in different ways, but they have, in each case, had to deal with their fate.... But there are no grounds to make their lives even more difficult and to rob them of their livelihoods. We have not condemned the *Sippenhaft* [detention as punishment for the offences of other family members] of that time if we allow it to take on a new lease of life today.[26]

The incident generated much public excitement and many letters to the West German press, such as the following from a victim of Nazi persecution to the *Frankfurter Allgemeine Zeitung*:

> I personally see the detestable crimes and cruelties that her husband is accused of as indisputable. They have to, and hopefully will, fill the conscience of every upright German with repugnance—perhaps also with the admission of moral complicity. I hold that her husband ... should always be held up as an example.
> ... In [Mrs Sommer's] treatment by her institutional leaders, I see a shocking return to our recent past in the practice of a system that has been co-responsible for the execution of thousands of innocent members. To lose work and bread—as in her case—or to forfeit freedom through prisons or concentration camps—as in my case ... makes little difference to me.[27]

The *Süddeutsche Zeitung* also published a letter from a former concentration camp prisoner on this subject. Once again, the reader appeared to be in tune with the wide condemnation of Mrs. Sommer's dismissal by the press:

> As a so-called 'Mischling' racially persecuted in the Nazi era, as well as the son of one of those violently abducted and imprisoned, and the nephew of two uncles murdered in the concentration camps . . . I cannot understand how the hospital administration could take up measures against a young and inexperienced woman who married a man like Martin Sommer out of love. All decent people must be in agreement in the loathing against the inconceivable crimes of Martin Sommer. Nevertheless, it needs attention if the wife is treated with regard to who she married and who is the father of her daughter. It is unworthy of a liberal and democratic state if measures like those of the hospital administration are allowed to repay human crimes that were committed by another family member.[28]

Shocked and angered by the terrible revelations emerging from the Sommer trial, many West German publications were forced to question why it had taken so long to bring this defendant to account, given that details of his crimes had been available since the end of the war.[29] There was some contemplation of the number of other war criminals who remained at large, with the example of Buchenwald physician Dr. Eisele, recently fled to Egypt, proving a popular point of reference in the press. Consequently, the Association of Jewish Refugees in Britain was confident that this war crimes case was having a significant impact on the West German people:

> The few names mentioned in the Bayreuth and Ulm trials represent a numerically large category of persons who were ordinary citizens before Hitler's day, then became mass murderers, and are now submerged in German society as 'respectable citizens'. Around many a German 'Stammtisch' sit people like Sommer and there is more than one doctor now vaccinating school children, having put aside the syringe with which he administered lethal injections until fourteen years ago. One would only too willingly believe that these deeds, revealed in a trial before a German court, have not only shocked the German in the street, but have also awakened his conscience.[30]

Others, though, seemed less convinced by this rhetoric of the 'murderers among us'. Noting the seemingly endless line of war crimes trials in recent months, the *Hamburger Echo* began to probe this difficult subject:

> Inevitably . . . the question emerges why the proceedings were opened so late, and whether it still has meaning thirteen years after the war's end to initiate the investigation of events that were part of a time even

Recalling Resistance 59

longer ago. Shouldn't one be better off drawing a final line under the whole bloody Hitler era?[31]

The newspaper deliberated on this issue over the space of half a page before finally conceding that the Sommer trial probably was a good idea as it could help to restore West Germany's reputation in the eyes of the world. The implication was that trials constituted little more than a useful exercise in public relations, a means of underscoring the distinction between the Federal Republic and the Nazi regime, rather than a necessary judicial task to punish the atrocities committed under the Third Reich. The fate of the Buchenwald inmates alone, it seems, did not warrant sufficient grounds for the renewed legal proceedings. The newspaper did, however, concede 'before we can draw a line under the past, we have to reckon with it clearly. That is the purpose of the trials'.[32]

The conclusion of the Sommer case provided a further opportunity for reflection among the West German newspapers. The court's decision to bestow a life prison sentence on the accused was welcomed by observers, and many publications saw the result as serving an important educational purpose for the rest of the population. The *Rhein-Zeitung* was typical, arguing that one of the greatest achievements of the trial would be in providing a valuable lesson in the dangers of totalitarianism, nothing that 'perhaps this trial . . . contributes to the knowledge of the values that our Federal Republic affirms and protects'.[33]

Other newspapers went further, revealing a deep sense of shame and sorrow for the crimes committed during the Nazi era. The *Kasseler Post* was typical:

> We must all be ashamed that the terrible evils should have been able to take shape in Germany, completely independent of reason, circumstances and the fact that the greatest majority of our people can only be reproached for complicity. . . . Many have not wanted to believe what is now revealed in a whole series of trials, and many have also been afraid to see the dreadful truth. . . . But no one can avoid this truth any more. We have to deal with our 'unfinished past' and to draw a lesson for all time.

Nonetheless, an apologetic mode of thinking remained evident even here. The newspaper explained people's responses to the trials in terms of victors' justice and the sense that similar judicial measures had not been taken against Allied war crimes, referring to the 'arbitrary character and the hypocrisy of these proceedings', before finally concluding with the following:

> As deeply painful as it is for all of us to be confronted with the most shameful period of our history in these trials, we have to bear and affirm it because otherwise our honour cannot be re-established.[34]

While the media grappled with the relative merits of the trial, the cumulative effect of all this emotive reporting may have actually worked against a closer public reflection on the case, with gruesome descriptions of Sommer's actions discouraging people from paying any further attention to the trial, or perhaps desensitising them to the horrors of National Socialism. Indeed, in the midst of the proceedings, one woman from Coburg complained to the *Neue Presse* about its relentless coverage of the Sommer trial:

> We always hear reports on these cruel deeds. One always reads what the Germans have committed in this war. Bring us something gay, cheerful or things from which we see that goodness and beauty still occur in the world.[35]

Her letter was reprinted at the top of a special editorial in which the newspaper seized the opportunity to launch a scathing attack not only on this individual reader, but upon all those who still refused to engage with the legacy of the Third Reich:

> What serious newspaper does not prefer to report on goodness and beauty? But this world is not only good and beautiful and it is the task of the newspapers to report on everything that is important for the general public. A newspaper should also enlighten. However, they do not fulfil these tasks if they allow the evil and nastiness to fall under the table. On the contrary, if we all—journalists and readers—continue to put many known evils and nastiness before this world, it can perhaps represent a turn for the better![36]

Switching its focus to the dismissal of Barbara Sommer from the Bayreuth hospital and the wider question of responsibility for the Nazi past, the newspaper then attacked all those who continued to give precedence to German suffering:

> As the war was ending, the wife of the Hangman of Buchenwald was ten years old. What could she know of the crimes that were committed in her childhood in the concentration camps of her homeland, where most of the adults themselves did not know, or want to know. Today everyone knows what happened at that time. And that is good.
>
> But there are always still many who confuse the cause and effects. What happened to the Germans in the war and after the war—with the air raids and the deportation of millions from their homeland—was the effect. The cause was the human persecution by the most terrible Nazi regime. Martin Sommer had murdered in Buchenwald long before the war. And many of his murderous cronies still live among us. . . . We think on that and we do not forget it.[37]

Recalling Resistance 61

The extent to which people were responding to the Sommer trial was subject to further scrutiny by pollsters for the Allensbach Institut für Demoskopie. Between 1 and 8 August 1958—just weeks after the Bayreuth court had sentenced Sommer to life imprisonment—the organisation interviewed 2000 people over the age of 18 across the Federal Republic. The survey sought to determine their reactions to both the particulars of the Sommer case and the necessity of continued Nazi war crimes trials as a whole.

The results of the Allensbach survey revealed that 79 percent of those questioned had heard or read about the Sommer case, highlighting the extent of the trial's resonance across the country. Most agreed that Sommer's life prison sentence was a satisfactory result to the proceedings although, as was frequently the case with war crimes trials, there was also a minority who would have preferred an even harsher sentence—namely the death penalty—for the defendant, despite the lack of any provision for capital punishment within the Federal Republic.[38] Those who had heard of the Sommer trial were also more likely to support the prospect of further war crimes proceedings in the future. The IfD presented the following two quotes regarding the Nazi past to respondents and asked them to select which they most agreed with:

> If it comes to light today that someone had committed a crime at that time he still has to be punished today. I do not see why someone who tortured or killed other people should go unpunished.

> I find that one should once again stop putting people before the courts for deeds they had committed many years before. I think it would be good to finally draw a line under the past.

Of those claiming to have been following the Sommer trial, 62 percent opted for the first statement, accepting the need for more trials, compared with 37 percent of those who had not been paying attention to the case.[39]

It could thus be argued that the revelations emerging from the Bayreuth courtroom during the summer of 1958 seemed to play a significant role in convincing a greater proportion of the West German population of the need for continued prosecutions and that there could still be many more former killers like Sommer within society. A core element of the West German population (around one-third of those questioned), however, opted for the second statement, regardless of whether or not they had been following the events of the Sommer trial.[40] This would suggest that, despite all the efforts of public prosecutors, survivor groups and liberal newspaper editors to emphasise the importance of these proceedings, there remained a sizeable group of people that wanted to focus solely on the future, rather than persistently raking over the embers of the recent past. Interestingly, the fact that the IfD used two separate statements placed in quotation marks when exploring this subject could be seen as encouraging a more open and honest

62 West Germans and the Nazi Legacy

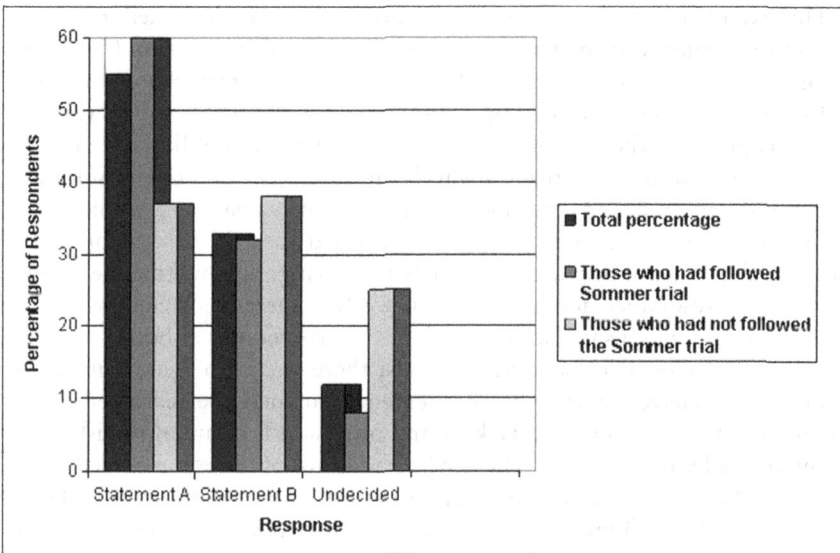

Figure 3.1 Graph showing attitudes to the Nazi past, based on awareness of the Sommer trial, 1958.

Source: Data sourced from 'Die Stimmung im Bundesgebiet: Die KZ-Prozess', *Institut für Demoskopie Allensbach am Bodensee*, October 27, 1958.

set of replies. Rather than simply giving the perceived 'correct' answer to a loaded question, interviewees may have been granted a sense of security and freedom to express their opinions by the apparent sight of someone else calling for an end to war crimes trials. They did not have to feel themselves alone in taking a similar stand against the continuing prosecutions.

People's attitudes to trials also affected their opinions on Sommer's sentencing. Those supporting the notion of further legal proceedings against former Nazi personnel were far more inclined to accept life imprisonment as a 'good' conclusion to the case or to call for the introduction of the death penalty in their anger at his crimes. However, the 37 percent of those following the trial who nonetheless preferred to see a final line drawn under the Nazi era were, perhaps unsurprisingly, inclined to see a life sentence as too harsh.[41] Opponents of further war crimes trials frequently questioned the wisdom of placing frail, ageing suspects in the dock, an argument with special resonance in the Sommer case, given the repeated photographs of the defendant, confined to a wheelchair since the end of the war, being carried into the Bayreuth court from an ambulance.

The responses gathered by the IfD did not seem to be particularly affected by gender, but political affiliations of the interviewees did complicate matters. Although supporters of the CDU and SPD questioned in the survey held identical views on Sommer's punishment, with 72 percent of people in each case agreeing with the final sentencing, more diverse responses emerged when discussing the two statements regarding the handling of the Nazi past. While the majority of people supporting the three main political parties appeared to accept the need for further prosecutions, SPD followers proved the most adamant in their convictions, with 62 percent calling for any remaining war criminals to be brought to account.[42] This result is in keeping with the party's post-war pressure on the conservative Adenauer government to be seen to confront the past, from granting reparations to Israel to tackling the issue of former Nazis who had retained high office in the new republic. By contrast, 40 percent of the respondents from the more right-wing, nationalist FDP—itself a haven for many former Nazis after the war—demonstrated a much stronger desire to draw a line under the past, compared with 32 percent of the CDU and 29 percent of SPD supporters.[43]

Interestingly, the IfD also took into account the responses of people who had been linked to Nazi organisations, either personally or through relatives, based on whether interviewees claimed to have suffered as a result of denazification at the end of the war. Having highlighted their own 'injuries' during the survey, it is perhaps unsurprising that 52 percent of them opposed any new wave of investigations into suspected war criminals. Nonetheless, with an emphasis on German victimhood implicit among this group of respondents, the majority—65 percent—still agreed that Sommer had warranted life imprisonment, a prison sentence merited, after all, through his abuse of German concentration camp prisoners.[44]

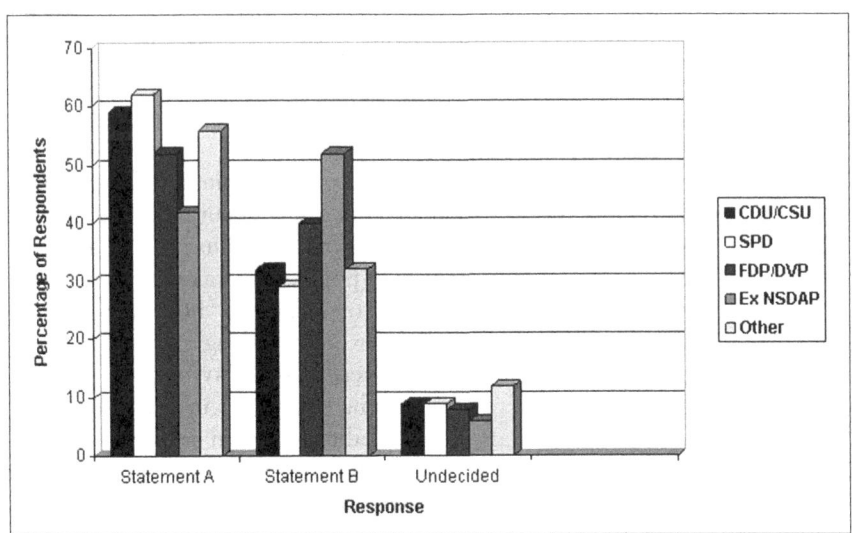

Figure 3.2 Graph showing attitudes to the Nazi past by political affiliation, 1958.
Source: Data sourced from 'Die Stimmung im Bundesgebiet: Die KZ-Prozess', *Institut für Demoskopie Allensbach am Bodensee*, October 27, 1958.

The results of this opinion poll therefore show that interest in the Sommer trial was not confined to the media but was, to a large extent, generally shared by the West German population, whatever their stance on the war crimes issue. An analysis of responses within Bayreuth itself, meanwhile, underlines further the tensions that the case was generating between different sectors of society.

REACTIONS IN BAYREUTH

Since 1945, Bayreuth had been forced to work particularly hard to disentangle its cultural heritage from the taint of National Socialism. Attempts by the Wagner family to revive the traditional summer opera festivals after the war proved controversial, not least because the composer's daughter-in-law, Winifred Wagner, had been categorised as a 'major offender' under the Allied denazification programme as a result of her close friendship with Adolf Hitler.[45] It thus fell to her children to try and restore the family name, but reviving the festival required money, and the local Bavarian authorities were unwilling to spend what little funds they had on such a venture. The idea of recreating the annual pilgrimages to Wagner's *Festspielhaus*, though, did prove popular among local conservatives and former Nazis who established a special fund-raising committee, The Society of the Friends of Bayreuth, in 1949. A major figure in the committee was Gerhard Roßbach, a veteran of the First World War and former member of both the Freikorps and the SA. As one of Hitler's earliest supporters, Roßbach had been involved in the 1923 Munich Putsch and was at the time a prominent industrialist.[46] The Bayreuth festival therefore continued to be linked, at least financially, to the old regime. Questions may thus be posed over the extent to which attendance at the festival came out of a genuine desire to hear the music or from a desire to recreate the 'good old days' of the 1930s.

While some of the money pouring into the cause originated from some rather dubious characters, Wagner's heirs were keen to ensure that the music itself was released from its former Nazi connotations. During the 1950s, Wieland Wagner re-staged some of the most popular operas with new sets, direction, choreography, singers and conductors. The only holdovers in the *Festspielhaus* staff were the costume designer and lighting expert.[47] These deliberate changes led to the coining of the term 'New Bayreuth', a phrase which not only gained popular currency among opera fans in relation to the new artistic ventures, but could also be applied to the town as a whole in its efforts to dissociate itself from the Nazi regime. The first post-war festival opened in July 1951, complete with posters fixed to the walls of the opera house signed by Wieland and Wolfgang Wagner with the following message:

> In the interest of the smooth conduct of the festival, we kindly request that discussions and debates of a political nature should be avoided. Art is what matters here![48]

West German press coverage of this first festival of the Federal Republic duly obeyed, carefully avoiding speaking about the recent past and focussing firmly on the opera.[49] Rather than being held up as a symbol of German, or Nazi, supremacy, Wagner's music was now, in the words of Frederick Spotts, presented as 'a bridge between nations', an important means of international reconciliation after the Second World War.[50] The theme, signalled by the family's determination to employ foreign—and especially Jewish—musicians and conductors was apparently endorsed by the Bayreuth Stadtrat. In contrast to the swastikas flown during the Third Reich, the 1951 festival saw the town council decorating the route to the opera house with the flags of other nations for the first time.[51]

The connection between Bayreuth and the Third Reich, however, would not simply go away, particularly when the Sommer trial was heard just days before the 1958 festival was due to open. The juxtaposition of these two events was made manifest in several issues of the local *Bayreuther Tagblatt*, which placed articles on the trial alongside snippets of information about the forthcoming festival and photographs of the opera stars set to fill the leading roles for that year.[52] On the one hand, the newspaper fulfilled its moral obligation to provide its readership with information about Nazi crimes. On the other hand, the *Bayreuther Tagblatt* carefully provided subtle evidence of the 'other' Germany with all its glorious cultural traditions—a side of the nation in which the people could still take some pride. It was a theme picked up upon by another local newspaper, the *Fränkische Presse*, at the end of the Sommer proceedings:

> Unfortunately for Bayreuth it was a bad coincidence that such a trial took place here. The name of the town was in these days named before the whole world together with that of the Killer of Buchenwald. Bayreuth prefers it if its name is taken in connection with the operas now beginning as a cultural town and not with the excesses of the past.[53]

The juxtaposition of these 'two Germanys' raises further questions about local responses to the Sommer trial. Did news of the 1958 festival, placed so close to the trial reports, prompt people to reflect upon and question their previous support for Hitler's regime? Alternatively, did news of the festival cushion some of the impact of the trial's revelations? The *Bayreuther Tagblatt* certainly appeared keen to discourage any notions that Sommer had anything in common with the local townsfolk. In a very apologetic article, the newspaper stressed that it was just a matter of fate that Sommer was now being tried in Bayreuth rather than another area of the Federal Republic:

> It is thanks to blind chance that the name Bayreuth had been repeatedly cited during the past months in the world press in connection with violent crimes which happened 15 or even 20 years ago in the era of the Third Reich and were born out of the spirit of that time. None of these deeds . . . occurred in our area or even in Bayreuth itself.[54]

To some extent, it is thus possible to see a sense of duty hanging over this trial, a sense that the town had to quickly get this unpleasant Sommer business out of the way before it could relax and get on with enjoying that year's opera performances.

On the face of it, the local residents did display a desire to exorcise the ghost of the Nazi past and engage with the Sommer trial. Each day, people scrambled to catch a glimpse of the infamous defendant for themselves, with crowds gathering outside the court to the extent that, on at least one occasion, Sommer had to be whisked through a side exit at the end of the day's hearing to avoid the crush.[55] Inside, the *Deutsche Woche* noted how the courtroom was 'permanently overfilled', with every seat in demand.[56] As the trial progressed, and witness testimonies revealed disturbing details about Sommer's activities in Buchenwald, spectators struggled to retain a sense of decorum, with several shouts of 'Hang the swine' emanating from their ranks.[57]

Much of this attention is explicable by the fact the Sommer trial dealt with crimes committed in Buchenwald. The concentration camp was, after all, located within Germany and had been reasonably well known to the population thanks to reports in the National Socialist press throughout the 1930s.[58] Moreover, the fact that Buchenwald had contained a large number of political opponents enabled Germans to reflect upon their own suffering under Hitler. Observers could recognise their compatriots among Sommer's victims and empathise with the camp's survivors. In addition, details of Sommer's barbaric treatment of the Buchenwald prisoners may have helped to ease people's consciences about their own behaviour under the Nazi regime. The trial reasserted the concept of a totalitarian state run on terror, a state in which any act of opposition could have resulted in a stay in Sommer's notorious cell block. Any former complicity with the Nazi regime could thus be explained away on the grounds of self-preservation.

While historians have long concluded that the extent of resistance to Nazism was, in reality, never that great, the *idea* of widespread opposition had an obvious utilitarian value after 1945. In the East, the term 'victims of fascism' promulgated a Soviet emphasis on National Socialism as the product of capitalism, while also enabling people to unite in a sense of suffering. In September 1948, for example, the Day for the Commemoration of the Victims of Fascism was characterised by large demonstrations by the Association of Victims of the Nazi Regime (VVN) in Berlin. The VVN was distinctively left-wing, founded at the end of the war by resistance fighters and concentration camp survivors. Mainstream political parties would routinely condemn it as a Communist organisation and there were regional bans in West Germany amid the Cold War tensions of the 1950s. The aims of the VVN, however, were clear and would ensure that the organisation would remain an important force for keeping the Nazi past in the public eye. Initially formed to provide material restitution to all former victims, the VVN was determined to fight any re-emergence of fascism. Over the years, it has frequently disrupted SS reunions and denounced Neo-Nazi activities. It has also played a key role in highlighting the crimes of the Third Reich.[59] With branches all over the country, it is thus easy to see how members of the political Left and labour movements, persecuted from the very start of Hitler's chancellorship, were able to find an outlet for sharing their memories of the past and produce a strong response to anyone wishing to gloss over the Nazi era.

It is, of course, important to consider what sort of behaviour we could reasonably expect from the local populace in relation to the trial. These people, after all, had their own lives to lead and their own jobs to do. They could not be expected to attend every day of the trial in person. Many people may also have felt disinclined to go to the hearings owing to the genuine distress that the trial's revelations could cause. Nevertheless, the attitude of the Bayreuth population came in for criticism among some observers. Writing for *World Jewry* in 1958, Eleonore Sterling suggested that the levels of public interest displayed in the case may have rested in the opportunity provided for 'some Germans to unburden themselves of their own guilt by taking up a position of moral superiority'. Sterling argued that 'one could not but suspect that the eagerness with which many expressed their horror over Sommer's crimes served to cover up their own bad consciences'.[60]

It is impossible to determine precisely the identities of those heckling and abusing Sommer outside the Bayreuth court, yet an examination of some of the letters sent to the court during the proceedings suggests that there was a significant counter memory culture circulating in the region at the time, one which recalled all too painfully the suffering of the political Left under National Socialism. As Helmut Paulus outlined in his account of the proceedings, the Bayreuth court received 280 letters during the course of the trial from people all over the world anxious to express their views on the case. Such letters underscore the extent to which the Sommer trial became a popular talking point in the Federal Republic and constitute an invaluable means to get closer to the thoughts and feelings of the 'ordinary' population. It is possible to identify the issues causing the most popular concern during this period while noting some striking similarities among these texts, suggestive of an active circle of former concentration camp prisoners determined to draw attention to their experiences of the Third Reich.

The vast majority of correspondents began by noting how they had read about the Sommer proceedings in the newspapers, illustrating the media's important role in disseminating details of the war crimes trials—together with reminders of the Nazi past—to a wide audience. Particular reference was repeatedly made to the populist publication *Bild-Zeitung*, a factor which might also explain the preponderance of a sensationalised style of writing within so many of the letters. Just as the press had drawn heavily upon animal imagery to dehumanise the defendant or had emphasised his behaviour as an 'excess' perpetrator, those writing to the court also tended to utilise demonic vocabulary when referring to the accused. Sommer was consequently described repeatedly as a 'monster', a 'creature' or a 'beast in human form'. Several writers stressed his 'brutal' and 'bestial' nature and seized upon the popular nickname, 'The Hangman of Buchenwald'.

The majority of letters, though, came from former Buchenwald prisoners, people who had been in a position to observe or experience firsthand the violent abuse unleashed by the defendant. The trial thus became an opportunity for them to have their story heard. Within these letters, Sommer continued to be rendered distinct from both the rest of the West German population and his fellow members of the SS. Several writers emphasised how Sommer often administered severe beatings and lethal injections on his own initiative, effectively destroying the defendant's claims that he had been following orders. One man admitted that he could say a lot more about Sommer's crimes, but found it difficult to put the atrocities into words.[61]

Similarities in the very phrasing of these letters revealed a strong left-wing discourse running through them. Several writers made reference to their 'murdered comrades', a term that suggested the presence of an active survivors' group made up of former political prisoners, which sought to draw attention to the level of resistance that had existed against the Third Reich, thus underlining the extent of German suffering under Hitler and refuting any notion of a collective German shame. One writer noted:

> In these proceedings, I see a derision and contempt of all killed, murdered and still living comrades of the concentration camp Buchenwald and I raise, in their names, a public protest to the High Court to cancel, in the memory of all killed and still living resistance fighters and anti-fascists, the preferential treatment granted to the accused.[62]

Another correspondent simply concluded his letter with the statement 'I have not forgotten my murdered comrades who were with me in the camp'.[63]

A counter memory can thus be seen as circulating in West Germany which recalled all too clearly experiences of opposition and persecution under the Third Reich. These writers drew upon an alternative political tradition present in Bayreuth, a tradition of left-wing politics and trade unionism rather than the conservative right-wing nationalism that has dominated popular representations of the region.[64]

Another popular theme among the letters sent to the Bayreuth court concerned the devising of various methods to punish the accused. One writer, calling for the highest possible punishment and ruing the lack of the death penalty under West German law, insisted that even 'hanging is much too good for him! It would be far better and more just to behead him after the pronouncement of the judgement!'[65] Another correspondent suggested utilising Sommer's own methods of torture to give him a taste of his own medicine, carefully detailing how he too should be hanged from the surrounding trees and beaten, with a burning cigarette pressed into his face. Reflecting upon the state of Sommer's health, the writer added:

Today the accused is still a wreck, so I would like to remind him that he himself carried out these sentences on his prisoners, who were also just wrecks. Whether the accused comes away [from this] with his life, we leave up to him.[66]

Correspondents also engaged with the prevailing scandal over the character of Barbara Sommer, a woman apparently unruffled by her husband's past activities. Several people expressed their indignation at the fact she had even been allowed to accompany him throughout the proceedings. One man expressed his amazement at what he saw as Sommer's 'preferential treatment' and demanded that he be stripped of such perks as receiving letters and family visits:

[This is] a repeated request in the name of the memory of all war victims, all Nazi victims and all the tortured, to show Sommer that he is inhuman before God and decent humanity and can expect no more privileges.[67]

The overwhelming majority of letters sent to the Bayreuth court approved wholeheartedly of the Sommer trial and agreed with the need to bring other former criminals to account. One man went further than most as he looked beyond the particular circumstances of the Sommer case to argue for more concerted investigations into other alleged war criminals, especially among members of the West German medical profession. The writer, himself a doctor in the Federal Republic, demanded that greater action be taken in weeding out compromised individuals implicated in the crimes of the Third Reich. Acknowledging the attention that had already been made during the trial to the Munich-based Dr. Eisele, the writer petitioned:

We ask the honoured District Attorney's office to investigate on the basis of the shameless disclosures in the Sommer case—for their occurrences shame every respectful person with the vile Nazi era with the biggest embarrassment—all crimes that were committed in the concentration camps by others than Sommer. Above all, to condemn as quickly as possible the doctors Eisele from Munich-Pasing, Dr. Plaza etc and all others who committed crimes and killed people. Above all, these doctors may no longer be registered as doctors. It is a shame for all decent doctors if these doctors still remain![68]

The letter, raising questions about the number of former Nazi perpetrators who had been able to return to their professional life unobstructed in post-war West Germany, clearly embraced the notion of 'the murderers among us'. At the same time, though, it is questionable as to how far the writer acted out of a genuine sense of atonement rather than out of concern for his own professional reputation as a medical man. His regular distinctions between Nazi doctors and 'decent' doctors, Nazi criminals and 'decent, just people', impose a sense of distance between the criminals of the Third Reich and the rest of the West German population. However, there also remained a minority of people who were opposed to such trials. One letter stands out in this vein as the writer drew heavily on the anti-Communist rhetoric of the immediate post-war period to produce a polemical right-wing attack on Soviet atrocities that relativised Nazi crimes:

> In the opinion of all the enslaved and subjugated peoples in the East, the Marxist hangmen, murderers, oppressors and exploiters have bestially murdered and starved over 35 million Russians, Poles, Hungarians, Rumanians, Czechs, Lithuanians, Bulgarians, Germans etc since 1917 and were therefore punished in the name of God through Himmler, Hitler and Goebbels etc being gassed and exterminated....
> The Nazis destroyed 7 million people, the Marxists over 35 million! Over 10 million people still languish in the Marxist kzs and are tormented to death by Marxist beasts....
> Certainly, if leaders only ever speak of the crimes of the German people, far worse crimes in the rest of the world are covered up and glossed over. However, one cannot suffocate the truth![69]

A CRITICAL ENGAGEMENT WITH THE PAST?

The extent to which the 1958 prosecution of the former SS-*Hauptscharführer* Martin Sommer inspired a more critical West German engagement with the Nazi past is questionable. Eleonore Sterling, reporting on the case for *World Jewry*, claimed that the trial, together with some of the other judicial developments of 1958, was having a positive impact on popular attitudes to the past, stating:

> Recent West German trials against Buchenwald guard Martin Sommer and against ten former members of the SS-Einsatzkommando Tilsit, as well as the charges preferred against concentration camp doctor Hanns Eisele, served once again to instruct the German public about crimes committed during the Hitler regime.[70]

Similarly, reflecting at the end of the year upon the series of trials conducted in 1958, the *Frankfurter Allgemeine Zeitung* concluded that such proceedings were having a profound effect on popular West German opinion:

> The trials at Bayreuth, Ulm and Bonn will be followed by others. Terrible as it may sound, we should welcome this. Not because some murdering functionaries are belatedly subjected to their deserved penalties while many others escape them, but because, owing to the reports in

Recalling Resistance 71

the entire West German press, the gruesome facts of our recent history, the mass murder of Jews and Communists, of women and children, are at long last brought home squarely to all those of our fellow citizens who have ignored them up till now. . . . These concentration camp trials are thus the first, and perhaps the last, chance to bring about a moral and spiritual rehabilitation of Germany.[71]

The results of the Institut für Demoskopie's opinion poll and the letters sent to the Bayreuth Landgericht show that the Sommer case did, indeed, occupy a significant place in the public consciousness. In contrast to the events in Ulm, West Germany now had a trial which was able to attract a vast number of spectators to the courthouse itself and inspire public discussion, as a result of the attention thrust upon Barbara Sommer, on questions of wider complicity with the crimes of the Third Reich.

However, while descriptions of Sommer's activities in the Buchenwald cell block appeared to shock, anger and appal the West German people, the extent to which this trial produced any real change in the way people viewed the past remains debatable. The fact that it was the Sommer case, rather than the trial of the former Einsatzkommando members at Ulm, that seemed to produce the greater resonance during the summer of 1958 suggests that perhaps it was a certain type of criminality that would capture the public imagination: crimes perpetrated against Germans, in Germany, rather than those committed against Eastern nationals in areas now subsumed behind the Iron Curtain. Focussing on crimes committed in Buchenwald, a camp originally constructed to hold serial criminals and political opponents, perpetuated mythologised notions of resistance and victimhood that had prevailed in West Germany since 1945. Throughout the trial, there remained a continued emphasis on German suffering under Nazism with little attempt to place the history of Buchenwald within the wider context of the Holocaust, thereby continuing the pattern of earlier Western interpretations of Nazi crimes which downplayed the atrocities carried out in Eastern Europe during the Second World War. Similarly, the West German press spent more time on the 'human interest' story of the defendant's wife, rather than attempting to explain the structure of the National Socialist state or the development of genocide.

At the same time, Sommer himself was presented as an 'excess' perpetrator. The fact that details of his behaviour had emerged as early as April 1945 had rendered Sommer a particularly infamous figure even before his trial came to court, and could enable people to see him as one of the 'big names' of the Nazi regime whose punishment was long overdue. Such imagery could therefore encourage earlier West German attempts to limit the blame for Nazi crimes to a radical few and evade a contemplation of any wider responsibility.

Despite the level of public attention given to the 1958 trial of Martin Sommer, the way in which the defendant—and his crimes—were portrayed, both in the courtroom itself and the national press, continued to impose a sense of distance between the criminals of the Third Reich, and the rest of the 'ordinary' West German population—a psychological barrier that may have impeded any closer reflection on the past during this time. War crimes proceedings in Ulm and Bayreuth may have brought National Socialist crimes to the forefront of public discussion, but there was still much work to be done before the people of the Federal Republic of Germany entered into a widespread, critical engagement with the Nazi past.

4 Eichmann
A Nation on Trial?

Years after the collapse of the Third Reich, there remained great speculation as to the whereabouts of some of the most infamous figures of the Nazi regime such as Dr. Josef Mengele and Martin Bormann. In 1960, however, one high-ranking former Nazi was uncovered: former SS-*Obersturmbannführer* Adolf Eichmann was sensationally kidnapped from his post-war hiding place in Buenos Aries by Mossad agents, acting on information supplied by Holocaust survivor turned Nazi hunter Simon Wiesenthal.[1] Eichmann had worked in the Jewish Department of the RSHA and had been the central figure behind various emigration schemes, including the plan in 1940 to deport four million Jews to Madagascar. During the Second World War, Eichmann assumed a leading role in the deportation of over 500,000 Poles and Jews from western Poland and, notoriously, compiled the minutes of the Wannsee Conference in January 1942 where plans for the physical annihilation of the Jews were drawn up. He was subsequently responsible for timetabling the transportation of European Jewry to the extermination camps. Eichmann's name had already cropped up on numerous occasions during the 1945–6 IMT as defendants pointed to his central role in the organisation of the Holocaust, although his significance was not immediately recognised by the Allies. Seeing Eichmann's name in the judgement, Justice Francis Biddle had appended a telling annotation, asking 'Who was he?'[2] Throughout 1961, however, Eichmann's name gained far greater currency. His trial in Jerusalem, which began on 11 April 1961, commanded global attention; this was, after all, the biggest name to be prosecuted since Nuremberg some fifteen years earlier. By the end of the year, Eichmann had been found guilty and, following an unsuccessful appeal process, was duly hanged on the grounds of Ramla prison at midnight, 31 May 1962.[3]

The Eichmann trial has long fascinated scholars, although the focus of existing academic studies rests not so much with West German responses to the trial, but how it was received in Israel and the United States.[4] This, however, has not prevented scholars from making great claims for the trial's impact within the Federal Republic. On the contrary, many accounts fleetingly assert that the proceedings had a major part to play in West

Germany's ongoing efforts to 'come to terms' with its past. Lawrence Douglas argues that the 1961 prosecution of Adolf Eichmann constituted 'The Great Holocaust Trial'—a case that 'served to *create* the Holocaust' in the public consciousness.[5]

There are certainly a number of factors that would support such claims. For the first time, the specific plight of the Jews was at the forefront of public discussion. The Eichmann proceedings made extensive use of Jewish survivor testimony, enabling the story of the 'Final Solution' to be brought to life far more vividly for observers and giving a voice back to the victims of the Nazi regime. This stood in stark contrast to the trials conducted by the Allies in the immediate aftermath of the war, which had relied heavily on official documents created by the perpetrators. It is not coincidental that the aftermath of this case would prompt an outpouring of survivor memoirs, with authors feeling encouraged to share their own experiences and persuaded that the world was now more willing to listen to them.[6]

For some commentators, the Eichmann case also seemed to revitalise the war crimes issue back in West Germany. The political theorist Hannah Arendt attended the trial in her capacity as a journalist for the *New Yorker* magazine. In her iconic study, she credits the proceedings with giving the West German judiciary the much-needed impetus to improve its handling of the war crimes issue, noting 'for the first time since the close of the war, German newspapers were full of reports on the trials of Nazi criminals, all of them mass murderers'.[7] She insists that it was the dramatic and rather controversial arrest of Adolf Eichmann in 1960 that helped inspire the 'first serious effort made by Germany to bring to trial at least those directly implicated in murder', thereby ignoring the wave of war crimes investigations and prosecutions that had been set in motion within the Federal Republic since the late 1950s.[8] Interestingly, the *New York Times* also picked up on this theme, noting how, at the start of the trial—no doubt feeling sensitive to charges of inaction by foreign observers—'the Central Office for the Investigation of Nazi Crimes, normally fiercely tight-lipped about its work, issue[d] heaps of statistics implying that the Germans themselves are about to speed the wheels of justice against Nazi criminals'.[9] Rudy Koshar, meanwhile, argues that the Eichmann trial acted as a 'lightning rod for increased historical interest in both Israel and Germany', helping to create a more critical climate in which West German youth would begin to ask more questions about the past.[10]

But how far was this really the case? Arendt concedes that despite the lofty educational ambitions harboured by prosecutor Gideon Hausner, the spectators who filed into the Jerusalem court each day to follow the Eichmann trial firsthand largely comprised Holocaust survivors, rather than the envisaged legions of Israeli youth. The trial consequently found its greatest audience among a group of people who already knew only too well the suffering that the Nazis had wrought upon the Jews.[11] This chapter makes a closer examination of the Eichmann trial in terms of just how far these proceedings resonated within the Federal Republic itself, while filling in some of the remaining gaps within existing historiography.

WEST GERMANS AND THE CASE OF ADOLF EICHMANN

On the surface, the trial did seem to have a significant impact upon the West German public. It commanded a sizeable degree of media attention, with most major publications running daily reports from the court. The harnessing of the growing medium of television to screen nightly primetime summaries of the proceedings further enhanced the trial's resonance, enabling it to reach a far wider audience and, as Jean-Paul Bier argues, transformed the Holocaust into a 'painful actuality' for the West German audience.[12] It could also, of course, be said to have added to the novelty of the proceedings in the public imagination. In the early stages of the trial, Dr. Franz Meyers, President of the Bundesrat and Premier of North Rhine Westphalia, claimed that the Eichmann trial was having a bigger impact on the West German people than the IMT had ever been able to achieve.[13]

The high-profile nature of the events in Jerusalem inspired, in turn, a number of other cultural activities within the Federal Republic. Alongside the news footage of the trial itself, West German television relayed special programming on the history of the Nazi regime, such as the fourteen-part documentary series *Das Dritte Reich*, which attracted a sizeable audience. Seventeen million people—41 percent of the adult West German population—watched at least one of these programmes, with 30 percent following it over the course of several shows and 72 percent of the population claiming to have spoken about it with other people. The most interested sector of the population was the 30–44 year old age bracket, at least 50 percent of whom claimed to have seen at least one of the programmes.[14]

The world of theatre also felt the effects of the trial. Rolf Hochhuth's controversial play, *The Deputy*, generated much publicity as it depicted the Papacy's failure to intervene in the face of the atrocities being perpetrated against the Jews. Including the figure of Adolf Eichmann in one of the acts, it was performed in twenty-seven countries during 1961.[15]

Around the country too there were various local initiatives to foster attention in the Eichmann case. Days before the start of the trial, the city of Frankfurt published a pamphlet which refuted claims that the German population had known nothing of the persecution of the Jews. The twenty-four-page document was produced by Dr Willy Hartner, vice-chancellor of Frankfurt University, and declared that 'whoever denies this today is a liar'.[16]

In Munich, meanwhile, the West German writer Rolf Seeliger, together with the *Vereinigung der Verfolgten des Naziregimes* (VVN), one of the leading associations of former victims of National Socialism, organised a public exhibition on Eichmann and the Nazi past in the Bürgerbräukeller on Rosenheimer Straße.[17] The choice of venue was significant, having been the scene of both the NSDAP's ill-fated putsch against the Weimar government in 1923 and Georg Elser's assassination attempt on Adolf Hitler during the Nazis' commemorations of that event on 8 November 1938. The exhibition included photographs and documents relating to Eichmann's role in the Nazi machinery and was open daily to the public between 9 am and 8 pm, with entry costing fifty Pfennig. The show attracted a steady stream of visitors, particularly from the local schools. A Munich teacher was the first to write in the visitors' book, simply stating, 'This is deeply shocking'.[18]

On the face of it, then, the trial certainly seemed to make itself felt within the Federal Republic. Publicity alone, though, does not necessarily equate to a critical, careful reflection on the recent past. Indeed, for many people, the Eichmann exhibition proved 'deeply shocking' for a completely different reason. The show gained notoriety and public attention not so much for its overarching message about Nazi criminality, nor even as a result of the sensationalism attached to the figure of Adolf Eichmann himself. Instead, the resonance of the exhibition rested firmly in its peculiar association with one of the biggest political scandals of this period: the growing questions surrounding Konrad Adenauer's choice of State Secretary. The man filling this prominent government position, Hans Globke, had penned the commentary to the infamous Nuremberg Laws of 1935 that had severely curtailed Jewish rights in Nazi Germany. The fact that he was still able to wield such influence over West German politics had subsequently rendered him the subject of much criticism, especially from East Germany.[19] Certain documents displayed in the Munich exhibition clearly implicated Globke in the story of Eichmann's crimes. As a result, the first 'visitors' to the exhibition were members of the West German security police, who removed the offending items before the show could open to the public.

This measure, though, did not prevent Globke's name from being mentioned in the same breath as that of Adolf Eichmann. Not only did the confiscation receive substantial press comment, but the police themselves left Globke's name indelibly marked on the exhibition by substituting a letter, authorising them to remove the documents, in their place. Visitors to the exhibition could therefore continue to make the connection between their State Secretary and the crimes of the Third Reich, while the official letterhead no doubt served as a reminder of both the continued reluctance among key sectors of West German society to foster a more critical engagement with the Nazi past, and—in an interesting precursor to the *Spiegel Affair* that would erupt one year later—an apparent police hostility to the practice of free speech. The removal of the Globke documents became the talking point of the exhibition, dominating coverage by the local *Süddeutsche Zeitung* while details of the actual exhibition received only a paragraph towards the end of the article.[20]

Similarly, in terms of the press coverage of the trial itself, it is worth noting that despite the vast quantity of newspaper reports, just 1 percent of articles made headline news and only 13 percent ever reached the front page at all. Instead, the overwhelming majority tended to be 'buried' within the inner pages of the West German press, perhaps reported more out of obligation rather than any sense that such stories could be crucial, newsworthy events.[21] A closer examination of media content and public representations of the past is thus required.

Indeed, further analysis of popular responses to the Eichmann trial suggests that, contrary to conventional narratives, reactionary opinions, evasions and mythologies continued to circulate during this period. While the Eichmann trial certainly captured the public imagination, much of the discussion centred firmly on the Germans themselves amid widespread concern as to the effect these proceedings would have upon the Federal Republic's reputation abroad. These fears had already been expressed in the run up to the trial by some of the leading public figures of the Federal Republic. Chancellor Adenauer acknowledged, 'I have a certain amount of concern as to the effect . . . on opinion about us Germans as a whole' and, in a statement revealing how there remained some ignorance or confusion as to real nature of the Holocaust, he urged the world to remember that Nazism had 'committed just the same crimes against Germans as Eichmann did against the Jews'.[22] Further statements from the Chancellor repeatedly stressed West Germany's programme of reparations to Israel, his personal good relations with Prime Minister Ben-Gurion, and the argument that only a 'relatively small percentage' of Germans had been convinced Nazis and that a 'great majority' had, in fact, been 'happy to help their Jewish fellow-citizens when they could'.[23]

Nor were such sentiments confined to the political Right. The mayor of West Berlin, Willy Brandt (SPD), also issued a statement prior to the trial which underscored the distinction between the perpetrators of the Third Reich and the rest of the West German population:

> The people of the world must know and be told that Adolf Eichmann does not reflect the thinking of the German people. The crimes he committed do not reflect the basic tenets of the German Federal Republic. . . . A new Germany desiring to live in a democratic community has been born and lives in the hearts of the greatest majority of my people.[24]

It was also striking during this period that the West German Defence Ministry began to recall the role of German-Jewish soldiers who had fought for the country during the First World War, thereby helping to create a rather rosy image of Jewish/non-Jewish relations prior to the rise of National Socialism.[25]

The media were quick to pick up on these themes. During the trial, the *Frankfurter Illustrierte* set out to investigate what Israelis were saying about the case and, by extension, the (West) German nation. The following exchange with a Jewish cafe owner was held up as typical of the wholly positive responses the newspaper was clearly pleased to have encountered:

'I have lost my whole family', said Schmoel, but he said it without hatred. He opined that one could not hold the youth in Germany responsible for the deeds of their parents.[26]

Such findings, though, did not prevent the right-wing press from making its expected radical pronouncements on the case, with the *Soldatenzeitung* predicting that 'the opening of the Eichmann trial will mark the beginning of the biggest anti-German hate campaign known for the last five years'.[27] *Der Freiwillige*, the organ of Waffen-SS veterans, was also reluctant to concede that there could be any merit in taking legal action against Eichmann and continuing to rake over the past. In a statement that underlined the ongoing post-war efforts of Waffen-SS veterans to style themselves in the mould of the honourable German soldier (and thereby distance themselves from the Nazi genocide), the newspaper nonetheless implicitly acknowledged the crimes that had been committed under National Socialism:

> During the Eichmann year, press and film have conspired to defame the honour of the men who served as privates, officers and generals in the Waffen-SS. Nothing has been too absurd or far-fetched to incriminate us and to saddle us with responsibility for some degrading and infamous acts.[28]

Even some of the country's mainstream publications retained an apologetic view of the past. The *Rhein-Zeitung* asserted how the majority of the population had remained ignorant of Nazi crimes and made a clear distinction between 'the Germans' as a people and those who 'abused the German name' by committing such crimes, declaring:

> Our whole country is sitting in the dock. . . . Though it is a fact that most Germans did not know what was hidden in the phrase 'Final Solution', as deceptive as it was perfidious, it is just as much a fact that we know it now and shall have to take account of it down to its last details. We cannot brush aside, with a flick of the hand, the horrors perpetrated under the abuse of the German name. Nor can we do so by the mere assertion, correct though it is in itself, that the Federal Republic is no longer the Third Reich. Instead, we shall have to look things in the eye and make ourselves so strong together with all the forces of the free world, that nothing like this can ever happen again.[29]

American journalists reporting from within West Germany, meanwhile, noted the tensions that the trial was creating in wider society: 'The mass of Germans do not discuss Eichmann with foreigners and the deliberate turning away worries many of those who are concerned'. In general, it appeared that the older generation wanted to see a line being drawn under the past, while younger West Germans insisted that such matters did not concern them. Those who were involving themselves more fully with the case tended to be drawn from official circles, the media and a few public figures.[30]

Throughout the media coverage of the trial there was also a tendency, as was first visible during the immediate aftermath of the war, to demonise the accused. Adolf Eichmann was frequently described as a 'devil' or 'monster', and there were regular references to the glass security booth he was housed in during the proceedings for his own protection. Eichmann's *Glaskasten* became a trope of trial reports, conveying connotations of a dangerous wild animal being placed on display in a global zoo. The illustrated magazine *Quick* even included photographs of the 'cage' being constructed in the run up to the start of the trial.[31] Dehumanising Eichmann in this manner enabled a psychological—as well as geographical—distance to be imposed between the defendant and the rest of the West German population.

Throughout this period, however, there were several examples of more liberal minded journalists and editors who were prepared to accept a share of responsibility and shame for what had gone before and who were determined to inspire a wider, more critical engagement with the past among the wider population. Some used the opportunity to ponder the whereabouts of other war criminals and the need for continued legal action against them. *Revue*, publishing a series of illustrated articles on the Eichmann case under the banner 'The Trial of the Century', clearly felt there was still much work to be done in this matter and questioned what had become of Eichmann's accomplices. Pointing to the number of former Nazis who must still be living peacefully 'among us as harmless citizens', the newspaper printed photographs of many 'absent' personalities such as Bormann and Mengele, together with an overview of their position within the Nazi regime and the crimes associated with their names.[32]

Impassioned editorials in several newspapers urged others to reflect on the recent past and recognise the lessons that needed to be learned if West Germany, and the world, were to avoid a repeat of such horrors in the future. Reporting on events from Jerusalem, *Die Zeit* argued: 'Eichmann is an inescapable fact. He stands for our past, which we will have to accept with as much decency, honesty and dignity as we can muster'.[33]

The Eichmann trial certainly produced a strong sense of disbelief and bewilderment within the West German press as to how such crimes could have been possible. The *Frankfurter Rundschau* posed a series of questions as it sought to grapple with the enormity of the Holocaust:

> How was this all possible, how could it happen that six million people could be murdered out of hand, without visible cause or coercion, just because they were Jews? And how was it possible for these crimes to emanate from the leadership of a civilised people that owed a great deal to its Jewish component?[34]

Similarly, the *Bonner General-Anzeiger* reflected:

If Eichmann had slain 20, 30 or even 100 Jews these would be figures we could grasp. But what can one make of five or six million dead? Such enormous figures take on a somewhat abstract quality. . . . They tend to belong to the world of statistics. They are incapable of arousing emotions for a lengthy period. If it were otherwise, what human being could bear it?[35]

Such comments, together with the *Rhein-Zeitung*'s profession of popular ignorance, implied that the Eichmann trial was providing people with their first insight into the horrors of the Third Reich. These protestations, however, were rejected by the women's publication *Frau und Politik* which suggested at least some knowledge of Nazi crimes had been circulating in the Federal Republic before the 'revelations' of the Eichmann case:

No one will believe us when we say we didn't know about all that. And is it really the whole truth? Didn't we know there were concentration camps, about which terrible things were reported? Didn't we know that our Jewish fellow citizens, even before they had to wear the Jewish star, were terrorised in a way that can't bear thinking about? Did we not, for instance, know about the wiping out of so-called inferior lives?[36]

The extent to which such editorials succeeded in sparking private reflection on the crimes of the Third Reich, however, remains questionable. Writing in 1961, Jewish writer Joel Carmichael acknowledged the problematic nature of trying to measure people's responses to the trials:

For all we know, many Germans may simply have switched off their TV sets the moment the Eichmann trial came on. There are individual pockets of Nazi obduracy scattered throughout the country, to say nothing of the broader strata of old-fashioned nationalist, right-wing and patriotic opinion. The older Germany has not, after all, evaporated. Indeed, not only was there a tendency among right-wing extremists . . . to call the Eichmann trial a 'show trial' designed to 'defame' Germany etc., but in the very midst of the trial, a former top Nazi was elected Bürgermeister of a small town in Lower Saxony and a street was named after Ludendorff. . . . In odd spots, also, some anti-Semitic handbills were circulated and a swastika scrawled here and there; these may be traced to the influence of the Eichmann trial.[37]

While Carmichael admits that such activity was 'peripheral', there remained divergent viewpoints in the Federal Republic throughout this period, as well as some continued doubts as to the wisdom of continually raking over the embers of the Nazi past.

Some of the most interesting insights into popular attitudes to these trials can be gleaned from the numerous readers' letters that were sent to West

German newspapers in response to the extensive media coverage. Some wrote in response to a specific article, others to the unfaltering news coverage as a whole, reacting in the face of the international spotlight now trained upon the Federal Republic. Still others showed signs of having engaged closely with the trial, compelled to put pen to paper by certain arguments or testimonies set forth in the courtroom. Whatever the impetus behind these letter writers, though, it was clear that the prosecution of Adolf Eichmann was striking a chord among the West German population.

The majority of letters reprinted in the newspapers appeared to share the more critical views expressed in countless editorials, a factor which does, of course, raise the issue of editorial control over the selection of material for publication. A letter to *Die Welt* in March 1961, though, took issue with the fact that debates over Israel's very right to arrest and try Eichmann continued to dominate much of the public discussion on the case. The writer implored:

> Almost half of all Israeli families still mourn relatives who died because there was a Nazi Germany. Must not matters of procedure seem of less than secondary importance in the face of the immediate and constant recollection of the million fold murder that weighs on the people of Israel?[38]

The use of rhetorical questions was a consistent feature of readers' letters on the Eichmann trial, suggesting that editors and journalists were not alone in trying to galvanise public interest in the case. Emotive appeals as to how such crimes could ever have happened, what could be done to prevent a recurrence and what others would do if they had been in a similar position all sought to inspire a serious reflection upon the legacy of the Nazi past. Much less constrained than professional writers in terms of what they could and could not say, these correspondents embarked upon a far more passionate, dramatic and critical representation of the trial. A letter to the Hamburg-based newspaper *Die Zeit* on 31 March 1961 was typical. The newspaper had previously urged people to 'follow this case with extreme consciousness ... analyse it coldly ... and manfully swallow the pain ... for the Germans have really never been cowards'.[39] Now one of its readers rejected out of hand any notion of observing the events in such a clinical and restrained fashion:

> Is that all? Shouldn't a glance into a past like that rather make the entire people leap up with a single shriek? Keeping calm in the face of such atrocities can only be done by characters like Eichmann. And for that matter, what *were* all those 'Yes, sir!' and 'Aye, aye, sir' characters, and all those countless people on the bandwagon, if not cowards? That's why I think we should not be so worried about the consequences about our reputation abroad; instead we must ask ourselves over and over again: How could it ever have come to that? What must we do so that it doesn't happen again?[40]

Other letter writers questioned the failure of the German people and, in particular, the German churches, to prevent the occurrence of the crimes in the first place. A writer to the Munich-based *Süddeutsche Zeitung* acknowledged the failure of any large-scale resistance movement against the Nazis and demonstrated a strong sense of shared responsibility for the atrocities that had been committed:

> It was not the Eichmanns—it was ourselves, and therefore I consider the whole German people guilty. . . . No one said from a pulpit: 'remain human!' Here and there a Catholic priest or a Protestant pastor grew indignant. But what I would like to know is why the entire body of bishops and all the pastors did not rise up and say: 'We withdraw from all the organs of the state, including the armed forces!'[41]

A high proportion of letters sent to West German newspapers during the Eichmann trial emanated from ex-military personnel. Some expressed an awareness of their own culpability in Nazi war crimes, others engaged excitedly in wider legal debates about the ability to refuse an order from a superior officer, and many more described some of the appalling sights they had seen while serving in Eastern Europe. In contrast to the notions of widespread silence that have characterised historical depictions of the 1950s or, indeed, the post-war legacy of the Wehrmacht, the staging of war crimes trials at the start of the 1960s became explosive moments, giving rise to a desire by many former soldiers to talk about the past and acknowledge, however implicitly, that criminal activities had taken place.

One such correspondent to *Die Welt* was a former Luftwaffe sergeant who considered it part of his good fortune not to have spent the war among the mobile killing units or concentration camp personnel. Nevertheless, the revelations emerging from the Eichmann proceedings seem to have forced him to reconsider past allegiances and subject himself to some serious soul-searching:

> I must speak up, I cannot help myself! I must tell what I felt and what I still feel in reading your reports of the Eichmann trial. Shame, shame, shame! And nothing but a wild and desperate shame!
> . . . Shattered, I keep asking myself over and over what I really would have done if . . . I had been ordered to participate in these bestialities. Would I have had enough character, enough humanity, to have turned my gun around and shoot those who were tearing children away from their mothers and simply smashing them? Would I have had the same bad character to shoot down wounded women and children who were painfully and agonisingly dragging themselves out of the mountains of corpses?
> My God! It is frightful! I don't know, I cannot say. I can give no binding answer, no convincing one. It is only the shame, the burning

Eichmann 83

shame that remains, no one can extinguish it any more, for I once did call these fellows 'Comrade'! There are still, after all some left of those that did the shooting, of those that obeyed those orders. Were they really ordered to be so bestial? For that matter were they ever soldiers? Do none of those who are still alive and who committed such bestialities stand up—for our honour—beat his breast and confess: "I was there too, I also let myself be swept along!"

And this Eichmann! Spread everything out in front of him, piece by piece, deed by deed, for he never soiled his fingers, he only gave the orders! He gave the orders, and we obeyed—we idiots![42]

The letter is full of self-condemnation, to the extent that by the end of the piece, the writer has identified himself entirely with those perpetrators who implemented the systematic mass murder of European Jewry. As the letter progresses, the author moves away from simply recounting his overwhelming sense of shame, typical of many other thoughtful readers' letters of this period, and starts to ponder far more deeply on the nature of collaboration and participation in the atrocities. Taken as a whole, the letter reads like the writer was in a close enough position to at least observe, if not commit, the crimes being described. The repeated use of rhetorical questions, combined with the short, sharp dramatic statements, give the impression of a man wrestling with his conscience and trying to deal with the reality of his past participation in the Nazi regime. The whole letter also stands in contrast to the newspaper editorials which claimed most Germans had been ignorant of Nazi crimes. Instead of the Eichmann trial being seen as the provider of brand-new information, here we have a sense that the high-profile Jerusalem proceedings actually provided an opportunity for members of the West German population to break their silence and to express publicly the knowledge they had already been harbouring in private.[43]

A closer examination of readers' letters is afforded through a study of the populist Hamburg-based newspaper *Bild-Zeitung* which, on 1 June 1961, printed extracts from sixty letters it had received over the course of the Adolf Eichmann trial from people all over the Federal Republic.[44] Some had clearly suffered at the hands of the Nazis themselves with several references to their own imprisonment in concentration camps that illustrated the presence of a counter memory on the Left. The majority of correspondents, though, appear to have been 'ordinary' members of the Third Reich, neither active in the resistance nor perpetrators at the heart of the Nazi genocide.

The views expressed by this section of the population varied enormously. An initial look at the letters sent to *Bild-Zeitung* suggests, unsurprisingly, that the majority of its readership wholly approved of its handling on the Eichmann trial. 'What you achieve with your Eichmann reporting!' exclaimed a reader from Kreuznach—and he was not alone in this sentiment. Another proclaimed, 'Your comments on the Eichmann trial show a love of the truth. It would be good if one was to learn once again how many innocent children were murdered with the six million Jews'—implying that many West Germans had already forgotten, or had failed to take on board, the details of the Holocaust that had emerged in the immediate aftermath of the Second World War.[45]

Opinion, though, clearly divided over the merits of having so much column space in the national press devoted to a figure like Eichmann. Several writers were wary of the dangers of giving him a platform to expound his views; others felt he was simply unworthy of such celebrity-like status. One reader stated bluntly, 'Much too much is spoken about Eichmann. He deserves to hang.'[46]

In fact, the issue of a suitable punishment for Eichmann became a popular theme within readers' letters to *Bild-Zeitung*. One correspondent stated, 'In my view there is only one sentence: the death penalty!'[47] As is often the case with high-profile trials dealing with particularly callous or disturbing acts, such calls for capital punishment became a popular rallying cry throughout the Nazi war crimes trials of the 1960s. Other readers, though, felt even this was too good for a figure like Eichmann, arguing that he be made to feel for himself what it was to suffer. Former concentration camp victims were particularly keen to devise ways to give Eichmann a taste of his own medicine. The very news that the defendant was currently able to enjoy the use of comfortable slippers angered one correspondent from Haubersbronn:

> Eichmann's felt slippers—they remind me of my time in Dachau where we had to wear wooden shoes. Couldn't one give these to Eichmann as well so he feels at least a little discomfort?[48]

While Eichmann's potential punishment excited much debate, the other major theme to dominate the letters printed in *Bild-Zeitung* concerned the accused's defence counsel, the West German lawyer Dr. Robert Servatius. Many readers found it outrageous that Eichmann could even warrant a defence lawyer; others took issue with the tactics being employed by the defence, accusing Servatius of 'whining' and even calling for him to face his own trial after the conclusion of the Eichmann case. The very fact that the lawyer in question was of West German nationality also proved a grave cause for concern. A reader from Munich called upon his fellow citizens of the Federal Republic to distance themselves from Servatius, not wishing to be similarly seen as 'clients of Eichmann'. Another correspondent denounced it as 'a scandal that a German lawyer volunteers to defend this monster!'[49]

Thus, while the majority of comments published in *Bild-Zeitung* revealed how many West Germans were following the events in Jerusalem closely enough to be able to name the lawyers involved, along with a general recognition of the need to deal with Nazi war criminals, there remained a significant proportion of correspondents who continued to focus their concern upon the Federal Republic's reputation and the desire to separate themselves from the crimes of the Third Reich, rather than any careful consideration of the legacy of the National Socialist past. One woman rued the fact 'one has to shame oneself before the entire world'; another exclaimed passionately, 'Eichmann is not the German people!' Likewise, a reader from Flensburg insisted that 'the German people wanted neither the war nor the persecution of the Jews'.[50]

Another criticism of the continuing war crimes trials came from a correspondent in Jügesheim who contrasted Eichmann's apparently comfortable stay in custody with the Allies' earlier treatment of the ordinary German population, asking 'Why does one interrogate all the upright people, while one treats brutes like Eichmann like a raw egg?'[51] The defensive tone adopted in this statement bears the implicit sores of the denazification process in the immediate post-war era and underscores the popular notion of German victimhood. Another reader, meanwhile, took offence at the moralising tone adopted by *Bild-Zeitung* and its implicit condemnation of those who failed to act against the persecutions, retorting 'I ask you: What, then, did you do against Hitler?'[52]

At the same time, though, there were readers who welcomed the newspaper's handling of the trial and attacked the apologetic reactions being displayed among many of their compatriots; a woman from Berlin-Charlottenburg emphasised how 'just too many [people] deny these shocking crimes today'.[53] With readers taking issue with those members of the West German public who had hoped to 'forget' or distance themselves from Nazi war crimes, we can see the emergence of a more critical engagement with the past. A discussion also seems to be taking place, if only across the pages of *Bild-Zeitung*, as to what constitutes guilt and responsibility for Nazi atrocities. One man from Berlin-Halensee argued that 'everyone who withdrew his head at that time has to feel like an accessory—if they have a conscience!' Another reader from Berlin insisted, 'Whoever continues to excuse Eichmann today makes himself guilty'.[54]

The letters sent to *Bild-Zeitung* also revealed a particular interest in discussing (and refuting) the issue of following orders imposed from above, a popular post-war line of defence adopted by so many war crimes defendants. Once again, there were a number of comments proffered by ex-service personnel only too keen to demonstrate how they had been able to disobey orders without reprisals. One such reader from Langenfeld also seized the opportunity to criticise the level of popular consensus that had underpinned the Nazi regime, stating 'I myself denied a Himmler order to shoot an entire village because of partisan activity. Every dictatorship would be finished if it did not find so many willing helpers.'[55] A former military figure from Reidlingen was similarly keen to present himself as a 'decent' German. He refuted any notions that they had been powerless in the face of orders from above and separating himself from criminals like Eichmann: 'As a soldier, I would not have come out so well with my prisoners if I had followed all orders'.[56]

The fact that such comments were offered for publication in the national press says something about the level of security these readers were enjoying and, indeed, had come to expect in their post-war lives. By pointing to examples where they claimed to have disobeyed orders, or inviting a discussion with former victims, these men presented themselves wholly in accordance with the notion of the honourable German soldier, freely admitting they had been at the scene of some of the crimes but highlighting the small acts of resistance and examples of basic human kindness that could elevate them above their former comrades. There appears to be no question in these men's minds that this very public admission of being in contact with prisoners of the Third Reich could expose them to facing their own war crimes charges.

There was a sense, though, among the readers' letters to *Bild-Zeitung* that men like Adolf Eichmann were just the tip of the iceberg and a realisation that there was still much to be done in terms of both bringing remaining perpetrators to account and generating greater public awareness of Nazi crimes. While many people seized the opportunity to recall the suffering of German prisoners in German concentration camps, one reader deplored the fact that 'no one speaks about the extermination sites in the Baltic'. The peculiarities of the Holocaust thus remained somewhat hazy in the popular West German consciousness. In the midst of all those letters to *Bild-Zeitung* debating the necessity of following orders, a suitable comeuppance for Eichmann and the impact the proceedings were having on the West German name, a question posed by a Düsseldorf reader struck a particular chord. While his fellow correspondents confined themselves to discussing legalistic and perpetrator-oriented issues, this writer asked simply: 'During the Eichmann trial shouldn't one spend a minute each day remembering the victims?'[57]

Further insights into West German responses to the Adolf Eichmann trial can be gleaned from contemporary opinion poll data. Observers noted that interest in the Eichmann trial diminished as time went on—and that many people had been surprised (and, it is implied, somewhat disappointed) by Eichmann's 'lacklustre' performance in the proceedings; memories of Göring's behaviour at the IMT were, perhaps, revived here. Commentators likewise noted that the number of readers' letters being sent to the press had also tailed off after July 1961. The *New York Times* correspondent Gerd Wilcke quoted a Bonn teacher who stated that 'most persons, after the initial shock felt at the opening of the trial now cannot wait to have Eichmann sentenced. They know Eichmann is guilty but they cannot bring themselves to admit their own share of the guilt'.[58] The newspaper also cited an opinion poll conducted by the Institute of Applied Social Sciences in Bad Godesberg which found 40 percent were 'satisfied' with the media coverage of the proceedings, while 32 percent felt 'the press were overdoing it'.

As with the IMT and the Ulm Einsatzkommando proceedings, the Eichmann case prompted much interest in popular West German responses both among foreign observers and social research institutions and media within the Federal Republic. As early as April 1961, Sydney Grusen, foreign correspondent for the New York Times, concluded that 'perhaps there is only one emotion that practically all Germans share about the trial, the wish that it was done and finished with'.[59] Having conversed with a number of people in Bonn on the matter, Grusen highlighted the comments of one individual who despaired: 'How long and how often do you want us to beat our breasts? Does it make you feel better if we repeat it every day that Nazism was evil, that, if you want, we were evil? What we are trying to tell you is that we know it, we understand it and that we are not now evil'.[60]

A survey by the Institut für Demoskopie in Allensbach in June 1960 found that 90 percent of those questioned had heard about Eichmann's arrest.[61] One year later, as Eichmann's prosecution was underway in Jerusalem, a similar survey saw this figure rise to 96 percent.[62] The majority of the West German population therefore claimed some knowledge of the trial, and in August 1961, the Institut für Demoskopie set out to explore popular responses to the proceedings in more detail. Two thousand West German citizens over the age of 16 were presented with eighteen statements on Eichmann and the Nazi past and asked to say whether they agreed or disagreed with their content. These statements were themselves based upon comments that had previously been offered by members of the public to the Institut on this matter. The results of this survey can be found in the graph below and reveal the extent to which reactionary, apologetic or defensive viewpoints continued to dominate popular ways of thinking about the legacy of the Third Reich during this period.[63]

One of the main problems associated with the use of opinion poll surveys as an historical source concerns the use of leading questions, and the statements posed by the Institut für Demoskopie would certainly fit into this category, pointing as they do to a morally correct response and, in each case, receiving the obvious answer. The first statement put to the people argued, 'People like Eichmann have to be punished all the same, whether they were soldiers or not'. A huge majority of respondents—72 percent—agreed. The scale of consensus is not surprising, given that the question was being asked in the midst of one of the most publicised war crimes trials in history. Those participating in the survey were, in all likelihood, aware that the rest of the world was taking a keen interest in how the country was responding to the Eichmann case, particularly given the ongoing concerns, expressed by the media and politicians alike, about the effects on the country's reputation. Responses to this initial statement may therefore have been automatic, with people quickly affirming their support for the continued prosecution of Nazi criminals and saying what they believed the interviewer, and the rest of the watching world, wanted to hear from the West German people. Similarly, a preponderance of people (47 percent) also rejected any notions of ongoing anti-Semitism when asked whether they thought the word 'Jew' was 'still a bad sounding word'.[64] Meanwhile, by referring distinctly to 'people like Eichmann', the accused seems to be

88 West Germans and the Nazi Legacy

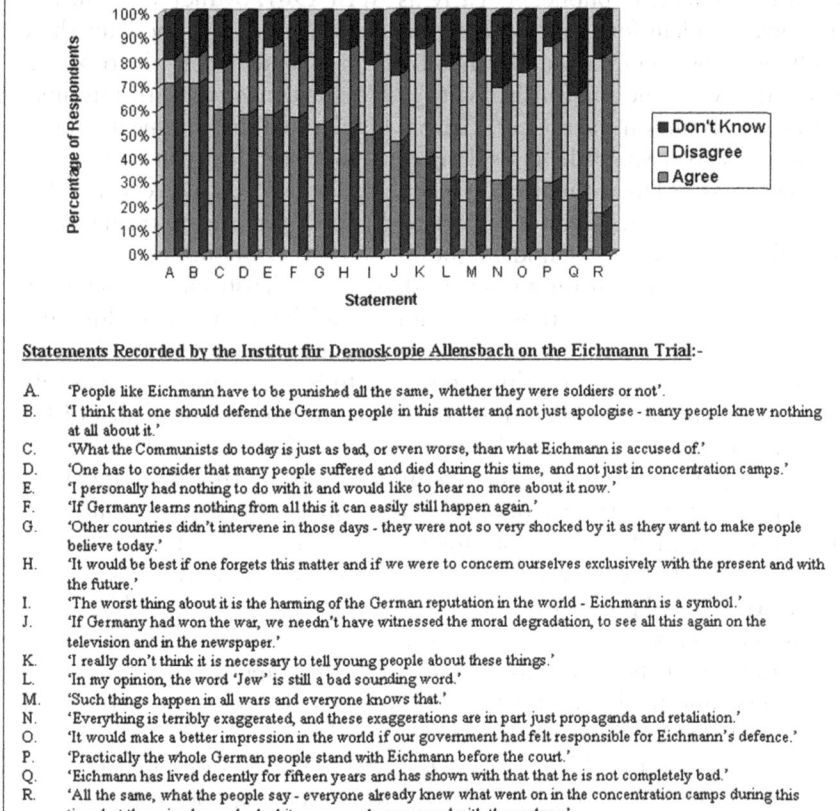

Statements Recorded by the Institut für Demoskopie Allensbach on the Eichmann Trial:-

A. 'People like Eichmann have to be punished all the same, whether they were soldiers or not'.
B. 'I think that one should defend the German people in this matter and not just apologise - many people knew nothing at all about it.'
C. 'What the Communists do today is just as bad, or even worse, than what Eichmann is accused of.'
D. 'One has to consider that many people suffered and died during this time, and not just in concentration camps.'
E. 'I personally had nothing to do with it and would like to hear no more about it now.'
F. 'If Germany learns nothing from all this it can easily still happen again.'
G. 'Other countries didn't intervene in those days - they were not so very shocked by it as they want to make people believe today.'
H. 'It would be best if one forgets this matter and if we were to concern ourselves exclusively with the present and with the future.'
I. 'The worst thing about it is the harming of the German reputation in the world - Eichmann is a symbol.'
J. 'If Germany had won the war, we needn't have witnessed the moral degradation, to see all this again on the television and in the newspaper.'
K. 'I really don't think it is necessary to tell young people about these things.'
L. 'In my opinion, the word 'Jew' is still a bad sounding word.'
M. 'Such things happen in all wars and everyone knows that.'
N. 'Everything is terribly exaggerated, and these exaggerations are in part just propaganda and retaliation.'
O. 'It would make a better impression in the world if our government had felt responsible for Eichmann's defence.'
P. 'Practically the whole German people stand with Eichmann before the court.'
Q. 'Eichmann has lived decently for fifteen years and has shown with that that he is not completely bad.'
R. 'All the same, what the people say - everyone already knew what went on in the concentration camps during this time, but they simply overlooked it or were only concerned with themselves.'

Figure 4.1 Graph showing West German public opinion on the Eichmann trial, 1961.
Source: Data sourced from Elizabeth Noelle & Erich Peter Neumann eds., *Jahruch de Öffentlichen Meinung, 1958–1964* (Allensbach & Bonn: Institut für Demoskopie Allensbach, 1964).

bracketed in a separate division along with other notorious members of the National Socialist hierarchy. The statement presupposes that there will be few who could be considered on a par with Eichmann and thereby imposes a sense of distance between him and the rest of the West German population. It was easy to agree with the continued prosecution of Nazi war criminals if one believed the number of culprits to be small and that, with 'people like Eichmann' hard to find, continued war crimes trials would, in the run long, prove unnecessary.

Once again, concerns for the Federal Republic's standing in the world proved uppermost in the public consciousness, with 51 percent of those questioned agreeing that the worst thing about the trial was the damage that the proceedings would do to the country's reputation.[65] Many of those questioned feared that foreign observers would forever associate the (West) German nation with Eichmann, with 57 percent opposing any claims that the whole of the German people were standing before the court with Eichmann.[66] In addition, 45 percent of people also opposed the idea of the Federal Republic involving itself in Eichmann's defence. Instead, there was a sense that the interviewees wanted to remind the world of the real Germany, to present the Third Reich as an aberration in an otherwise healthy history and to reject firmly any notion of collective guilt.

The remaining statements employed by the Institut für Demoskopie were also inherently defensive and apologetic, clinging stubbornly to notions of German suffering—as opposed to the suffering of foreign victims—while pointing out the failings of other nations. For example, 55 percent of the survey participants agreed that 'other countries didn't interfere in those days, they were not so very shocked by it as the people today want to believe', while, speaking in the midst of the Cold War and against the background of the construction of the Berlin Wall, 61 percent of those questioned were only too keen to affirm that 'what the Communists do today is just as bad as, or even worse, than what Eichmann is accused of'. The resonance that this particular statement produced among the respondents demonstrates how the present political climate influenced responses to the past and allowed a narrative of German suffering to be perpetuated that encompassed the 'misleading' and seductive propaganda of the NSDAP and Allied action against Germany during the Second World War, through to the denazification process and the division of the country. There remained some sense that the Federal Republic was being unfairly targeted, the result of victors' justice or wildly exaggerated propaganda stories.[67] A majority of respondents—59 percent—also agreed that 'one has to consider that many people suffered and died during this time, and not just in the concentration camps'—a comment that carried connotations of the fate of the German soldier on the front line, the number of German civilians killed by Allied bombing raids on the cities and the later violent reprisals carried out by the advancing Red Army.[68]

Such statements would not have been out of place within the dominant representations of the immediate post-war period, highlighting as they do the popularity of resistance and victimhood myths among the 'ordinary' population, and apparently seeking to maintain some degree of silence over the whole affair. That the majority of respondents during this 1961 survey continued to subscribe to such sentiments complicates claims, offered by numerous historians, that it was the Eichmann trial that constituted the definitive turning point in popular attitudes to the Nazi past.

Finally, a majority of the interviewees insisted that they had not learned about Nazi crimes until the end of the war. Such protestations of ignorance enabled people to evade any sense of shared guilt or responsibility for Nazi war crimes and served as a useful basis for then disassociating themselves from any obligation to address the past. For example, 59 percent of those questioned concurred with the statement 'I personally had nothing to do with it and would like to hear no more about it now'. Similarly, 53 percent agreed that 'it would be best if one forgets this matter and if we were to concern ourselves exclusively with the present and with the future'.[69] There thus remained a determination among a large section of the West German population to draw a line under the Nazi era and to concentrate on looking towards a better future, rather than dwelling on uncomfortable and painful reminders of the recent past.

The overwhelming impression gleaned from this opinion survey is, therefore, one of a public continuing to adhere to exculpatory and evasive myths or fictions concerning the legacy of the Third Reich. At the same time, though, it was perhaps possible to identify the stirrings of a more enlightened response to the problems of the past. 58 percent of participants in the survey agreed that Germany needed to learn something from the Eichmann trial in order to prevent any recurrence of such crimes in the future. However, the question of whether the younger generation should actively be taught about the Nazi past proved much more of a sticking point. Just 46 percent felt it was necessary to 'tell young people about these things', while 40 percent disagreed.[70]

It is the division over this one statement that perhaps most accurately sums up the state of West German opinion during this period. Many citizens remained reluctant to rake over the embers of the Nazi past, with vivid memories of their own sufferings still uppermost in their minds. On the other hand, there was a growing awareness that the nation needed to do more to address the legacy of the Third Reich and a growing frustration among the younger generation concerning their elders' silence. It is in this debate over the need to teach younger people about the Holocaust that we can find the long-term origins of the student unrest that would come to characterise the latter half of the decade.

The results of the Eichmann trial were varied. On the one hand, there were many attempts during this period to engage with the legacy of the Nazi past. Exhibitions, books and plays all helped to keep the message of the trials within the public eye. The number of unpunished war criminals within the Federal Republic also remained the subject of some disquiet, thanks to a series of high-profile political scandals, while it is also notable that the Eichmann trial coincided with renewed attempts to crack down on the number of former Nazis who were able to draw state pensions.[71]

On the other hand, though, ostensibly open responses to the trials were infused with evasive distortions. Earlier post-war mythologies persisted, as did a strong sense of distance between the accused and the rest of the West German population. While such trends continued, it would be easy to dismiss Nazi crimes as the work of a radical, sadistic few and for the people of West Germany to separate themselves from such demonic figures. The perpetrators of the Holocaust were not yet recognised as the 'ordinary' men described in subsequent historiography.

The trial received wide press coverage, yet surveys of public opinion showed how the majority of West Germans during this time failed to see the necessity of continued war crimes proceedings. Trials remained a highly controversial issue throughout this period, not least due to the ongoing political and legal debates over the Statute of Limitations. The prospect that trials *could* feasibly be brought to a swift end hardly proved conducive to persuading people to support them wholeheartedly in the meantime. We need to go beyond these large-scale high-profile trials to look instead at how people reacted when events were brought much closer to home, when the defendant really was drawn from their own midst and when the trial was conducted in their own backyard.

5 One of Us

By the start of the 1960s, the legacy of the Nazi past appeared to be gaining increasing recognition within public West German discourse. The new wave of war crimes proceedings was now underway, along with various educational and commemorative activities, while a series of high-profile scandals had prompted many to question the way in which former Nazis had been able to quietly revert to their pre-war positions in public life. At the same time, though, the new decade brought with it some all too clear reminders of the fact that divergent voices persisted within the Federal Republic when numerous synagogues, churches and other buildings were daubed with swastikas. The graffiti began on Christmas Eve in Cologne but quickly spread across the country, sparking condemnation at home and abroad amid fears that the 'old spirit' had not gone away after all.[1] While the West German government swiftly blamed the incidents on misinformed youths and debated possible improvements to Holocaust education, it was clear that efforts to inspire a closer public reflection on the Third Reich remained slow, hesitant and far from perfect. The number of people who were prepared to engage with the past in a genuinely critical way remained limited. Instead, many were still keen to assign the blame for Nazi atrocities on a distinct set of 'excess' perpetrators who had little in common with the everyday West German citizen. How, though, would people react when the accused in a war crimes trial was neither a sadistic concentration camp killer like Martin Sommer, nor a high-ranking bureaucrat like Adolf Eichmann, but was actually someone drawn from their own ranks, an apparently 'ordinary' individual well known within the local community? This chapter explores the impact of such a case: the 1962–3 prosecution of former SS-*Stabsführer* Martin Fellenz in Flensburg, Schleswig-Holstein—an area of Germany which already had its own peculiar association with the Nazi regime to contend with.

This northern, predominantly rural state had experienced a close affinity with the National Socialist movement since the agricultural depression of the late 1920s. Between 1926 and 1928, farm prices declined steadily while farmers' debts and underemployment increased. Sons who had aspired to the professional classes increasingly had to stay on the land, producing a sector of frustrated young men who, as Timothy Tilton has stressed, were more likely to join the SA.[2] Between May 1924 and March 1933, a period marked by a total of seven Reichstag elections, Schleswig-Holstein also repeatedly demonstrated its allegiance to the NSDAP through the ballot box, featuring consistently among the top ten electoral districts for the party. In November 1930, the state gave the Nazis 27 percent of the vote— their highest national figure at this time. In July 1932, this figure rose to 51 percent and, while support fell to 46 percent by November that same year, echoing a national decline in NSDAP fortunes, the region nonetheless continued to provide the Nazis with their biggest success.[3] Thirteen years later, amid the final throes of the Third Reich, the region also became a refuge for many leading personalities of the Nazi regime, most notably Hitler's named successor, Grand Admiral Karl Dönitz, who established his provisional capital in the border city of Flensburg in May 1945.

At the start of the 1960s, Schleswig-Holstein continued to be associated with the Third Reich thanks to a series of 'revelations' as to the number of former Nazis who had retained public positions in the state after the war. In January 1961, the local newspaper, the *Schleswig-Holsteinische Volkszeitung*, published an article listing seven key names that had dominated public discussion in the region over recent months. In addition to Martin Fellenz, the subject of this chapter, the list also featured a teacher from Lübeck who had denounced Anne Frank's *Diary* as a forgery, two former members of the Nazi judiciary now drawing state pensions, and three members of the state medical profession with compromised pasts.[4] The latter included former 'euthanasia' doctor Werner Heyde, who provoked the biggest scandal as it emerged that, despite assuming the post-war alias of Dr. Fritz Sawade, several people in the state administration and elsewhere in the community had known his true identity, yet failed to report him to the authorities. Indeed, it transpired that Heyde/Sawade had even talked about the Nazi medical system within the intimacy of his local *Stammtisch*, providing details that only someone closely involved with the 'euthanasia' programme could have known.[5] It was enough for the *Schleswig-Holsteinische Volkszeitung* to describe Schleswig-Holstein as 'a state of Neo-Nazis', adding:

> Through chance, flight or even appointment, wanted accomplices in the monstrosities of the NS-regime come to this state and seek to conceal their disgraceful deeds. . . . The state of Schleswig-Holstein is associated with their names. From month to month it is proven more clearly that justice has narrow limits—as shown by the fact that even judges and district attorneys themselves, just as administrative officials, have come under suspicion, proudly protecting old Prussian comrades who have become murderers and who 'one' could not denounce.[6]

Foreign observers were also critical. The *New York Herald Tribune* launched a particularly scathing attack, commenting:

The small North German state of Schleswig-Holstein is acquiring the reputation of being a happy hunting ground for former Nazis. . . . It is the picture of a society whose fabric is permeated by covert and tenacious pro-Nazi favouritism and protection.[7]

The newspaper labelled the state capital of Kiel as a 'Nazi quagmire', and argued that the local population 'votes for Dr. Adenauer's democracy every four years, but shows a high degree of tolerance to convicted Nazi war criminals during the intervals'. Referring to the Heyde controversy, the paper suggested there was an 'extensive conspiracy of silence that enabled him to prosper in their midst for years'.[8] Indeed, the main bone of contention during this period was not so much the number of former Nazis residing in Schleswig-Holstein—although the sheer preponderance of them appeared striking—but the layers of knowledge that seemed to surround their recent history and the apparent degree of support that they continued to enjoy in the face of such knowledge. The press, in both the Federal Republic and abroad, regarded Schleswig-Holstein as a region with a peculiar lack of interest in the recent past, a region that was content not to inquire too deeply into people's backgrounds but instead keen to perpetuate the wider silences surrounding the Nazi era. If the truth should nevertheless emerge, as in the Heyde case, it also appeared to be an area that was willing to try safeguarding the compromised individuals from prosecution and enable them to hold onto positions of power and responsibility.

In reality, of course, regional responses to the Nazi past were rather more complicated than sensationalist media reporting would suggest. A counter memory had developed in the state, almost immediately after the war's end, which actually sought to draw public attention to the crimes of the Third Reich, even if its efforts were sometimes frustrated. In 1955, for example, the *Wiener Library Bulletin* recorded an incident that had occurred during a meeting of the Association of Former Internees and Victims of Denazification—a group comprising former Nazis—on 12 June in Neumünster. On the one hand, the very staging of this meeting is interesting; the 600 delegates in attendance underlined the previous levels of support the National Socialist regime had enjoyed in the region, as well as just how many locals had subscribed to notions of German victimhood since 1945. However, the evening was also notable for an opposing demonstration staged by trade unionists who gathered outside the town hall, only to be charged at by police brandishing rubber truncheons. An earlier appeal by the trade unions to prevent the meeting taking place at all had been rejected by the Schleswig state government, which insisted that such a rally was 'insignificant and unobjectionable from the political point of view'.[9]

There were, then, already sectors of the local population seeking to redirect public attention towards the suffering unleashed by the Nazi regime against the Jews and political Left. The stage was thus set for a battle between these competing versions of the past, between those wishing to draw a line under the whole Hitler era, and those seeking to foster a more critical public engagement with Nazi crimes. A study of the prosecution of local resident Martin Fellenz offers further insights into these conflicting responses.

SS- STABSFÜHRER MARTIN FELLENZ

Martin Fellenz was born in 1909 in Duisburg near the western border of Germany. During his early adult life he worked as a banker but in 1930 became one of the millions unemployed as a result of the Great Depression. At the start of 1931, Fellenz travelled to Berlin to study music, pursuing an interest originating from his school days. It was during this time that he joined the NSDAP and it was here, in 1936, that he met SS-*Sturmbannführer* Katzmann, a man who would later play a leading role in the Holocaust in Galicia.[10] Katzmann secured Fellenz a clerical position in the Ministry of the Interior where he remained until 1938. Then, as the Third Reich began to annex territory as part of Hitler's quest for 'living space', Fellenz was moved to Neuruppin, where he became involved in the policing of the newly acquired Sudetenland. At the start of the Second World War Fellenz was transferred to Poland, where he became part of the Warsaw police regiment.[11]

By April 1940, Fellenz had been promoted to the rank of SS-*Stabsführer* and was a police leader in the district of Cracow. Throughout 1942, his unit was among several police groups involved in the 'resettlement' of Polish Jews. Most notably, Fellenz was himself responsible for organising the evacuation of the Przemysl Ghetto over the course of 27 and 31 July and 3 August 1942 as part of the Aktion Reinhard programme. Consequently, 12,500 people were transported to Belzec extermination camp, while around a further 2500 Jews were shot in mass executions at the ghetto, having been deemed incapable of withstanding the journey eastwards.[12] Fellenz remained in this post until the end of December 1942, when he suddenly volunteered for front line military service.

Fellenz's transfer request would become a crucial issue during his 1962 trial. His defence claimed he opted for service on the Eastern Front because he could no longer reconcile himself to the atrocities being perpetrated against the Jews. Such claims, though, ignored the fact that Fellenz had already fulfilled much of his mandate in Poland. Indeed, by the time of his move, Belzec had ceased to operate, having seen around 500,000 people—90 percent of whom were Polish Jews—murdered in its confines.[13]

Having departed from Cracow at the end of 1942, Fellenz joined the SS 'Florian Geyer' cavalry division, only to fall from his mount and suffer a severe leg injury. He received medical treatment in the city of Schleswig, where he also took the opportunity to marry a local woman, before returning to the front line to see out the final phases of the conflict. In 1945, Fellenz was arrested by British forces and interned in a camp in Neumünster. During denazification proceedings in 1947, Fellenz concealed details of his role in the deportation of the Polish Jews, claiming he had merely been part of the auxiliary police and had only joined the Waffen-SS in November 1942. He was subsequently categorised as a *Mitläufer,* or 'Fellow Traveller', and released. He returned to his wife in Schleswig and reverted to his business roots, assuming the operation of his father-in-law's bakery.

Over the next few years, Martin Fellenz enjoyed a peaceful and rather privileged existence, immersing himself fully in the town's civic and cultural life. Continuing to develop his love of music, Fellenz involved himself in a number of local choirs, performing across the region and even making a record.[14] He did not shy away from the public spotlight and, in 1960, led a campaign to inspire a new generation of choir leaders.[15] He had also already carved out a niche for himself in local politics, standing for election to the Schleswig town council as a representative for the FDP in April 1955. Here, then, was an example of a former Nazi war criminal living openly under his real name and actively courting publicity. Fellenz, it appeared, had no reason to feel ashamed or lie low.

Fellenz's choice of post-war political allegiance is, in itself, interesting; the FDP was a well-known haven for former Nazis during the 1950s and 1960s. In the run up to the election, the local newspaper, the *Schleswiger Nachrichten,* produced a brief summary of each candidate, introducing them to the voting public. A paragraph outlined each man's early personal history, expertise and special interests and any experience he could bring to the job. Details of what each candidate did between 1933 and 1945, though, were usually omitted, this chapter in their lives being neatly airbrushed out with no awkward questions asked. In Fellenz's case, the newspaper merely stated:

> He entered the war after 1939 as a Troop Officer and as an officer of the Higher Staff. After being wounded in Russia and released from the Wehrmacht, he resided in Schleswig.[16]

There was no mention of his involvement with the police, the Przemysl Ghetto or the *Aktion Reinhard* programme. Indeed, there was not even any mention of his being in Poland during the war. Far from being cast as complicit in mass murder, Fellenz, with the reference to his war wounds, was now portrayed as a victim. Presenting Fellenz as a member of the Wehrmacht, rather than the SS, similarly invoked notions of the honourable German soldier and memories of the suffering experienced by the army on the Eastern Front. The very next sentence in the biography, meanwhile, recorded Fellenz's musical background, showing him to be an intelligent, cultured and ultimately harmless individual. The newspaper did not investigate whether there might be something more behind these otherwise innocuous life stories. Rather than raking over the Nazi past, it preferred to literally focus on the future in the form of the forthcoming ballot and what each candidate could do for Schleswig.

One of Us 97

Such was the local regard for Fellenz that he was also included among a thirty-strong delegation that travelled to Hayes and Harlington in Middlesex in June 1960 to celebrate the town's twinning with both Schleswig and the French town of Mantes-la-Jolie. Fellenz went to England not only as an official representative of the Schleswig town council, but also, drawing upon his musical talents, as the composer of a special tune to mark the occasion. Film footage of these events depicts what would seem to be the quintessential English summer fete, complete with a carnival procession and marching brass band. The scenes sum up the sheer ordinariness of Fellenz's post-war life, as well as the level of trust and confidence that his hometown had implicitly bestowed upon him by including him as their ambassador for this event.[17]

It was at the end of this trip, though, that Fellenz's hitherto tranquil life suddenly unravelled. Upon his return to Germany on 20 June 1960, Fellenz was arrested for his involvement in the crimes committed against the Polish Jews—charges brought about by investigations conducted by the Ludwigsburg Zentralstelle. Fellenz spent the next thirty months awaiting trial in a Flensburg prison. During his eventual prosecution, he categorically denied having ever issued orders for the shooting of the Jews and repeatedly protested his ignorance as to the true meaning behind the euphemistic phrase 'Resettlement'.

News of the arrest of Martin Fellenz, as the *Flensburger Tageblatt* admitted at the time, produced the 'strongest echo' in England, sending shock waves through the residents of Hayes and Harlington who had received him just days before.[18] Locals there were furious, not only at the revelation that one of their guests had been a mass murderer, but also at the base deception practised by Fellenz, a man who had actually introduced himself to his hosts as a former concentration camp prisoner. In reality, the only camp Fellenz had been held in was the British detention centre in Neumünster while awaiting his denazification proceedings between 1945 and 1947. The *Daily Express*, in an effort to characterise Fellenz's initial appearance, employed the word 'gentle' five times in the space of a single article, thereby setting up a deliberate contrast with the reality of his involvement in the Nazi genocide. The newspaper introduced the story, noting 'there was no doubt about it at the time—the gentle German with the soft voice and shy smile was the charmer of the party visiting Hayes, Middlesex on a goodwill mission'.[19] Elsewhere in the article, Fellenz was referred to as 'the perfect guest' with a cultivated manner.[20]

While the British tabloids latched eagerly onto the story, news of Fellenz's arrest was treated far differently back in Schleswig-Holstein. Although the community appeared to be taken by surprise at this sudden turn of events, the case received relatively little attention in the regional press. Newspaper articles remained brief, limiting themselves to the bare facts of the case, and devoid of any editorial comment. The role of the Ludwigsburg Zentralstelle in orchestrating the arrest was noted repeatedly, enabling it to be seen as 'outside' interference in the affairs of Schleswig-Holstein, and all the local newspapers made an implicit comment on Fellenz's prominent social position, referring to him as a Schleswig town councillor in their headlines. However, none of these publications expressed any outrage that a man with such a brutal past had been able to entrench himself within the fabric of the local community.[21] Arguably, by this point, such revelations had become the norm; Fellenz could simply be seen as yet another in a long line of prominent individuals harbouring a compromised past, unworthy of any particular excitement.

At the same time, two of the local newspapers, the *Flensburger Tageblatt* and the *Südschleswigische Heimatzeitung*, immediately placed themselves on a defensive footing, stressing, before any questions could even be raised, how little had been known in the area about Fellenz's past up until that time: 'One only knew that, during the war, he had conducted a music platoon and that he had been imprisoned automatically by the English after 1945 as a member of the Waffen-SS'.[22] Like the biography provided for Fellenz's 1955 election campaign, such descriptions presented an extremely sanitised version of the accused's wartime activities while suggesting that his denazification proceedings had been unwarranted, perpetuating the notion of Fellenz's own victimhood. Such protestations of ignorance concerning Fellenz's behaviour under the Third Reich enabled local people to deny any culpability in protecting him after the war, while a further line of defence was constructed around the reassuring fact that Fellenz had been born in Duisburg and only settled in Schleswig after 1945. This important detail was repeated throughout the early newspaper reports on the case and enabled the region to avoid any sense of responsibility for Fellenz's early political and ideological development.[23] It was a move that fitted into a wider post-war trope that presented National Socialism as coming from 'somewhere else'. Silences remained, though, as to the level of popular support that the region had previously given to the NSDAP.

The national media, though, were less than convinced by such claims and continued to criticise Schleswig-Holstein's handling of former Nazis. The *Frankfurter Rundschau* argued that Fellenz had, actually, been known to people for years but no one had turned him in.[24] *Die Zeit*, however, ruefully noted that such silences were not confined to Schleswig-Holstein but were typical of wider West German society at the time:

> He had discarded his [past] with his SS uniform. He was just a peaceful citizen of a peaceful and peace-loving city who strove to be finished with the results of the war as quickly as possible and as well as possible.... Who knew that the businessman—and in the interim also a popular citizen of the city—had earlier been an SS man? Many had been in the SS. And no more was spoken of them.[25]

The local press was not alone, though, in its reluctance to offer public comment on the case. Fellenz's colleagues on the Schleswig town council recorded Fellenz's absence from their next meeting as a matter of formality for the minutes, but offered no sense of their own opinions on his arrest. Instead, it was noted that there had been some public interest in the matter; councillor Dr. Carl Wehn, a representative of the CDU, agreed he would issue a brief statement on it, and the council then moved onto the seemingly more pressing issue of discussing the proposed plans for a new car park.[26] The minutes of any organisation, of course, only include the elements of meetings that the participants want on record, yet here it would seem that the council lost a valuable opportunity to show observers that they were taking the situation seriously.

A public statement issued by the FDP, meanwhile, refuted any suggestion that Fellenz's past had been an open, tolerated secret. The Party stood by its representative and, at the same time, seized the chance to attack the very continuance of war crimes investigations, clinging to the popular belief that those implicated in the Nazi genocide had merely been compelled to follow orders imposed from above. The statement emphasised:

> A) Herr Fellenz not only has the greatest confidence of his friends, but that of the whole public as justified by his behaviour in the last ten years.
>
> [and]
>
> B) The state committee of the FDP holds that the arrest for war crimes fifteen years after the war's end is only still justified if there are well-founded suspicions that he really was responsible for the accusations and was not just the executor of received orders.[27]

Wider reactions within Fellenz's hometown of Schleswig certainly appear to support the first half of this statement and suggest that favourable impressions of Martin Fellenz continued to circulate within the local community long after his arrest. Letters preserved in the Landesarchiv Schleswig indicate that he had no shortage of friends and colleagues wishing to visit him in his Flensburg prison cell or willing to outline their support for the prisoner to both the judicial authorities and Fellenz himself. One man, while asking for permission to visit Fellenz in custody, stressed how he and his wife had been friends with Fellenz for 'many years' and both now felt it was 'important to be there' for him.[28] Many acquaintances revealed their amazement at the recent turn of events. A member of Fellenz's choir petitioned the authorities in an effort to find out how long Fellenz was likely to be held in custody. He highlighted the crucial role that Fellenz had played in their choir, and insisted that no replacement could possibly be found for him.[29] Another chorister wrote directly to Fellenz himself, affirming that he still had a lot of support in the local community:

> Try to make the best of your situation as far as you are able. You can be sure that our thoughts and wishes are constantly with you. . . .

Denunciations go astray, so each of us could, today or tomorrow, fall into your situation. But we and you have already been through so much hardship and suffering in our generation that this will mean little. . . . I assure you that I am utilising every possibility to get you out of detention until the opening of a trial. At the same time, I—like everyone who has belonged to your circle over the past fifteen years—would bet my last shirt that the allegations one brings against you will not suffice to let it come to a trial![30]

Fellenz's standing in the Schleswig community, therefore, was such that the majority of those who knew him found the allegations about his horrific crimes in Poland incomprehensible, or unimportant. The correspondence outlined above illustrates how, in the summer of 1960, many people felt that Fellenz's arrest was simply all a big mistake, and that the charges levelled against him by the Ludwigsburg Zentralstelle could never amount to much in a court of law. The first local reaction to these events, then, was to close ranks around Fellenz, to safeguard his position—whether in the FDP or in his choir—and to make a big show of support for 'their man'.

MEDIA INTEREST IN THE FELLENZ TRIAL

Despite the doubts expressed by his supporters, prosecutors were able to press ahead with their case against Fellenz. The resultant trial, conducted between November 1962 and January 1963 and involving 120 witnesses, was reported faithfully every day in the local Schleswig-Holstein newspapers, although it lacked the national appeal of either the Ulm or Bayreuth proceedings.[31] The latter feature may be explicable by the novelty of revived war crimes proceedings starting to wear off. While the 1958 prosecution of the Einsatzkommando Tilsit had attracted a vast degree of media interest because it constituted the first major trial of Nazi personnel to be held under the jurisdiction of the Federal Republic, there were now many similar proceedings taking place right across the country, all of which were competing for column space in the West German newspapers. Nearly twenty war crimes cases were being heard at Landgericht level in 1962 alone; in November 1962, just as the Fellenz trial was getting underway in Flensburg, there were also proceedings taking place against former Sachsenhausen guard Kurt Eccarius in Coburg and former Lemberg police officer Oskar Waltke in Hanover. The charges levelled against the latter figure were also similar to those facing Fellenz, with Waltke accused of shooting Jews being transported out of the ghettos between 1942 and 1944.[32] Taken as a whole, therefore, the sheer number of prosecutions and investigations then underway could be seen as producing a sense of 'trial fatigue' among newspaper editors and the wider population alike. Similarly, it could be argued that the level of interest in both the Fellenz case, and West German proceedings as a whole, may have suffered as a result of the recent media frenzy that had surrounded the Eichmann trial the year before.

The failure of the Fellenz case to hit the national headlines may also owe something to the nature of the crimes being discussed in Flensburg. Like the Ulm trial, it failed to produce a media resonance anywhere near akin to that of the 1958 prosecution of Martin Sommer in Bayreuth because of the fundamental fact that it was dealing with war crimes perpetrated against Polish Jews in Poland, rather than offences committed against German nationals within Germany itself. There was a continued unwillingness within West Germany to consider the extent to which the majority of the victims of National Socialism had actually been foreign Jews and East Europeans. Instead, there remained a popular desire to focus solely on the plight of the German people under Hitler, in places that bore more familiar-sounding names, and to continue thereby to construct myths of German victimhood.

Furthermore, it is significant that such local media reporting which did occur on the Fellenz case was noticeably lacking in the sort of sensationalism and emotive drama that West Germans may have come to expect from war crimes reporting. While Sommer was held up to be the personification of evil and a peculiarly sadistic killer, and Eichmann was shown to be the 'banal' bureaucratic face of Nazi criminality, there was no attempt to demonise, critique or otherwise ponder Fellenz's character, a factor which may owe much to the defendant's standing within the local community. People appeared unwilling to consider that a man they had respected, trusted and even elected into local political office could have a darker side to him. Emphasising Fellenz's high standing within local Schleswig life, *Die Zeit* commented:

> He did much that gave him a name in the little city. . . . To be sure there were some in Schleswig who called him arrogant and thought his qualities were overestimated. But nothing changed [the fact that] he was [an] esteemed citizen in this city.[33]

If any picture did emerge of Fellenz's character during his trial, it was one which continued to hold him up as a fundamentally decent, gentle and cultured individual. One witness, Dr. Ernst Jansen, a lawyer from Düsseldorf, was admittedly rather dismissive of him as he described the defendant as 'a coffee house violinist' and an ambitious person who 'had liked to be or appear to be someone', yet the sentiments of his testimony nonetheless seemed to fit in with this comforting image of a very ordinary man.[34] Likewise, the press leapt upon the testimony of Dr. Sachs who, having described Fellenz as 'colourless', argued he had appeared not as the 'prototype soldier, but as an artistically interested person'.[35] He had, it seemed, been wholly unsuited for his wartime role in Poland. Another witness, meanwhile, recalled how Fellenz had been a 'good comrade', a phrase bearing connotations of strong loyalty and the existence of a close-knit community of former SS personnel.[36] Such comments, together with the number of former SS members who were now appearing to testify on Fellenz's behalf, did not exactly help to relieve images of Schleswig-Holstein as a 'Nazi nest'. In fact, it became clear during the course of the trial that the defendant had remained in fairly close contact with some of his former colleagues after 1945, with the prosecution displaying a keen interest in a good luck card that Fellenz had sent to the witness Wilhelm Kunde for a party during the post-war era. The court wanted to know more about the pair's post-war relationship and, although neither the witness nor the accused was able to recall precisely when the card had been sent, the image was nonetheless created of the solidarity still persisting among former SS personnel.[37]

There was little attempt to provide editorial comment on these events. The devices employed by prosecuting and defence counsel, together with the language used by the (predominantly former SS) witnesses, were allowed to speak for themselves. This matter-of-fact reporting, usually running across the space of at least half a page, reduced the trial to a routine, and rather sterile, legalistic exercise. That so many former SS men had been allowed to testify for their old 'comrade' was accepted without question. Similarly, while Fellenz's decision to request a transfer to the front line at the end of 1942 proved to be a popular talking point throughout the proceedings, there was no attempt to iron out the apparent discrepancy between this petition, the result of Fellenz allegedly feeling sickened by the treatment being meted out to the Jews, and his subsequent denial of ever having known about what was happening to the Jews being transported. Instead, the *Flensburger Tagblatt*, which referred to Fellenz's transfer four times over the course of its coverage, recorded how the former SS-*Scharführer* Wilhelm Kunde (now employed as a customs secretary in Bremen) had told the court, 'Fellenz himself was very agitated over the shootings of hundreds of Jews in Michalovice and stated he no longer wanted anything to do with it and reported to the Front'.[38] The newspaper also relayed the words of another former Nazi, Sepp Müller, who recalled Fellenz as having stated, 'This Beyerlein [the man responsible for the Michalovice 'evacuation'] is a dirty swine! I've had enough! I want to get away . . . as soon as I can!'[39]

During the trial coverage, there were recurring references to the fact that many survivor witnesses frequently became confused or forgetful during their testimonies, rendering an implicit attack on the problems of continued war crimes trials so long after the events in question. That many former SS personnel had become 'hazy' about the details of the 'Resettlement' programme, or the extent of their own awareness of it, was, however, allowed to pass unchallenged by the local press.

Even when Jewish survivors came to testify thirteen days after the start of the trial, the *Flensburger Tagblatt* remained surprisingly calm in its handling of the trial. Much of the horror of the 'Resettlement' action was consequently glossed over, sparing the residents of Schleswig-Holstein the process of having to engage with the reality of the Holocaust. The most dramatic coverage the *Flensburger Tagblatt* provided was to use the headline 'My Relatives Are Not Coming Back', a phrase that stood in stark contrast to the sensationalism employed in the national newspapers such as the *Frankfurter Rundschau*, which ran with the line 'I Just Saw Blood and Bodies', or *Die Zeit*, which proclaimed how the victims had been 'Shot Like Hares'.[40]

The Fellenz case did not become front page headline news in the local press until the final sentencing on 17 January 1963. Fellenz was convicted on two counts of complicity in murder and sentenced to a total of four years in prison, the court unable to determine beyond doubt whether Fellenz had really understood the implications behind the euphemistic phrase 'Resettlement' and whether, as a result, he had knowingly sent five transports of Polish Jews to their deaths in Belzec. The court had also been unable to prove whether he had personally committed four acts of murder—as alleged by the prosecution—with the shooting of Jews from the Przemysl Ghetto. However, the Flensburg court did take into account the lengthy period that Martin Fellenz had spent in custody while awaiting his trial, adjusting the sentence in a manner that secured his immediate release and enabling him to go straight home with his wife.

It was this result which ensured the case suddenly found an echo within the national West German press, being widely regarded as yet another example of a judicial reluctance to punish former Nazi war criminals effectively. The sudden condemnation of the trial suggested that the press had been keeping an eye on the events in Flensburg, even if they had not actually been printing many articles on it. The *Rheinischer Merkur*, for example, criticised the court's willingness to accept Fellenz's protestations of ignorance about the fate awaiting the transported Jews, as well as the eagerness with which evidence from other former SS members had been heard, opining:

> This sorry comedy will persist as long as fellow criminals are allowed to pass as witnesses, safe in the knowledge that their highly perfected gift for total amnesia will not expose them to perjury prosecution.[41]

Several West German newspapers made a point of noting the Jewish response to the Fellenz verdict in what could be seen as attempts to shock the wider population into taking more concerted action with regards to the National Socialist legacy. The *Frankfurter Allgemeine Zeitung* was typical, highlighting how the sentence had been sharply criticised in Jewish circles and stressing how there was 'a danger that the results of the trial will minimise the mass murder'.[42] The *Frankfurter Rundschau*, under the headline 'Exasperating Verdicts', quoted a Jewish witness, Morris Gottfried, who had appeared during the proceedings:

> Had I known that criminals are allowed here to testify on oath, I would not have troubled to come and give evidence. But then, nothing has changed in Germany, things are what they have always been.[43]

Die Zeit, meanwhile, expressing amazement at how 'once again, a German court proved inexplicably mild vis-à-vis the crimes of the Nazi era', puzzled over how Fellenz could receive a four year prison sentence for participating in mass murder while a Munich man sentenced that same day for strangling his wife was given six years imprisonment.[44] The newspaper sarcastically suggested that the Flensburg judges 'saw no sense in tearing an "esteemed" citizen from his family and profession for a long time' and bemoaned the implicit conclusion that the notion 'wrongs must be *atoned* is clearly no longer obvious'.[45]

Local media responses to the Fellenz sentence seemed mixed. While the more conservative *Flensburger Tagblatt* persisted in the detached tone it had adopted throughout the proceedings, the *Südschleswigische Heimatzeitung* was much more excitable, declaring that 'this type of justice brings us back down into the cold cruelties of those years when millions of people were tortured, gassed, shot and hanged. We are ashamed!'[46]

This sense of shame, though, was not merely out of concern for the victims of Nazi persecution; the reputation of Schleswig-Holstein and the national German character were also being called into question. Recalling the circumstances of Fellenz's arrest, *Die Welt* questioned the impact that the trial would have on West Germany's standing in the world:

> It is to be feared that the residents of Hayes and Harlington will no longer want to know the Germans. One cannot receive them again: who even knows what's what in the Federal Republic now? The complete mess that has gathered around numerous trials for the 'overcoming of the past' in past years has become scandalously large. It has gone so far that Jewish citizens ask if they should distance themselves from such trials because they only render satisfaction for the guilty and their sympathisers.

Reflecting on the lack of widespread public interest in Nazi war crimes proceedings, *Die Welt* added, 'Many see their indifference justified because nothing comes out of these trials'.[47]

How far, though, were such sentiments the preserve of the more liberal newspapers? How far had the revelations of the Fellenz trial served to shock the local people of Schleswig-Holstein into altering their opinion of the accused? Were they too now ashamed to have had anything to do with the accused? Or would Martin Fellenz be able to emerge from these proceedings with his reputation still intact?

PUBLIC INTEREST IN THE FELLENZ TRIAL

For the most part, the muted reception that had characterised media coverage of the Fellenz case was echoed among the wider population of Schleswig-Holstein. There were none of the crowd scenes outside the court that had typified the Sommer trial in Bayreuth, nor was there any apparent desire to observe the proceedings firsthand. *Die Zeit* noted the consistent emptiness of the public gallery inside the courtroom:

> It was a trial which for some weeks, day after day, dealt with the most brutal mass murder known in recent German history: the systematic extermination of the Jews in the General Government. In the course of this action, two million of the three and a half million Jewish inhabitants of the so-called General Government were exterminated. Shot, beaten, gassed. But only a few have taken notice of this trial. The audience benches in the Flensburg court were often empty.[48]

Amid her work on the Eichmann trial, Hannah Arendt cited the Fellenz case as being typical of a widespread lack of German interest in Nazi crimes, insisting that the hearings had occurred 'in an almost empty courtroom'.[49] Similarly the British *Guardian* newspaper, referring to Schleswig as 'a part of Germany which has had more than its fair share of war criminals', commented:

> Germans are losing the ghoulish interest which they took in earlier trials and the number of people who attend in order to learn about the Nazi era was probably never very large.[50]

This apparent lack of public interest in the case certainly seems surprising, given the defendant's standing within the community, yet responses to the Fellenz trial may have been rather more complicated than a few rows of empty courtroom seats might otherwise suggest.

Firstly, the very timing of the trial may have affected people's willingness to attend the proceedings in person. Held towards the end of 1962, the people of Flensburg were getting ready for Christmas and probably had neither the time nor inclination to immerse themselves in the gruesome details of a war crimes trial. The local press certainly observed the striking contrast between the cheerful, festive scenes being played out throughout the rest of the city and the tales of human suffering that dominated the courtroom. The *Schleswig-Holsteinische Volkszeitung* noted that, while the rest of the city was filled with bright Christmas lights, the courtroom was overshadowed by 'the darkest chapter of our history'.[51]

Secondly, it is important to note that there were moments during the Fellenz trial when the hearings did play out before a small public audience, with several school classes being brought to the court to follow the events for themselves. The *Schleswig-Holsteinische Volkszeitung* noted how teachers were often sitting with their classes until quite late into the evening and was clearly pleased at such scenes, declaring these educational activities to be the 'best vaccine' against continuing racism in West Germany.[52] While the extent to which the pupils were able to absorb the enormity of Fellenz's crimes and comprehend the legal terminology and complex arguments that were being employed in the court remains questionable, it is clear that there were individuals in Schleswig-Holstein during this period who were attempting to foster a more critical engagement with the Nazi past. The teachers of the late 1950s and early 1960s played a crucial role in helping to draw attention to Nazi crimes and in challenging some of the silences surrounding the country's recent history that had otherwise seemed to permeate the older generation across the Federal Republic.[53]

A similar situation occurred in the winter of 1965–6, when Fellenz found himself the subject of a retrial in the state capital of Kiel.[54] Dr. Hans-Jörg Herold was a young history student at the time when his lecturer, Professor Erdmann, organised a trip to the court to watch the proceedings. He recalls that the trial was presented to his class as a valuable educational opportunity, enabling them to engage closer with the ongoing debate over the Statute of Limitations and to discuss the methodological problems associated with oral history. Dr Herold recalled recently:

> I attended the sessions because I was interested not only in the mentioned problems, but also in the consequences for our society since the Ulm Einsatzgruppen trial [of] 1958 and the employment of the 'Zentrale Stelle der Landesjustizverwaltungen zur Aufklärung nationalsozialistischer Verbrechen' in Ludwigsburg. . . . In Kiel, I wanted to see into the eyes of one of the Nazi culprits.[55]

Fellenz himself continued to appear as an unexceptional character. Dr. Herold described him as being attentive, disciplined and well-dressed, "in short, a normal citizen, not remarkable". The sight of this innocuous-looking figure in the dock enabled Dr. Herold to feel some sense of sympathy with the accused: "I felt sorry for him when the prosecutor spoke his sentence and Fellenz pressed his lips and went white. Only a few days before Christmas".[56] Like the press reports on Fellenz's original trial in Flensburg, Dr. Herold noted how there were few spectators in the courtroom for the hearings aside from his university classmates. However, Professor Erdmann's conviction that the trial constituted an important learning tool for his students was such that he even arranged for the trial prosecutor to come and talk to the class in his own home about the West German legal system.

Herold's experiences, together with the presence of school classes during the 1962–3 proceedings, suggest the existence of alternative modes of thinking about the past in Schleswig-Holstein during this period—interpretations that marked the emergence of a more critical confrontation with the legacy of the National Socialist era. At the same time, though, some pupils within the state continued to be exposed to more "conventional" interpretations of the Third Reich and the Second World War. At the start of 1963 as the Flensburg Fellenz trial was coming to an end, the town of Geesthact near Hamburg came under scrutiny within the international press—and even during the course of a House of Commons debate in Britain—when Hitler's successor, Karl Dönitz, addressed a group of high school pupils. While Dönitz steered clear of delivering any overtly Nazi ideas to his audience, he did stress the need for military personnel to obey orders and how soldiers were not entitled to question the rights and wrongs of their actions, an argument that was in keeping with the debates circulating at the heart of the Fellenz case.[57]

Further evidence that the first Fellenz trial was having an impact on at least some sectors of the local population is apparent through readers' letters sent to the newspapers. Although lacking within the local Schleswig-Holstein press, comments did appear on the results of the Fellenz trial among those following events in the national press. Writing to *Die Zeit* in the aftermath of the trial, one reader from Langen expounded at great length on Fellenz's lenient sentencing and the continuing failure of the West German judiciary to deal effectively with the crimes of the Third Reich:

> This discrepancy between the District Attorney's proposition for lifelong imprisonment and the verdict for the SS officer Martin Fellenz that is tantamount to a parole, further shakes the already heavily marred confidence in the justice of the Federal Republic. With this judgement, the judges justify the Nazi genocide and deride the victims and the survivors. Today it can no longer be said: he hadn't wanted it, he knew nothing about it, he was powerless against the 'evacuation policies'. Today the silent accepting of this type of verdict means—an approval. The Fellenz government from Flensburg is the best breeding ground for the discriminations of a Khrushchev, for the propaganda of the [East German] zone rulers.[58]

Additional insights into the popular resonance of the Fellenz case can be gleaned from letters sent by members of the public to the Flensburg court itself, although again far fewer were generated by these proceedings than during the 1958 Sommer case. Fundamentally, these letters can be divided into two main groups. On the one hand, there were correspondents who were clearly outraged at both the lenient sentencing and the fact Fellenz had been able to live unheeded in the region for so long. On the other hand, there were those who seemed pleased at the way in which Fellenz had effectively evaded punishment and hoped this could now be the end of the matter once and for all. At the end of the trial, the local newspaper, the *Südschleswiger Heimatzeitung*, sought to explain such contrasting opinions in terms of a generational divide between trial observers. The newspaper recorded that there were a number of older spectators in the public gallery, many of them apparently friends and colleagues of Martin Fellenz, who had gathered as a sign of continuing support on the final day of the proceedings. As the sentence was handed down, these people smiled and waved at the defendant, clearly displaying their pleasure at his imminent release. Younger people present in the court, though, were angered at what they were witnessing and were more inclined to believe that Fellenz had merited far harsher treatment. The newspaper commented that 'a dark chapter of German history was played out before the young trial observers, without being satisfactorily illuminated'.[59]

A closer examination of the letters sent to the court, however, enables us to look beyond the ages of trial observers and identify even greater shades of opinion and several key themes that were dominating popular ways of thinking about the legacy of the Nazi past.

The sentencing of the accused was certainly a popular talking point, with many correspondents calling for improvements to be made within the West German justice system. One writer, Herr C., argued:

> For these deeds, there should be only one punishment—the death penalty. . . . One is overtaken by a sense of satisfaction when one thinks about the death penalty in the judgement of the Eichmann trial. It is not the joy at the death of this man, but in the name of just punishment for all the bloody deeds of these people. . . . One should reintroduce the death penalty for murderers. Otherwise one can't talk about justice in Germany any more.[60]

Another writer, Herr B., expressed similar dissatisfaction with the results of the Fellenz trial. Drawing attention to the fact he considered the recipient of his letter—Amtsgerichtsdirektor Otto—unworthy of the usual courtesy of the polite *Sehr gehrter Herr* form of address, he rejected arguments that the inability to prove whether Fellenz understood the meaning of 'Resettlement' rendered a lenient sentence a necessity: 'You could also declare not guilty a murderer who maintains not to know what a murder is and that a murder is punishable', he retorted.[61]

A far more outspoken letter, meanwhile, came from Herr W., who launched a furiously scathing attack on the Fellenz verdict, as well as Schleswig-Holstein's handling of the National Socialist legacy as a whole, playing upon fears engendered by the Cold War—and recently heightened as a result of the Cuban Missile Crisis:

> These Nazi swine in the German justice deliver us to the Communists and Russians. All of Schleswig-Holstein appears to be a Nazi nest. Sawade case, Fellenz case, Dusenschön case in Hamburg—one justice scandal follows the other!
> . . . It stinks to the Heavens in the German justice system. One has to be ashamed to be a German!
> . . . Have we deserved nothing better than these shocking justice scandals that rush us over to the Russians and the Communists?????????
> . . . It is disgraceful to have to live in this Nazi state. . . . How can we still hope to be free of these Nazi swine? The Nazi swine have delayed

these trials for two decades, no one remembers everything anymore. What do increases in taxes, economy, prosperity etc. mean against this swelling plague of Nazi swine. It stinks to the Heavens![62]

The very language employed by Herr W. throughout his letter is significant. The phrase 'Nazi nest', utilised at the start of the letter to describe Schleswig-Holstein, conjures up connotations of another expression that was enjoying popular usage during this period—*Nestbeschmutzen*. This term was used to admonish those seeking to redirect attention to Nazi crimes during the early post-war years, accusing them of 'dirtying their own nest'. Herr W. can thus be seen as turning such language against itself as he calls for a more strident judicial handling of the recent past.

Although it was the sentencing of the accused—and the results of war crimes trials as a whole during this period—that dominated the letters sent to the Flensburg court, there was at least one person who had been clearly encouraged by the course of the Fellenz trial to reflect on the recent past. Having followed the details relayed in the press about the deportation of Polish Jews to the extermination camps, Herr C. pondered the fate of the German Jews he had once lived alongside in Kusel and began to express his own deep sense of shame for not intervening on their behalf:

> There were Jewish families who had been resident in Kusel since the times of their grandparents, who were shopkeepers and who cared as much about their customers as Christian merchants. . . . Just thinking of them makes my heart ache. They wanted to keep their homeland and they couldn't even save their lives. All the men, women and children were put into concentration camps and out of all these people not a single one has returned. Sometimes I am caught in a deep remorse and I'm telling myself that one could have helped them because where there's a will, there's a way. One could have got papers for them. If they could only have got out of Germany.[63]

However, despite all his professed shame and desire to atone for the past, there remains a strain of apologia running through this letter. By pointing to the degree of assimilation in Kusel, Herr C. could underscore local traditions of tolerance, reject any notion of inherent racism and present National Socialism as having been imposed from the outside, a movement which had little to do with his own community. At the same time, he highlighted the Jews' own responses, pointing out that 'most of them . . . lacked the money to emigrate and they themselves didn't think that all this would come to such a horrific end'.[64]

Another letter writer had also felt compelled to reflect upon his own experiences of the Third Reich, albeit as a means to offer assistance to Fellenz's defence attorney. In contrast to the emotional outpourings of those critical of the trial's results, Herr P. noted quite coolly:

It is stated that there is no known case where someone was placed before an SS court or shot for refusing an extermination order. As a former SS member, I once had to guard a comrade who was arrested for refusing an order and was eventually transported with an unknown number. I am prepared to repeat this statement before the court.[65]

The author of this letter apparently felt no shame about his past, nor any sense of a social stigma attached to him as a result of his past allegiances. Indeed, he appears sufficiently confident to be able to relate his experiences with the SS in public without any fear of reprisals, whether in the form of judicial proceedings against himself or a moral outcry from the rest of the population. It demonstrates the eagerness of former SS personnel to perpetuate claims that they had to follow orders out of self-preservation and exemplifies the degree of camaraderie that existed between former SS members after 1945, with veterans willing to help by testifying on one another's behalf.

Letters sent to the Flensburg court also underlined how there remained some people who still sought to relativise the atrocities committed by the Nazis. Herr Br. rejected any notion of collective guilt for the crimes of the Third Reich as he stressed that 'the German people are no worse and no better than the people of other nations'. Like many people, he continued to place the blame for the atrocities firmly on the Nazi leadership, particularly Hitler and Himmler, and held firm to the belief that disobedience at that time meant risking one's own life.[66] A passionate Herr S. also explored this theme at some length as he displayed his vehement opposition to the prospect of continuing war crimes trials. His letter also emphasised notions of German suffering, describing the damage wrought by Allied air raids on German cities, and implying how the 'ordinary' German population had been misled by the Nazi leadership:

> The almost twenty year hunt for war criminals has been made among the war defeated. But [there are] still no proceedings against the former enemy sides. I have never had anything against the Jews in my life, although I have seen and experienced with much anger the scandals of the Jews. . . . 6 million Jews is a malicious invention of propaganda, just as one can say 6 million women, children and elderly people were burned alive by the Morgenthau gangster. . . . No Churchill, no Harris, no Morgenthau have known a neutral court. In the last weeks of the war alone, over two thirds of the 350,000 refugees from the East were burned alive in Dresden. . . . Have [ever] a people suffered more than the Germans? . . . Please finally finish with war crimes.[67]

* * * * * * * *

The case of former SS-*Stabsführer* Martin Fellenz consequently provides an interesting insight into the conflicting public responses that a Nazi war crimes trial could engender. It exemplifies the cases of former Nazis who managed to assimilate themselves back into the very fabric of post-war West German society—and the level of public support and respect they continued to enjoy even when accusations of mass murder were raised against them. Questions can thus be posed as to the extent to which the much-discussed notion of 'the murderers among us', so clearly personified by Fellenz, actually facilitated a critical dialogue with the recent past. Does the phrase indicate an awareness of the scale of Nazi atrocities and a desire to see those responsible brought to account, or does it remain a rather abstract concept, referring to unknown quantities of shadowy, faceless individuals distinct from the 'ordinary' population? It is possible to demonise defendants on trial in faraway courtrooms or associated with particularly grisly acts, but this becomes a much harder process when the accused plays an intimate part in the local community; he cannot be depicted quite so easily as a 'monster' when he is known to be 'one of us'.

However, rather than posing deeper questions as to how cultured, intelligent and seemingly 'harmless' men could participate in genocide, the example of Martin Fellenz reveals a community largely in denial, unconvinced by the allegations levelled against him and certain it has all somehow been a big mistake. Fellenz, it could be argued, can be seen as innocent by association. Similarly, with the court proceedings focussing very much on the complex nature of the Nazi hierarchy, the deliberately obscure language utilised by those involved in orchestrating the 'Final Solution' and the necessity of following orders, Fellenz's wartime behaviour could be quickly explained away, the result of forces beyond his control. Once again, the extent of Nazi war crimes—and the level of consensus behind the Third Reich—could be sidestepped.

The Fellenz case did manage to create something of a split in Schleswig-Holstein—not just between the prosecution, who called for life imprisonment, and the defence, who sought an acquittal, but between the older generation and the young, those wishing to 'draw a line' under the whole Nazi era and dismiss all charges and those seeking atonement, engagement and some acknowledgement of a wider responsibility for the crimes of the Third Reich. The latter sentiment was present in the state, but, when brought face to face with a suspected war criminal drawn from their very own midst, the majority of Schleswig citizens continued to firmly stand by their man.

6 Draw a Line?

By the mid 1960s, any previous doubts about the West German judiciary's inclination to prosecute Nazi war crimes were assuaged by the sheer number of proceedings taking place across the country. The most famous of these was the Frankfurt Auschwitz trial, conducted between December 1963 and August 1965. Twenty former extermination camp personnel faced charges relating to the gassing of hundreds of thousands of Jewish men, women and children as well as the brutal murders of Polish civilians and Soviet prisoners of war between 1941 and 1945. Chief among the accused was former SS-*Oberscharführer* Wilhelm Boger, notorious for having devised the so-called 'Boger Swing' for the torture of Auschwitz prisoners. Other defendants included former medical personnel who were charged with performing human experiments and administering lethal injections. The eventual sentences passed down by the court saw the defendants receiving prison terms ranging from life to just three-and-a-half years.[1]

The scale of the trial, together with the emotive testimony of Holocaust survivors, ensured that it commanded worldwide media attention. In Frankfurt itself, police units were put on standby and special gates were erected to protect the defendants from violent crowds outside the courtroom—yet, despite the dramatic nature of the case, no crowds appeared.[2] The sixty-space public gallery remained relatively empty throughout the proceedings, a popular presence at the trial only really occurring with the prosecution's summing up and the pronouncement of the verdicts in the summer of 1965.[3] For the most part, interest seemed limited to members of the younger generation. Even these observers, however, failed to comprehend the seriousness of the situation at times. In her *Auschwitz Trials: Letters from an Eyewitness*, Emmi Bonhoeffer, whose husband Klaus had been murdered by the SS for his role in the resistance, noted:

> I am shocked by the apparent callousness with which young people listen in occasionally on the hearings. Quite frequently the judge has to call them to order as they sit there among the audience in shirt sleeves, with legs crossed high and chewing gum as if they were looking at a movie thriller.[4]

This sense of detachment in the face of arguably the most infamous set of crimes of the twentieth century illustrates how, twenty years after the war's end, the Federal Republic was still struggling to come to terms with the legacy of National Socialism. War crimes trials too were becoming an increasingly controversial issue as time went on. Examining individual cases in the earlier stages of this book has already thrown up repeated examples of people's desire to leave the Nazi past firmly behind them or, at the very least, questioning the courts' ability to assess crimes so long after their commission. As the 1960s progressed, these concerns were given added weight by ongoing parliamentary debates over whether to implement the Statute of Limitations for Nazi crimes. In this climate, more and more people began to hope that a final line might yet be drawn under the whole Nazi era.

At the same time, though, there remained special interest groups and key members of West German society who continued to press for a more critical public confrontation with the lessons of the Third Reich. This was a period in which the Holocaust also really started to take centre stage in representations of National Socialism; war crimes trials increasingly focussed specifically upon crimes of mass extermination—and these cases, in turn, gave rise to any number of cultural, commemorative and educational initiatives discussing the persecution of the Jews. This chapter explores these conflicting trends against the backdrop of three trials concerning war crimes at Auschwitz, Treblinka and Sachsenhausen which collectively underscored the industrial scale of the 'Final Solution' while attempting to direct public attention to the Eastern European dimension of the Nazi genocide.

The central figure behind the Frankfurt Auschwitz trial was Fritz Bauer, Attorney General for the state of Hesse. Bauer had himself spent three years in a Nazi concentration camp as a political opponent, before fleeing to Denmark and later Sweden where he involved himself in antifascist activity.[5] Returning to West Germany in 1949, he proved a determined supporter of war crimes trials and a fierce critic of the Federal Republic's handling of the past, illustrating how members of the legal profession played a crucial role in keeping these issues alive throughout the post-war era. Frankfurt itself had long been an important political and cultural centre in the western part of Germany, a liberal stronghold during the *Kaiserreich* and a city with a significant Jewish population prior to 1933.

The first Treblinka trial was held in Düsseldorf between December 1964 and September 1965 with ten defendants facing charges relating to the gassing of at least 70,000 Jewish men, women and children, as well as the fatal 'mistreatment' of many other prisoners in this purpose-built extermination camp. Chief among the accused was Kurt Franz, a man who had actually been born in Düsseldorf and had returned to his hometown after the war. This local figure had worked quietly as a chef until his arrest. The trial spanned 94 days and called upon 153 witnesses. Four of the defendants, Franz, Heinrich Matthes, Willi Mentz and August Miete, were sentenced to life imprisonment; another four received prison terms ranging from twelve to four years. One defendant died before the end of the proceedings; another was acquitted.[6]

Overlapping both the Treblinka and Auschwitz cases was the Sachsenhausen trial conducted in Cologne between October 1964 and May 1965. This case also involved ten defendants, headed by Otto Kaiser. The accused were charged with the mistreatment of prisoners, as well as the mass shootings of hundreds of Russian prisoners of war inside the camp during the autumn of 1941. Kaiser was eventually sentenced to fifteen years in prison, one man was acquitted and the remaining eight co-defendants received prison terms that amounted to little over a year.[7]

Like Frankfurt, both Düsseldorf and Cologne had given relatively limited support for the NSDAP during the 1920s as, indeed, had the state of North Rhine Westphalia in general. The nation's industrial heartland had long been characterised by a political allegiance to the left-wing SPD or to the Catholic Centre Party, and while much of the country swung to the extreme Right to vent their frustration in the midst of the Great Depression, the Rhineland had moved closer to the extreme Left. In September 1930, for example, the KPD received 25 percent of the Düsseldorf vote compared with the Nazis' 13.6 percent.[8] Neighbouring Cologne behaved in a similar fashion and even as late as March 1933, with Hitler already in power as German Chancellor, the Nazis received less than one-third of the vote in that city.[9]

Nevertheless, the region had occupied a significant position within National Socialist rhetoric. One of Hitler's key aims was to achieve the remilitarisation of the Rhineland as part of his long-standing plans to overturn the hated Treaty of Versailles. This was finally achieved on 7 March 1936 in clear defiance of both the Versailles and Locarno treaties. In addition, as the home of German heavy industry and high-profile firms such as Krupp Steel in Essen, the area would play an important role in providing the necessary armaments for the Nazi war effort—and suffer greatly from the Allied bombing campaigns during the conflict as a result.

During the 1950s, North Rhine Westphalia returned to its Leftist political roots and much was done to cultivate an anti-fascist history. Indeed, while many West German cities remained silent with regards to the Nazi era after 1945, Cologne proved quite vocal on the past, not least as a result of Chancellor Konrad Adenauer's own public statements on the city's recent history. Adenauer had been born there in 1876 and served as mayor of the city between 1917 and 1933, before being forced from office by the Nazis. 'Nowhere was Nazism resisted so openly until 1933 and nowhere was there so much spiritual resistance after 1933', he declared in 1946.[10] Adenauer's statements aided in the construction of a powerful post-war myth of Cologne as being a solidly Catholic area which had remained wholly resistant to the Nazi regime. A notion of dual victimhood was created which stressed both the NSDAP's poor performance in the Reichstag elections and the impact of the Allied bombing campaigns during the war.[11]

Other cities in the Rhineland could similarly point to healthy political traditions and a liberal outlook as a means of refuting any claims that they had provided popular support for the Nazi regime. Düsseldorf, for instance, had experienced a long history of Jewish immigration and, in contrast to the anti-Semitism and hostility that had existed against the Jews in other areas of the country at the start of the twentieth century, had been characterised by a relatively peaceful coexistence between its Jewish and Gentile citizens. Anthony Kauders has argued that the town enjoyed a history of tolerance and openness, stressing how the provincial assembly in the Rhineland was the only one to advocate equal rights for the Jews prior to 1848.[12]

Some silences did remain, particularly regarding the deportation of the Jews and the use of Jewish housing as compensation for the bombed-out German population during the Third Reich. Nonetheless, the state of North Rhine Westphalia had one of the highest concentrations of war crimes proceedings in the post-war period. In theory, the combination of all of these factors would render this region quite distinct from areas such as Schleswig-Holstein which, as outlined in the previous chapter, continued to struggle with a compromised past. In reality, though, responses to both the Düsseldorf Treblinka trial and the Cologne Sachsenhausen case reveal that this part of the country was also experiencing division or even apathy over the problem of Nazi war criminals.

The Auschwitz, Treblinka and Sachsenhausen trials dealt principally with mass crimes perpetrated against non-German nationals, involving some of the most notorious concentration camp figures and resulting in some of the heaviest prison sentences of this era. The fact that they were conducted more or less simultaneously allowed members of the press, at least, to draw comparisons between the cases and to build a more detailed picture of the organisational structure behind the Holocaust. The Rhineland trials, however, have been largely been ignored within the region's war crimes historiography, with scholars instead generally drawn to the second Treblinka trial held in Düsseldorf between February and July 1970 which involved the former camp commandant, Franz Stangl, or the Majdanek case (also held in Düsseldorf) which became the longest-running war crimes trial in West Germany, continuing from November 1975 to June 1981.[13] The Frankfurt Auschwitz trial, on the other hand, has been well documented in recent years. As with the 1961 Eichmann prosecution, it is frequently cited as a key turning point in the process of *Vergangenheitsbewaltigung*, owing to both its size and the fundamental fact that it took place on West German soil. Ian Buruma, for example, has insisted that the 1963–5 Auschwitz trial 'was the one history lesson that stuck' for the West German people.[14]

However, as with the previous case studies discussed in this book, responses to all of these trials were rather more complex than conventional historical narratives of 1960s West Germany allow. This was not simply a period of ever-greater critical engagement with Nazi atrocities, but one which continued to witness some reluctance, or even antipathy towards raking over the past. While all three trials, for instance, received daily mention in the West German press, they failed to make front page headlines at any stage; just 6 percent of reports on the Auschwitz case were positioned on the front page at all which raises questions as to just how important editors believed these proceedings really were. Furthermore, such reporting as did occur tended to be sensationalist and not necessarily conducive to inspiring a sober reflection on the past. An excited tone was struck by the *Kölnische Rundschau* weeks before the commencement of the Sachsenhausen trial in its own city as the newspaper eagerly reminded readers of its 'imminent' start.[15] This enthusiasm then continued unabated throughout the proceedings with the regular use of dramatic, sensational headlines and an opening paragraph in bold font to grab readers' attention. In covering the neighbouring Treblinka trial, the same newspaper likewise did its utmost to emphasise the scale of Nazi atrocities, on one occasion repeating the figure of 70,000 victims for which the defendants were being held responsible five times in the space of two small paragraphs.[16]

Newspaper articles on each of these trials reprinted harrowing witness testimony and much emphasis was placed on those members of the camp hierarchy who seemed to have gone beyond the call of duty in order to satisfy their own peculiar bloodlust. During the Auschwitz trial, the *Frankfurter Allegmeine Zeitung* ran a series of dramatic, macabre headlines screaming 'A Mountain of Children's Bodies' or '25,000 Murdered in 24 Hours'.[17] In her recent acclaimed study of the Auschwitz trial, Rebecca Wittmann has thus concluded that 'it was almost a pornography of the Holocaust, that both sold papers and distanced the general public from the monsters on the stand whose actions were reported in graphic detail'.[18] It was therefore possible to persist in longstanding efforts to render the criminals of the Third Reich distinct from their fellow countrymen rather than recognising them as 'ordinary' human beings. Indeed, Wittmann holds this trend responsible for the failure of the Auschwitz trial to impact upon the public consciousness, arguing that 'the public felt a lack of interest in the trial and its possible lessons because the press presented the perpetrators as monsters and sadists'.[19] The people were unable to relate to the defendants and were thus unable to discern any message or lesson emanating from the proceedings that could be held as relevant for them.

Similar tendencies were evident in the Treblinka trial. In the course of one brief article, the *Frankfurter Rundschau* reported how one defendant had been labelled 'Frankenstein' and another had become known as 'The Shooter', as well as how one witness had referred to defendant August Miete as being 'the very worst' of all the extermination camp personnel.[20] The *Frankfurter Allgemeine Zeitung* made repeated references to Miete as 'The Angel of Death', and noted how chief defendant Kurt Franz had been acknowledged in court as being 'a criminal of the first grade'.[21] Much was also made of Franz's photograph album which had been discovered

Draw a Line? 117

during his arrest and found to contain images of his wartime activities in Treblinka, complete with his handwritten caption, 'Those were the days!'[22] When it came to depicting Nazi perpetrators, little seemed to have changed since the emotive and dehumanising coverage of the 'Beast of Belsen' back in 1945.

Admittedly, some elements of the media did try to balance such imagery with reminders of the 'ordinariness' of these men. The *Kölnische Rundschau* individualised the ten Sachsenhausen defendants by listing their names, ages and post-war occupations on the opening day of the proceedings; these former extermination camp personnel were thus cast in the innocuous roles of carpenters, decorators and businessmen. The newspaper continued this process over the next few days of the trial, providing summaries for each defendant that detailed the main developments in their lives and the point at which each had joined the SS. Describing defendant Willi Wöhne, for instance, the *Kölnische Rundschau* recorded that he was a 50 year old electrician from Ludwigsburg who had been born in Berlin. He had lost both his parents at an early age and had been abused by his stepmother. Despite his professional training, Wöhne had been unable to find much work and had thus eventually joined the SS in 1940 and arrived in Sachsenhausen.[23] Not only did such details go some way to rehumanising these defendants, they also underlined the extent to which former war criminals had been able to reintegrate themselves into post-war West German society. Again, the *Kölnische Rundschau* reflected upon this theme:

> Who are these people who are accused of the mass murder and cruel torture of innocent victims of the violent National Socialist regime? Criminals with sadistic inclinations? None of the accused have previous convictions. All have returned to their civilian life without difficulty. They also appear outwardly as completely upright men.[24]

Furthermore, it is striking that media coverage of these trials seemed to make much greater use of photographs of the accused than previous proceedings. Usually, if a photograph was included in such reports, the majority of publications would generally opt for images of defendants sitting before the court. In this way, readers could see for themselves what a war crimes trial looked like, while the accused themselves were shown to be quite 'ordinary' middle aged figures. During the Treblinka trial, however, two newspapers stood out by adopting a different tactic. The *Stuttgarter Zeitung* tried to furnish a picture of what the 'Final Solution' looked like as it printed a scene of an armed guard standing beside a train and a pile of bodies while a local Düsseldorf newspaper, *Der Mittag*, reproduced a photograph of Kurt Franz in his SS uniform—an image which stood in stark contrast to the local cook now appearing before the Düsseldorf court.[25]

Among the principal points of interest during the Treblinka trial, however, was not so much the defendants or the crimes they were accused of, but the appearance of the West German State Secretary, Hans Globke, as a witness. It has already been noted how Globke's Nazi past had been the subject of some scandal since the end of the 1950s and how the seizure of documents relating to his role in the Third Reich had overshadowed the Munich Eichmann exhibition in 1961. Now, in 1964, Globke's physical presence at a war crimes trial furnished another direct link between Nazi atrocities and a high-ranking member of the cabinet—and unleashed a wave of excitement in the watching media.[26]

The press were also very much aware that the high-profile nature of the Auschwitz trial was placing the entire West German judicial system under the international spotlight, and that the very manner in which this case was conducted would be subject to foreign scrutiny. At the end of the trial in 1965, the independent *Stuttgarter Zeitung* took the opportunity to review the comments generated within the international media, while the liberal *Frankfurter Rundschau* hit back at foreign criticisms, levelled primarily by the East German press, over the leniency of the final sentencing. The newspaper noted defiantly that 'these people, who suffered so unspeakably under the dictatorship . . . should be happy that the law is once again being upheld'.[27]

For the most part, coverage of these trials contained little in the way of editorial comment which might have encouraged people to think more deeply about either continued war crimes trials or the legacy of the Nazi past. Instead, the articles that were produced tended to confine themselves to the bare facts of the case, summarising each day's events and relaying witness testimonies. One attempt to foster contemplation was offered by *Der Mittag*, which placed a black column at the heart of one its articles on the trial in which the central question was posed to the readers: 'Treblinka: how was it possible?'[28] The *Rheinische Post*, meanwhile, suggested that the Treblinka proceedings were already having an important effect on popular responses to the past:

> Lupins grow over the site of the extermination camp in Treblinka. But no grass grows for long over the crimes that were committed against the Jews. The process goes on—in the Düsseldorf court and in our engagement with the past.[29]

The extent to which West Germans were actually engaging with this past, however, was the subject of debate among contemporary observers. In October 1965, as both the Auschwitz and Düsseldorf Treblinka trials came to a close, the Association of Jewish Refugees in Britain declared:

> One may assume that the leading men of the Federal Republic of Germany who themselves condemn the Nazi horrors in no uncertain terms, have understanding for the difficulty of the situation on the Jewish side. It seems, however, that the bulk of German public opinion is not

favourable to the continuous reminder of the sinister past and also that some are not prepared to join in the unconditional rejection of Nazism. Young people hardly realise the full implication of events which happened before their time.[30]

Journalist and historian Gitta Sereny also noted the varied responses exhibited towards the first Treblinka trial. In an article for the *Daily Telegraph Magazine*, she relayed a conversation with the prosecutor, Alfred Spiess, who noted how his wife 'is entirely in favour of these proceedings and my part in them', his 17 year old daughter has 'read widely about it and has been to the trial with her school and alone', and how his 13 year old son 'wants to know all about this'.[31] Such responses are, perhaps, not surprising within the home of a leading West German prosecutor where a questioning of the recent past could be reasonably expected. However, among the wider population, the situation seemed rather more complicated. Sereny commented:

> The trials are reported almost verbatim by the German press and by radio and tv. Of the 1,460 newspapers and 30 magazines published in West Germany, an approximate 85 to 90 percent are said to be in favour of continued trials. However, the average German's almost automatic reflex upon seeing or hearing the term *NS Prozess* is to turn the page or the knob.[32]

The scenes within the Düsseldorf courtroom echoed the patterns of attendance for the Frankfurt Auschwitz trial. The *Stuttgarter Zeitung* noted how every last seat was taken in the public gallery as the sentences were finally passed down, yet the occupants of these seats were more likely to be members of the press corps rather than 'ordinary' West Germans.[33] The Cologne Sachsenhausen trial, meanwhile, did manage to attract a wider audience, but for all the wrong reasons. Reporting on the opening day of the trial, the *Kölnische Rundschau* underscored the level of support that chief defendant Otto Kaiser continued to enjoy among the wider community. As was the case with Martin Fellenz in Flensburg, Kaiser was surrounded by a loyal band of supporters, including friends, relatives and colleagues, who refused to believe anything wrong of him despite the hearings' domination by tales of his 'excess' behaviour towards the camp prisoners. The *Kölnische Rundschau* remarked:

> There is the rather stocky locksmith Otto Kaiser (51) from Bergisch-Gladbach. His hair is grey at the temple, he has two deep furrows around the corner of this mouth. His friends, neighbours and work colleagues have presented a petition to the court in which they refer to him as a 'highly respectable, brave, hardworking and reliable man'. But even this Otto Kaiser should be placed next to the slave drivers

Schubert, Sorge and Bugdalle, already sentenced to life imprisonment, as one of the fiercest block leaders of Sachsenhausen.[34]

The defendants in these trials thus seemed to fall into one of two categories: those that were clearly branded as 'excess' perpetrators, monsters upon whom all the blame for Nazi crimes could easily be placed, and those individuals who had managed to immerse themselves so fully into post-war society that it was difficult to perceive of them as being anything other than 'ordinary' men. Dr. Viktor Capesius was among the accused in the Frankfurt Auschwitz trial. During the war, he had administered lethal injections to prisoners, but since 1945, he had settled in the town of Gruppingen and run a pharmacy. In the spring of 1964, a special edition of the BBC programme, *Panorama*, asked locals there for their thoughts on the trial and it quickly emerged that Capesius continued to hold the respect of the local community. Neighbours told the programme how he was a 'popular' figure in the town, 'a very good businessman interested in civic affairs' and 'a great nature lover'. Indeed, the only criticism to be heard against Capesius was that he was a 'social climber'. One woman, questioned as to whether she felt the trial was right after all this time, commented 'it is hard to answer. . . . I do not know what he did in Auschwitz and why he went there'.[35]

Her expression of ignorance was in keeping with opinion polls conducted between May and June 1964 by the market research institute DIVO, which found that 40 percent of those surveyed had never heard of the Auschwitz trial, although the institute felt this figure may have been inflated by people professing ignorance in the hope of evading any closer reflection or pangs of conscience that might have come with further questions. Among the 60 percent who had heard of the proceedings, though, just over half agreed with the prosecution of such crimes twenty years after the war.[36] As the Auschwitz trial neared its conclusion in August 1965, journalist Eleonore Sterling recorded the reception she received when trying to initiate a conversation about the likely verdicts on a 'packed' city tram:

> Most of the faces round me looked back at me blankly, but a tough-looking working man said: "I wonder how many years those fellows will get", and another man exclaimed: "Swine!"[37]

Despite these assessments of public apathy to the war crimes trials, and despite some of the limitations of the related newspaper coverage, there was, in fact, some evidence that these cases were resonating at the local level of society. Writing for *World Jewry* in 1965, another contemporary observer, Hermann Langbein, argued that the Auschwitz case *was* having an impact. Indeed, he found it 'regrettable' that the Treblinka trial was not receiving a similar degree of public attention:

Opinion polls may reveal the ignorance of many Germans about Auschwitz or the trial, but there is not doubt that the number of those who feel the need to come to terms with the unimaginable horrors of Auschwitz has increased considerably since the trial began.[38]

While Sterling and Langbein produced conflicting interpretations of the trial's effects, *Die Zeit* decided to investigate matters for itself and in April 1965, after the case had reached over 150 courtroom sessions, went out onto the streets of Frankfurt to determine whether 'the trial [is] just a part of the daily routine for the citizens of this town, or not even that?' The responses it received agreed with Sterling's conclusion that the trial had failed to generate public interest. A policeman admitted that he did not know anything about the defendants in the case, while a local woman stated quite frankly, 'I still haven't read anything about it'. During the survey, the very need for continued war crimes trials became a popular discussion point. One man told the paper:

> You know, I no longer read the [press] reports. It is time that one finally stopped with these trials. No one is served by it twenty years after the war.[39]

One woman, though, proved to be the exception to the rest of those questioned, seizing the opportunity to launch into a fierce diatribe against the Auschwitz defendants:

> Wilhelm Boger was a Devil. He indiscriminately killed people at the "Black Wall", he drowned a clergyman, he invented the "Boger Swing" and beat numerous people till they were crippled. He killed children, mothers and old men. And Kaduk the Butcher? A wild beast is a human being compared with him. I have read much—everything that has been written about him. He put a cane over people's necks and placed it there so long until they were throttled. He indiscriminately killed Jews and Poles. He was worse than an animal. I have read everything—do you want to know more?[40]

In the wake of so many apathetic responses to his questions, the journalist conducting the survey was clearly taken aback by the woman's detailed response, exclaiming 'I was amazed. This woman *knew*'.[41] The reason for her knowledge, her intense interest in the case and the passionate nature of her reply, though, quickly became apparent. This interviewee had experienced at firsthand the brutality of concentration camp personnel during her time in Thereisenstadt. Thus, as Arendt and Douglas have argued in their accounts of the Eichmann trial, the people who seemed to take the greatest notice of the Auschwitz proceedings in Frankfurt were precisely those people who least needed to learn the lessons of the Nazi past: the survivors of Nazi persecution.

Not surprisingly, Holocaust survivors were especially vociferous campaigners to keep memories of the past alive during the 1960s and keen to ensure that war crimes trials would serve a lasting purpose. Together with local government officials, these people constituted an important pressure group in the process of *Vergangenheitsbewältigung*. One year on from the end of the Auschwitz case, a series of school and public lectures were given in Frankfurt by survivor and trial commentator Hermann Langbein. The lectures were part of a wider state programme for political and cultural education and revealed further evidence of a generational divide within West German society. Older people who attended the sessions frequently drew upon the popular apologia of the early post-war period, while younger West Germans repeatedly questioned how such crimes could ever have been possible and what could be done to prevent any recurrence in the future. Rebecca Wittmann has highlighted the significance of these events, stressing how the public debate revealed 'the growing dissonance between young and old in West Germany . . . that would lead to enormous protests later in the same decade', and underscoring how within the state of Hesse there appeared to be an official policy—at least within the Education Department—for dealing with the Nazi past.[42]

In Cologne, too, there was a clear link between the Sachsenhausen case and efforts to improve Holocaust education. Towards the end of the hearings, two of the trial witnesses, one Polish, the other a member of the local Cologne population, were invited to speak to pupils at a nearby school. The juxtaposition of these witnesses offered a reminder of German suffering in the city during the Nazi era, thereby recalling resistance mythologies, but also demonstrating a keen awareness of the fate of other nationalities at the hands of the regime. The visit was reported in the local press, and it emerged that the class concerned had already conducted some background research into the subject by reading *Der Sternkinder*, a book which, like Anne Frank's *Diary*, dealt with the plight of Dutch children during the occupation of Holland. The classroom itself was 'overcrowded' for the occasion and at the end of the session, one child was reported as saying:

> We were always shaken anew and could not grasp at all that people planned and carried out such atrocities. We all want to contribute so that such terrible events are no longer possible in the future. We thank you for coming.[43]

The school, however, did not envisage this meeting as an isolated event. The teacher responsible for organising the visit expressed his desire to establish a much closer relationship with the victims of the Third Reich and, in particular, to foster ties between his school and Polish youth groups as a means of creating an open dialogue between the two. In this way, it could be ensured that interest in the Nazi past was not a passing fad, a temporary phenomenon arising from a relatively high-profile war crimes trial staged on their own doorstep, but would in fact continue to be fostered for many years to come. The Sachsenhausen case thus seemed to be bestowing an important educational legacy to youngsters in the Rhineland and although the local newspaper did question the extent to which other members of the teaching profession shared such noble ambitions, this was not the only example of people recognising the pedagogic potential of war crimes proceedings. Already in early 1963, the German Trade Union Movement in Düsseldorf had published a special volume on the Eichmann trial with the express desire of teaching the younger generation about the past. The preface stated:

> We decided it must be our task to instruct them objectively upon this dark chapter in German history so that the German people shall never again be led under a dictator or perpetuate in his name such monstrous crimes.[44]

The Frankfurt Auschwitz trial also managed to secure a lasting cultural legacy with the production of Peter Weiss's play, *The Investigation*. The author had personally observed the daily courtroom sessions and based his work upon the actual dialogue spoken by the defendants and witnesses during the process, as well as Bernd Naumann's reports in the *Frankfurter Allgemeine Zeitung*. On 19 October 1965, the play was performed simultaneously on over twelve stages across the Federal Republic free of charge and broadcast on the radio, a move which granted it added publicity and enabled a far wider audience to hear its message.[45] West German television had also already begun to dramatise war crimes proceedings. In April 1964, Westdeutscher Rundfunk screened the play *Hund des Generals*, which dealt with the problem of establishing guilt in a war crimes trial, and in November that same year, Süddeutscher Rundfunk broadcast *Dreht euch nicht um!* which depicted concentration camp survivors having to recall their own painful memories to secure the conviction of a perpetrator.[46] The specific results of the Auschwitz trial were also further relayed with the publication on 20 August 1965—shortly after the trial's conclusion—of Martin Broszat and Helmut Krausnick's *Anatomy of the SS State*. Both scholars had appeared as expert witnesses during the course of the Auschwitz proceedings, outlining the development of the extermination camps and the nature of the Nazi state. The two-volume book enjoyed immense public interest and was out of stock within two months. The title was reissued in the autumn of 1967 as a more affordable paperback and became a best-seller in both the Federal Republic and abroad.[47]

The 1960s were also characterised by a series of public exhibitions detailing the history of the German Jews and their persecution under the Third Reich. Frankfurt, again, proved particularly prolific in this trend.

Between 23 November 1963 and January 1964, it hosted an exhibition on the Warsaw Ghetto, and between 18 November and 20 December 1964 it staged another on Auschwitz itself. Both exhibitions were held in the Paulskirche while the prosecution of the former Auschwitz personnel was ongoing in the local courtroom. The venue was significant in itself, having been the seat for the German Parliament in 1848. It thus constituted a powerful symbol of the democratisation of West German society, as well as a reminder of the existence of healthier German political traditions prior to the rise of National Socialism. The Auschwitz display made a clear link between itself and the war crimes proceedings then in progress, organised jointly by the *Frankfurter Bund für Volksbildung*, Fritz Bauer and two of the trial prosecutors, Henry Ormond and Christian Raabe. It also incorporated photographs of the accused arriving at the courthouse as part of its story, together with excerpts from the indictment. Elsewhere in the exhibition, images of Nazi parades, book burnings and boycotts of Jewish shops sought to trace the evolution of the 'Final Solution'. Both Frankfurt exhibitions attracted a large number of visitors, with the Warsaw Ghetto display drawing a crowd totalling some 61,000 people and the Auschwitz exhibition receiving 88,000.[48]

Cologne, meanwhile, had produced a massive exhibition, *Monumenta Judaica: 2000 Years of Jewish History and Culture along the Rhine*, that went on display between October 1963 and March 1964. The exhibition was divided into five broad themes: representations of Jews in early Christian art; the political, social and economic history of the Jews in Germany; Jewish contributions to art, literature and science; Jewish spiritual life in the Rhineland and the Jewish year.[49] The exhibition, comprising paintings, photographs, sculptures and documents, was opened in a blaze of publicity by the President of the West German Parliament, Dr. Eugen Gerstenmaier, and proved to be extremely popular with the West German public. By February 1964, *Monumenta Judaica* had attracted 67,000 visitors—an average of 4200 every week since its opening. Some days saw a total of twenty-five guided tours around the display and the accompanying guidebook had to be reprinted to meet the unprecedented demand.[50] The local *Rheinische Merkur* proudly proclaimed that 'nothing similar has ever been attempted before. Here at last the sources are shown in an unbiased way, without having been screened for the sake of propaganda'.[51] The *Stuttgarter Zeitung* likewise declared 'the Monumenta Judaica exhibition is a humble memorial for the 11,000 murdered citizens of this city and for all their fellow sufferers. . . . It is good that nothing has been suppressed or embellished of the suffering the Jews had to endure at the hands of the Christians'.[52]

The *Kölnische Rundschau* echoed this view, stating:

> Much talk is going on about the past which has to be liquidated. Here we are confronted with the past happenings. There has been a Jewish Question also before Hitler, Himmler and Eichmann, the exhibition

makes us aware of this fact. We have to realise that actually we are not faced with a Jewish Question, but with a Christian Question.[53]

This was, indeed, an issue that the West German churches were starting to address. Since the end of the Second World War, the Church (Catholic and Protestant) had come under repeated attack for failing to set a moral example during the Third Reich by intervening in the face of Nazi persecution of the Jews and other minorities. Christian groups, in response to their compromised past, had spent much of the post-war era emphasising the suffering that had been wrought upon the churches by the Nazi regime and highlighting cases of church-led resistance.[54] The rise of a younger generation of church historians in the 1960s, though, changed this as a closer analysis was undertaken of the early acclaim that had been given to Hitler after his appointment as German Chancellor, the enthusiastic support displayed for his aggressive foreign policy and the silences that had accompanied the Nazis' violent persecution of the Jews.[55]. Indeed, the Church would become another key force for encouraging a wider, more critical engagement with the past during this period.

Throughout the post-war era, for example, there were moves towards a new spirit of co-operation and reconciliation between Christian and Jewish movements. The Council of Christians and Jews paved the way, establishing a series of chapters across the Federal Republic.[56] Back in Britain, the organisation's newsletter, *Common Ground*, took an active interest in any instances of interfaith dialogue that were taking place in West Germany, especially among members of the younger generation. A host of Christian-Jewish youth groups were formed during the 1960s, the first of which was established in Düsseldorf at the start of the decade. In spring 1962, *Common Ground* was pleased to note that a similar youth group had been set up in Bielefeld, although it was, admittedly, smaller than its Düsseldorf counterpart and 'somewhat hampered by there being no local Jewish youngsters to meet in discussion'. Undeterred, the Bielefeld youth group focused itself on practical activities, with fifteen young members undertaking the repair of a Jewish cemetery in a village near Detmold.[57] In reality, this was not the first evidence of an active younger generation taking the initiative on the matter of the past. *Common Ground* ignored the fact that a Christian-Jewish youth group had actually been operating in Bielefeld since 1956, at the height of public interest in the story of Anne Frank. The group had reprinted extracts from her *Diary* in their own newsletter, prefaced with the following statement:

> It is our conscience with which we are concerned in this issue. Why? Because 11 years after Germany's defeat, 12 years after July 20 1944, 17 years after September 1939, 18 years after November 9 1938, 23 years after January 30 1933, German boys and girls know hardly anything about those dates. Because no German should ever forget those

dates. Because those days are memorials of our bad conscience. Because those days are the beginning or end of a sea of blood and tears. Because those days ought to make our face blush with burning shame.[58]

The group then proceeded to attack the state of history education within West German schools at that time, arguing that the children of the 1950s were still being taught in precisely the same manner as their parents and grandparents had been back in 1930 and 1900. The time had come, the group argued, for change. The early stirrings of a critical younger generation can thus be identified here, calling upon their compatriots to join together and to start probing the legacy of the Third Reich more deeply. In this way, it was hoped, some of the prevailing silences surrounding this era of recent German history could finally be shattered:

> Ask your teacher about Stauffenberg and Julius Leber, about the November pogrom and the Jew badge—they will not answer. Or will they? Just ask. Ask your parents about the concentration camps and the gas chambers. Ask them. And go to the libraries. Get yourselves the books that will tell you all about those days.[59]

Change, though, did not happen overnight. Three years later in November 1959, the Bielefeld youth group was planning a special public discussion to commemorate the anniversary of the *Kristallnacht* pogrom, but the event had to be cancelled because local adults 'would not come forward to express their views'. Reporting on this situation, the *Jewish Chronicle* made the explicit link between this situation and the fact that, at the same time, Bielefeld had witnessed the acquittal of Ewald Sudau in his trial for the murder of 150 Jews and Communists in Poland during the Second World War, implying that this was a town still reluctant to face up to the past.[60] More success in organising an interfaith commemoration of *Kristallnacht* in the Rhineland came in Cologne in November 1961—the twenty-third anniversary of the pogrom. Local schools placed wreaths in the Memorial Hall of the Jewish Community Centre and lit candles to remember those killed under National Socialism.[61]

Attempts to address the legacy of Nazism during this period were not confined to Christian youth. In July 1961, and against the background of the Adolf Eichmann trial, a conference of the German Protestant Church involving Christians from all over the country issued a public statement which made manifest their arguments for a closer reflection on the Nazi past and for improvements in history education:

> Parents and teachers should break the silence so far kept on this matter as far as the younger generation is concerned. In the present state of affairs of world politics, the attempt to clear ourselves and to throw the

blame for our own failure on other people endangers not only one particular group of people, but the life of every one of us. Again and again, young people complain that they have been insufficiently informed (if at all) about the events in Germany relating to the Jews. We owe youth a frank enlightenment in this matter, even though in doing so we will be compelled to confess our own failure and our wrong thinking.[62]

At the same time, the Church's statement attacked the popular defence tactic concerning 'orders from above' and argued for a recognition of a wider responsibility for the crimes of the recent past:

Countless people try today to justify their evil deeds and thoughts by referring to a so-called state of emergency created by orders. 'We could not help acting as we did because we had to obey an order against which no resistance was possible unless one was prepared to risk one's own life'. It is necessary to see clearly that behind these excuses there is concealed the silent confession that one has done nothing to prevent such coercive conditions as long as there was still time to do so.[63]

The following year, the Chairman of the Council of the German Protestant Church, Kurt Schaerf, addressed a gathering of 2000 Christians in Oberhausen during which he bemoaned the often negative responses shown by the West German people to the Nazi war crimes trials. Schaerf stressed instead how the recognition of guilt and repentance was the only means for achieving a national recovery from the Nazi past and regaining foreign respect.[64] Meanwhile, the theologian Professor Hermann Schlingensiepen maintained regular correspondence with his fellow clergymen on the question of the Nazi past throughout the post-war era, following closely the impact of the Eichmann and Auschwitz trials and writing at length on the subject of German guilt and atonement.[65]

Having set a precedent for concerning itself with the impact of Nazi war crimes trials, it is perhaps unsurprising to see that the German Protestant Church also seized the opportunity provided by the concentration camp trials of the 1960s and, more specifically, the wider debates over the Statute of Limitations to engage further with these issues.

Under West German law, there was a twenty year time frame available in which to prosecute crimes of murder and a period of fifteen years to try cases of manslaughter. While the latter deadline was allowed to elapse quietly in 1960, the sudden realisation that many former mass murderers might be able to evade justice prompted a host of criticism both at home and abroad.[66] A much-publicised campaign to extend or even abolish the Statute was mounted by numerous interested parties, from political parties such as the SPD to former victims' groups. In 1963 and 1964, as the Treblinka trial got underway in Düsseldorf, members of the German Protestant Church

128 *West Germans and the Nazi Legacy*

(EKD) were also gathering in the Rhineland for two successive synods that added their weight to this cause.

The 1963 meeting in Bethel resulted in a seven-page document affirming how all Germans had been implicated in the crimes of the Third Reich and ruing the failure of the churches to take concerted action at the time. The official statement was disseminated to the wider public through the press (both religious and secular) as well as via the pulpit during Holy Week. Speaking about recent Nazi war crimes trials and the role of the courts, the EKD commented:

> We see, first of all, a shockingly large and heavy task placed before our courts. They have to look into the abyss to evil and inhumanity which surpass the normal bounds of the imagination. The guilt that is to be punished here surpasses that which can be conceived and punished with the usual standards and punishments of human justice. Our courts of law will have great difficulty, after such a long time, in discovering the exact facts and determining rightly to what extent the accused were responsible. In every single case they will have to bear in mind what a powerful influence was exerted at that time by the terror of the Party and the State, through cunning propaganda and suggestion upon consciences which had been systematically willed to sleep for years or systematically trained in the wrong direction and by the temptations presented by positions of uncontrolled power. But the personal responsibility of every accountable person, especially the great responsibility of those entrusted with authority to give orders to others, must be irrevocably insisted upon. Within the limits in which human jurisdiction is possible, in any society evil must be recognised as abominable and must be punished accordingly.[67]

The EKD drew heavily upon inclusive terminology throughout its statement, emphasising the widespread sense of guilt and responsibility that must be felt for the crimes of the Third Reich. It added:

> For months we have experienced in the Federal Republic and in West Berlin an increased number of legal proceedings in which crimes of the National Socialist time are condemned, a process that, until now, seems to have excited foreign countries more than our own people. In these trials—the largest among them will be the Auschwitz trial—crimes that were committed by members of our people against millions of Jews and other ethnic groups, against men, women and children, once again rise before us in their enormous extent and their entire brutality. It is imperative that, through this, we challenge the discussion of the NS past of our people that we have previously neglected or taken too lightly.[68]

The statements coming out of the EKD's Bethel synod did not pass unnoticed by the wider population. The *Kirchliches Jahrbuch* recorded that 'an abundance of, for the most part, passionate letters and comments, objections, doubts and sheer rejections were expressed. What's more, petitions of irrelevant and insulting character were also made'.[69]

The 1965 Synod, meanwhile, turned its attention to the increasingly pressing issue of the Statute of Limitations. During the meeting of 15 January 1965, Superintendent Munscheid led the synod in the formulation of an official statement to be issued regarding the limitation of National Socialist crimes:

> The debate over the expiration or extension of the statute of limitations for crimes of the National Socialist period poses a difficult decision for the German people, in that they have to both answer for past events and preserve the rule of law. The decision lies with the responsible organs of our state. In this situation, we remind our congregation of the word of the Council of the Protestant Church in Germany from March 1963. We ask the Council to help, by [issuing] a comment, so that the congregation and the public can find the right understanding for the impending decision, and for the continued, burdensome legacy upon us.[70]

The proposal was passed with thirteen abstentions.

The debate over the Statute of Limitations spilled over onto the pages of the local Catholic newspaper, the *Rheinischer Merkur*. Despite so far having remained largely silent on the staging of war crimes trials in its vicinity, the newspaper did report on the Protestant Church's activities—and prompted several letters from its readers as a result, anxious to express their thoughts on the issue. One man from Hanover wrote:

> Won't the Communist propagandists have the chance from 1 May 1965 to point to the mass murderers who will have the convenient opportunity to emerge and run around freely in the Federal Republic? Won't the general impression grow up that known mass murderers are untouchable?[71]

The same correspondent continued to address the problem in a further letter to the newspaper just one week later:

> The punishment of the culprit is not the essential matter. Each process against Nazi criminals before a German court also means a purification of the German name in which the unspeakable happened at that time.[72]

Other readers also engaged with in the debate. A woman from Cologne commented:

> The early limitation of the heaviest chapter of crimes is nothing but a prize for the perfect murder. On moral and political grounds, it should

be possible to clear this up quickly. The efforts of all judiciary grind slowly, as is inevitable in a democracy, but even I cannot share the optimism of our politicians who opine that all appropriate investigative proceedings will be initiated before the expiry of the Statute of Limitations for National Socialist crimes.[73]

Not everyone shared these sentiments, though. Observers within the British Embassy in Bonn discussed the issue of continued war crimes trials with the head of the Ludwigsburg Zentralstelle, Dr. Erwin Schüle, who acknowledged a widespread concern within the Federal Republic for the country's reputation.

What he [Schüle] did find when addressing public audiences was feelings of uneasiness and shame which translated themselves into the suggestion that such proceedings should be hushed up so as not to drag the name of Germany in the mud; this, of course, was absurd, since justice had to be public.[74]

The British Consul General in Frankfurt similarly highlighted the way in which the war crimes trial issue continued to engender conflicting emotions for many West Germans:

Few people would encourage them, but few would say that they should not be held. While very few Germans took the initiative to discuss the trials, they readily expressed their horror and indignation when the subject was broached.[75]

In the midst of the Auschwitz trial, it was reported that Robert Werda, a chief inspector in Stuttgart, had received letters from members of the public asking that investigations into Nazi war crimes be curtailed. There was a sense among many West Germans that such investigations were being directed mainly against the 'small fry'—individuals who felt they had little in common with the sadists on display in Frankfurt.[76] This in itself was a sentiment very reminiscent of the responses afforded to the Allies' original denazification programme in the late 1940s, illustrating the way in which older modes of thinking about the past still had some currency within the Federal Republic.

The debates over the Statute of Limitations for Nazi crimes rumbled on to March 1965 when, after prolonged parliamentary discussions, the Bundestag finally agreed upon a compromise measure to extend the Statute to 1969. This effectively reset the clock to start its twenty year countdown from the moment of the Federal Republic's foundation in 1949, rather than the war's end in 1945 as had previously been the case. The move was justified on the grounds that the German courts had been in no position to operate properly amid the upheaval of the immediate post-war era. The decision granted West German prosecutors an additional four years to conduct their investigations into wanted war criminals and initiate further legal proceedings, but the move was not universally popular. Opinion polls undertaken by various researchers during this period all showed that a majority of West Germans continued to hope that a *Schlußstrich*—a final line—could yet be drawn under the entire Nazi era.[77]

* * * * * * * *

A study of the concentration camp trials in the mid 1960s thus underscores the way in which the burden of the Nazi past continued to divide West German opinion and offer an ongoing source of tension. There were certainly many sections of the West German population during this period who were determined in their attempts to foster a more critical engagement with the Nazi past. Although the war crimes trials themselves did not seem to generate the same scale of popular interest as those held in other areas, failing, for instance, to inspire a deluge of letters from members of the public as with the Sommer or Fellenz cases, there were clear signs that Nazi atrocities were increasingly being discussed at the grassroots level. Churches, youth groups and school teachers echoed many of the liberal attitudes then being expressed within publications such as the *Kölnische Rundschau*, helping to ensure that the desire to deal with the legacy of the Nazi past did not remain empty rhetoric confined to the pages of certain West German newspapers, but was actually transformed into practical educational and commemorative activities on the ground. The special exhibitions staged on Jewish history and culture, the trial witnesses and Holocaust survivors invited into the classroom to talk about their experiences and the public discussions planned on the crimes of the Third Reich—even if not always successful—were indicative of the emergence of a more critical memorial culture. At the same time, though, older patterns of remembrance did not simply disappear. Narratives of German suffering and resistance continued to hold sway for many, and the sheer number of war crimes trials then taking place perhaps added to a sense of fatigue with regards to the Nazi past. As the debates over the Statute of Limitations demonstrated, most West Germans, given the chance, would have preferred to see an end to all such proceedings to finally enable the country to emerge from the long shadows of the Third Reich.

Conclusion

As Allied troops mounted their final assault on the Third Reich in early 1945, they were confronted with appalling evidence of Nazi atrocities. Immediately, the world was faced with the dilemma of how best to explain or represent these crimes. how to grasp the 'unimaginable'. The Holocaust was, and remains, a problem that all of humanity must confront, come to terms with and try to comprehend. It remains the primary point of reference for acts of genocide within international law and continues to inform global campaigns to combat racism and prejudice. In 2005, the United Nations voted to formally dedicate January 27, the anniversary of the liberation of Auschwitz, as International Holocaust Remembrance Day.[1]

The development of Holocaust commemoration has been a lengthy and highly politicised process. Allied nations have had to contend with questions over their failure to intervene when rumours of atrocities first began to circulate in the early stages of the Second World War, their own record on Jewish immigration in the 1930s and their willingness to turn a blind eye to certain war criminals after 1945.[2] Those countries that experienced Nazi occupation, meanwhile, have had to face up to varying records of collaboration, complicity as bystanders or active perpetrators of mass murder.[3] The shadow of the Nazi past has hardly been a uniquely 'German problem'.

Within the Federal Republic, though, the process of *Vergangenheitsbewältigung* has, necessarily, been especially complicated. The experience of total defeat in 1945 left the population shocked, traumatised and embittered by their experiences. Struggling to pick up the pieces in a country ravaged by war and contending with severe food shortages, disruptions to essential infrastructure and missing loved ones—as well as foreign occupation—people were in little mood to look beyond their own immediate plight. It would take time before these wounds could start to heal and for West Germans to start looking back on this painful chapter in their lives.

The shift towards a more liberal political culture during the 1960s certainly aided this process, and a period of détente in the Cold War created a climate in which it became 'easier' to contemplate the fate of East Europeans under Nazism, exchange vital evidence with the Soviet authorities and start to recognise the particular significance of the extermination camps in eastern Poland that had been liberated by the Red Army. The coming of age of a younger generation also prompted a greater questioning of the Nazi past. Yet, for all of these developments, attempts to foster an engagement with the crimes of the Third Reich met with continual reticence or resistance. Many clung to the necessity of having to follow orders in a war situation and notions of German victimhood still held great sway, whether in terms of the suffering inflicted by the Nazis' use of terror and 'misleading' propaganda; or in terms of Allied air raids, expulsion from the eastern territories and denazification.

The problem of what to do with Nazi war criminals remained a particularly contentious issue throughout the post-war period. When prompted, most West Germans readily agreed with the need for judicial proceedings to bring those responsible for the genocide to account. There was a keen awareness that the rest of the world was keeping an eye on the Federal Republic and that any apparent attempt to sweep the past under the carpet could harm the country's fragile reputation. It would also play all too easily into the hands of Communist agitators in the GDR who, given the number of ex-NSDAP members in high office, continued to denounce West Germany as a Nazi quagmire. Even here, though, there was an ongoing tension between being seen to do the right thing by maintaining war crimes investigations and a widespread concern as to the effects that more details of the atrocities would have on the Federal Republic's international standing. Either way, popular attitudes towards war crimes trials were bound up with a concern for Germany's standing and reputation in the wider world.

By the mid 1960s, a general apathy set in, no doubt stemming from the sheer number of war crimes trials that were held. Attempts to relativise Nazi atrocities by pointing to the bombing of Dresden or Hiroshima, or the rapes and reprisals enacted by the Red Army as it marched on Berlin persisted into the latter part of the decade when they were fuelled further by U.S. actions in Vietnam. Legitimate questions over the health and memory of both defendants and witnesses gained ground, and as the events of the Second World War grew more distant, not everyone saw the wisdom in continuing to rake over the past. Parliamentary debates over the Statute of Limitations in 1965, 1969 and 1979 gave credence to these doubts, and with each round of the Bundestag discussions, an increasing majority of the population expressed a desire to end war crimes trials (and, by extension, discussions of the Nazi past) once and for all. Several scholars argue that it took the popular, emotional impact of the 1979 television miniseries *Holocaust* to finally persuade politicians to rule in favour of the Statute's abolition.[4] While international pressure and high-profile campaigns from survivors' groups also played a crucial role in this process, *Holocaust* certainly did revive public discussion of the persecution of the Jews and contributed to Germany's continued prosecution of Nazi acts of murder to this day.

The war crimes trials that have been assessed over the course of this study encompassed a whole range of criminal behaviour, from acts perpetrated by concentration and extermination camp personnel in Buchenwald, Auschwitz, Sachsenhausen and Treblinka, to Einsatzgruppen massacres committed in the Baltic States and the role of the police in the deportation of the Jews. Such trials played out against the background of differing local political traditions, and in each case we can see a region desperate to dissociate itself as much as possible from the legacy of the Third Reich. Ulm, Frankfurt and Düsseldorf, for example, could point to the large, assimilated Jewish community that had existed peacefully in their midst up until 1933; Bayreuth drew upon a musical heritage that stretched back to the nineteenth century—a culture that was shown to have been appropriated and abused by Goebbels's propaganda ministry. Significant silences remained in each of these places. The very fact that a war crimes trial was taking place within these towns was frequently explained away as a matter of fate: Martin Sommer had been moved to the hospital in Bayreuth at the end of the war, while the chief defendant in the Ulm Einsatzkommando case, Bernhard Fischer-Schweder, had come to the town through the refugee camp. Even in Schleswig-Holstein, it was quickly noted that the prominent councillor and businessman Martin Fellenz had been born in Duisburg.

These trials engendered varying degrees of public interest. In some cases, crowds raced to catch a glimpse of the defendants, to verbally or physically assault them. In other cases, the courts remained eerily empty and even some of the high-profile trials that had anticipated a significant public presence ended up disappointed in their lack of audience. Given the immense media coverage that surrounded some of these proceedings, we might well question why anyone would go to the trouble of trying to follow hearings firsthand and just what responses could reasonably be expected from ordinary West Germans. People had their own lives to lead, and work and family commitments assumed a natural priority over spending time in the company of a mass murderer. The harrowing nature of the subject matter also deterred many from following the trials avidly.

These case studies nonetheless offer evidence that the West German population was prepared to follow, attend or even write about those trial proceedings which had personal meaning for them. Some sought an opportunity to recall their own persecution under the Third Reich and desired to see those responsible forced to face the consequences of their actions. For others, trials were an opportunity to rally round a friend or colleague in his hour of need and show contempt for the dreadful allegations levelled against him. Even people with no direct interest in a case seized the opportunity to draw upon their own war losses and reformulate their victim narratives. A number of enlightened individuals, now working as teachers, lecturers, clergymen or journalists, did display a genuine desire to learn more about the past and recognised the utility of war crimes trials to teach others about this 'darkest chapter' of German

Conclusion 135

history. Younger people were often compelled to attend a court session as part of their history education and many seemed to digest the experience in a sober and critical manner, although others, admittedly, displayed boredom or behaved inappropriately.

Whatever the precise nature of the response, though, it is clear that war crimes trials possessed the power to inspire a wider discussion about the past and, at a local level, prompted individuals to test comfortable postwar mythologies by digging into their town's own record under National Socialism. Trials thus presented an opportunity to speak out; victims, perpetrators and bystanders alike could articulate their versions of the recent past, challenging or upholding prevailing memory cultures accordingly. Post-war West German society had been constructed on the tacit agreement not to ask awkward questions about individuals' previous associations. Continued war crimes investigations threatened to unravel all of this and thus had a destabilising effect on preferred remembrance patterns. Trials that involved respected members of the local community challenged efforts to assign all the blame for Nazi atrocities to those at the highest levels of the regime, or to renowned 'monsters'. The thought that a personal acquaintance could have been complicit in such deeds was a disturbing one and shattered claims that Nazism had come from 'somewhere else' and had little to do with the ordinary population. As Donald Bloxham has argued, 'Whatever we may say of the trials . . . they were the greatest, most enduring attempts to investigate Nazism and its effects in something approaching a detached way'.[5] Extending far beyond the Allies' own short-lived re-education programme of the late 1940s, war crimes hearings offered a recurring reminder of the dangers of anti-Semitism and political extremism and could inspire wider cultural representations of the Third Reich.

War crimes proceedings could, as we have seen, generate much excitement, emotion and drama. Particular media attention was paid to the sensational cases dealing with 'excess' perpetrators, enabling some sense of distance to be retained between them and the wider population. Rebecca Wittmann argues that this produced a paradoxical result; media coverage did elevate the Nazi genocide within the public consciousness, but the representation of the perpetrators was such that these crimes were seen as part of a 'macabre fantasy world'.[6] Human interest stories surrounding the defendants themselves could also take precedence over any calm and measured reflection on the fate of their victims. The prosecution of Martin Sommer, for example, gained far greater notoriety in the press as a result of his wife losing her job than for the brutal manner in which he dispatched the prisoners who had passed through the Buchenwald cell block.

It is also notable that war crimes trials were almost always accompanied by a sense of shock at the 'revelations' that emerged over the course of trial testimony. There was thus a seemingly endless cycle of horror and outrage being expressed in response to Nazi crimes, followed by a period of flagging interest until the next incident came along to jolt people out of their complacency. Whether people truly took these 'revelations' onboard at each stage, or whether there was, instead, a process of desensitisation to the details of Nazi atrocities, forgetfulness or the simple suppression of horrific facts is unclear. What these patterns do demonstrate, though, is that the process of *Vergangenheitsbewältigung* was far from being a linear path towards ever-greater critical engagement with the past. Instead, West Germany seemed to be characterised by a whole series of moments of 'confrontation' whose effects were often short-lived.

An analysis of the responses that were afforded to war crimes trials thus provides some interesting insights into the complexities of West German memorial culture during the 1960s. Far from a decade of immediate and far-reaching reform in terms of the nation's handling of the National Socialist legacy, as traditional historical narratives have so often suggested, this was a period that continued to be dominated by silences, evasions and subtle distortions of the recent past.

In the early twenty-first century, Germany is widely commended for the way in which it has 'faced up' to its past. The country continues to memorialise the victims of racial persecution, even if that process is sometimes difficult and controversial, as demonstrated by the length of time involved in designing and constructing the Berlin Holocaust Memorial. One of the problems with the concept *Vergangenheitsbewältigung*, however, is that the term presupposes the possibility of an end point to dealing with the past. Despite that long-cherished hope, a final line is unlikely to be drawn under the Nazi era. It is a period which continues to fascinate and horrify, and the last surviving Nazi war criminals continue to cause problems for Germany.

Throughout the 1970s and 1980s, there remained examples where the West German courts delivered the highest penalty for acts of murder committed by former Nazis. In 1992, the newly reunified Germany saw a life prison sentence passed on Josef Schwammberger, a former overseer in the SS labour camps in occupied Poland who was responsible for the murder of numerous Jewish forced workers. The world's media quickly dubbed this defendant 'the last Nazi', apparently confident that no further major offenders could be unearthed so long after the Second World War.[7] This, however, has not proved to be the case and between 2001 and 2010, life sentences were also handed down on Anton Malloth, Josef Scheungraber and Heinrich Boere for the murder of Jewish prisoners, Italian civilians and suspected members of the Dutch resistance, respectively.[8]

On 12 May 2011, a court in Munich found former extermination camp guard John Demjanjuk guilty of involvement in the murders of over 28,000 people in Sobibor during the Second World War. Although sentenced to five years imprisonment, the judge ruled that Demjanjuk should not have to spend any further time in custody. The 91 year old was thus released and moved into St Lukas nursing home in the spa town of Bad Feilnbach. Many local residents expressed their unhappiness that this popular tourist location should come to be associated with such a notorious figure, and a number of would-be guests changed their holiday plans; others protested, perhaps a little too much, that his presence did not bother them. *Der Spiegel* described Demjanjuk as the 'ghost of Bad Feilnbach', and the tensions that he has unleashed within the community echo many of the strains witnessed amid the trials of the 1960s.[9] Altogether, it is indicative of the way in which the country continues to be haunted by its National Socialist past.

Notes

ABBREVIATIONS

NA—National Archives, London

NOTES TO THE INTRODUCTION

1. Dietrich Strothmann, 'Die Sache Harster und andere . . .', *Die Zeit*, January 27, 1967.
2. 'Six Years' Gaol for Harster', *Jewish Chronicle*, March 3, 1967, 18. For details on the Harster trial, see Christiaan F. Rüter & Dick W. de Mildt eds., *Justiz und NS-Verbrechen: Sammlung deutscher Strafurteile wegen nationalsozialistischer Tötungsverbrechen 1945–1999, Band XXV* (Amsterdam: Holland University Press, 2001) Case No. 645.
3. The following are typical of these conventional historical narratives: Wolfgang Benz, 'Nachkriegsgesellschaft und Nationalsozialismus: Erinnerung, Amnesie, Abwehr', *Dachauer Hefte*, Vol. 6: *Erinnern oder Verweigern* (1990) 12–24; Werner Bergmann, 'Die Reaktion auf den Holocaust in Westdeutschland von 1945 bis 1989', *Geschichte in Wissenschaft und Unterricht*, Vol. 43 (1992) 327–350; Ian Buruma, *The Wages of Guilt: Memories of War in Germany and Japan* (London: Vintage, 1995); Aaron Haas, *The Aftermath: Living with the Holocaust* (Cambridge: Cambridge University Press, 1995); Siobhan Kattago, *Ambiguous Memory: The Nazi Past and German National Identity* (Westport, Connecticut: Praeger, 2001).
4. On the relationship between the Nazi past and the protest movements of the late 1960s, see Rob Burns, *Protest and Democracy in West Germany: Extra-Parliamentary Opposition and the Democratic Agenda* (Basingstoke: Macmillan, 1988); Geoff Eley, 'Protest Movements in 1960s West Germany: A Social History of Dissent and Democracy', *Journal of Social History*, Vol. 38 No. 3 (2005) 776–780; Ronald Fraser, *1968: A Student Generation in Revolt* (London: Chatto & Windus, 1988); Detlef Siegfried, '"Don't Trust Anyone Older Than 30?" Voices of Conflict and Consensus between Generations in 1960s West Germany', *Journal of Contemporary History*, Vol. 40 No. 4 (2005) 727–744; Nick Thomas, *Protest Movements in 1960s West Germany: A Social History of Dissent and Democracy* (Oxford: Berg, 2003); Dorothee Wierling, 'Generations and Generational Conflicts in East and West Germany', Christoph Klessmann ed., *The Divided Past: Rewriting Postwar German History* (Oxford: Berg, 2001) 69–89.

140 Notes

5. On the Anne Frank 'phenomenon' see Robert Sackett, 'Memory by Way of Anne Frank: Enlightenment and Denial among West Germans circa 1960', *Holocaust and Genocide Studies*, Vol. 16 No. 2 (2002) 243–265.
6. See, for example, Harold Marcuse, *Legacies of Dachau: The Uses and Abuses of a Concentration Camp, 1933–2001* (Cambridge: Cambridge University Press, 2001); Rudy Koshar, *From Monuments to Traces: Artifacts of German Memory, 1870–1900* (Berkeley: University of California Press, 2000); Christoph Classen, *Bilder der Vergangenheit: Die Zeit des Nationalsozialismus im Fernsehen der Bundesrepublik Deutschland, 1955–1965* (Cologne: Böhlau, 1999); Jan-Holger Kirsch, *'Wir haben aus der Geschichte gelernt': der 8 Mai als politischer Gedenktag in Deutschland* (Vienna: Böhlau, 1999).
7. Typical examples are Neil Gregor, *Haunted City: Nuremberg and the Nazi Past* (New Haven, Connecticut: Yale University Press, 2008); Sven Keller, *Günzburg und der Fall Josef Mengele: Die Heimatstadt und die Jagd nach dem NS-Verbrecher* (Munich: R. Oldenbourg Verlag, 2003); Peter Reichel, *Das Gedächtnis der Stadt: Hamburg im Umgang mit seiner nationalsozialistischen Vergangenheit* (Hamburg: Dölling & Galitz, 1997).
8. Donald Bloxham, *Genocide on Trial: War Crimes Trials and the Formation of Holocaust History and Memory* (Oxford: Oxford University Press, 2001). See also Lawrence Douglas, *The Memory of Judgement: Making Law and History in the Trials of the Holocaust* (New Haven, Connecticut: Yale University Press, 2001); Mark Osiel, *Mass Atrocity, Collective Memory and the Law* (New Brunswick, New Jersey: Transaction, 1997); Marouf A. Hasian, *Rhetorical Vectors of Memory in National and International Holocaust Trials* (East Lansing: Michigan State University Press, 2006).
9. See, for example, Ulrich Brochhagen, *Nach Nürnberg: Vergangenheitsbewältigung und Westintegration in der Ära Adenauer* (Berlin: Ullstein, 1999); Alon Confino, *Germany as a Culture of Remembrance: Promises and Limits of Writing History* (Chapel Hill: University of North Carolina Press, 2006); Neil Gregor, '"Is He Still Alive, Or Long Since Dead?" Loss, Absence and Remembrance in Nuremberg, 1945–1956', *German History*, Vol. 21 No. 2 (2003) 183–203; Jeffrey Herf, *Divided Memory: The Nazi Past in the Two Germanys* (Cambridge, Massachusetts: Harvard University Press, 1997); Alf Lüdtke, '"Coming to Term with the Past": Illusions of Remembering, Ways of Forgetting Nazism in West Germany', *Journal of Modern History*, Vol. 65 (1993) 542–572; Marcuse, *Legacies of Dachau*; Robert Moeller, *War Stories: The Search for a Usable Past in the Federal Republic of Germany* (Berkeley: University of California Press, 2001); Peter Steinbach, 'Zur Auseinandersetzung mit nationalsozialistischen Gewaltverbrechen in der Bundesrepublik Deutschland', *Geschichte in Wissenschaft und Unterricht*, Vol. 35 No. 2 (1984) 65–85.
10. Wolfgang Benz, 'The Persecution and Extermination of the Jews in the German Consciousness', John Milfull ed., *Why Germany? National Socialist Anti-Semitism and the European Context* (Providence, Rhode Island: Berg, 1993) 94.
11. In 1959, amid a rising number of anti-Semitic incidents, including the posting of offensive letters to newspapers, state prosecutors and local government ministers in West Germany, the West German government initiated legal proceedings against those believed to be instigating racism. See 'Combating Racial Hatred', *Jewish Chronicle*, January 23, 1959, 13. This did not seem to act as a deterrent, though, and, in the midst of the Auschwitz trial five years later, it was reported that a total of 115 people had been arrested over the

course of 1963 for Neo-Nazi or anti-Semitic incidents. See '10,445 Sentenced for War Crimes', *Jewish Chronicle*, June 26, 1964, 20.
12. Claudia Koonz, 'Between Memory and Oblivion: Concentration Camps in German Memory', J.R. Gillis ed., *Commemorations: The Politics of National Identity* (Princeton, New Jersey: Princeton University Press, 1994) 265.
13. See, for example, Hanna Yablonka, 'The Development of Holocaust Consciousness in Israel: The Nuremberg, Kapos, Kasztner and Eichmann Trials', *Israel Studies*, Vol. 8 No. 3 (2003) 1–24; David Cesarani, *Eichmann: His Life and Crimes* (London: William Heinemann, 2004); Haim Gouri, *Facing the Glass Booth: The Jerusalem Trial of Adolf Eichmann* (Detroit, Michigan: Wayne State University Press, 2004).
14. Devin O. Pendas, *The Frankfurt Auschwitz Trial 1963–1965: Genocide, History and the Limits of the Law* (Cambridge: Cambridge University Press, 2006); Rebecca Wittmann, *Beyond Justice? The Auschwitz Trial* (Cambridge, Massachusetts: Harvard University Press, 2005). Studies on the Majdanek proceedings, the longest war crimes trial in West German history, are also adding to this field. See Ulrike Weckel & Edgar Wolfrum eds., *'Bestien' und 'Befehlsempfänger': Frauen und Männer in NS-Prozessen nach 1945* (Göttingen: Vandenhoeck & Ruprecht, 2003); Volker Zimmermann, *NS-Täter vor Gericht: Düsseldorf und die Strafprozesse wegen nationalsozialistischer Gewaltverbrechen* (Düsseldorf: Justizministerium des Landes NRW, 2001).
15. See 'Children's Ignorance', *AJR Information*, Vol. 15 No. 6 (1960) 2; Siegfried, '"Don't Trust Anyone Older Than 30"?', 727–744.
16. Celia Applegate, *A Nation of Provincials: The German Idea of Heimat* (Berkeley: University of California Press, 1990); Alon Confino, *The Nation as a Local Metaphor: Wurttemberg, Imperial Germany and National Memory, 1871–1918* (Chapel Hill: University of North Carolina Press, 1997).
17. Confino, *The Nation as a Local Metaphor*, 98.
18. Alon Confino & Ajay Skaria, 'The Local Life of Nationhood', *National Identities*, Vol. 4 No. 1 (2002) 10.
19. Akiba Cohen et al. eds., *The Holocaust and the Press: Nazi War Crimes Trials in Germany and Israel* (Cresskill, New Jersey: Hampton Press, 2002) 4.

NOTES TO CHAPTER 1

1. The Allies debated various ideas for dealing with the Axis war leaders in the aftermath of the war. These ranged from the Morgenthau Plan to strip Germany of her industrial capacity to the summary execution of those guilty of committing atrocities. Even those who did advocate a war crimes trial were unsure of exactly the format it should take. Questions over establishing an international tribunal rather than hearing cases before a German court and the issue of post-facto law continued to surround the treatment of Nazi war criminals for years to come. For details on the planning for the IMT see Shlomo Aronson, 'Preparations for the Nuremberg Trial: The OSS, Charles Dwork and the Holocaust', *Holocaust and Genocide Studies*, Vol. 12 (1998) 257–281; Arieh J. Kochavi, 'The British Foreign Office versus the United Nations War Crimes Commission during the Second World War', *Holocaust and Genocide Studies*, Vol. 8 No. 1 (1994) 28–49; S.S. Alderman, 'Negotiating the Nuremberg Trial Agreements, 1945', Raymond Dennett & Joseph E. Johnson eds., *Negotiating with the Russians* (Boston: World Peace Foundation, 1951) 49–100.

2. This figure does not include Martin Bormann, who was tried in absentia. The head of the German Labour Front, Dr. Robert Ley, committed suicide before the opening of the IMT, and leading industrialist Gustav Krupp was ruled unfit to stand trial. For details of the Indictment against the Nuremberg defendants, see *The Trial of German Major War Criminals: Proceedings of the International Military Tribunal sitting at Nuremberg, Germany* (London: HMSO, 1946).
3. Robert Jackson, 'Opening Statement', Proceedings of the International Military Tribunal, Day 2, November 21, 1945.
4. See, for example, Marcuse, *Legacies of Dachau*, 55–59.
5. Robert G. Moeller, *War Stories: The Search for a Usable Past* (Berkeley: University of California Press, 2003) 40, 122.
6. Municipal Museums of Nuremberg, 'Memorium: Nuremberg Trials. Initiative to Establish a Memorial in the Nuremberg Palace of Justice' (January 2006) 6.
7. Michael Marrus, 'The Holocaust at Nuremberg', *Yad Vashem Studies*, Vol. 26 (1998) 5. For a critical overview of the praise that has been heaped on the IMT, see Bloxham, *Genocide on Trial*, 1–3.
8. On this theme, see Donald Bloxham, 'The Missing Camps of Aktion Reinhard: The Judicial Displacement of a Mass Murder', Peter Gray & Kendrick Oliver eds., *The Memory of Catastrophe* (Manchester, 2004) 118–134; *Genocide on Trial*, 88–89, 124–126; Tony Kushner, *The Holocaust and the Liberal Imagination: A Social and Cultural History* (Oxford, 1994) 205–342; 'The Memory of Belsen', Joanne Reilly *et al.* eds., *Belsen in History and Memory* (Oxford: Frank Cass, 1997) 181–205; John Fox, 'The Jewish Factor in British War Crimes Policy in 1942', *English Historical Review*, Vol. 92 No. 362 (1977) 82–106; Joanne Reilly, *Belsen: The Liberation of a Concentration Camp* (London: Routledge, 1998).
9. Erich Haberer, 'History and Justice: Paradigms of the Prosecution of Nazi Crimes', *Holocaust and Genocide Studies*, Vol. 19 No. 3 (2005) 493.
10. Kushner, *The Holocaust and the Liberal Imagination*, 226.
11. Bloxham, *Genocide on Trial*, 145–146. See too Rebecca West, *A Train of Powder* (London: Virago, 1984) 3.
12. Christoph Burchard, 'The Nuremberg Trial and its Impact on Germany', *Journal of International Criminal Justice*, Vol. 4 (2006) 800–829.
13. 'Press in Germany Covers War Trial', *New York Times*, December 13, 1945, 13.
14. Ibid.
15. Cohen *et al.* eds., *The Holocaust and the Press*, 75.
16. Raymond Daniell was London correspondent for the *New York Times* throughout the Second World War and had followed U.S. troops into Berlin in 1945. He had warned of the dangers of National Socialism and urged his countrymen to fight it before the attack on Pearl Harbor in 1941. '"So what?" Say the Germans of Nuremberg', *New York Times*, December 2, 1945, SM3.
17. 'Germany Little Interested in Trial of War Criminals', *New York Times*, December 1, 1945, 22.
18. Ibid. Similar conclusions were drawn by James O'Donnell, 'German on der Strasse: What War Guilt Trials?', *Newsweek*, December 10 1945, who commented 'there is probably no city its size in the world where this trial is less discussed by the man in the street than Nuremberg, no country in the world where this trial is less is known about it than Germany', cited in Gregor, *Haunted City*, 89.
19. 'War Crimes Trial Dull to Germans', *New York Times*, January 2, 1946, 6. An economics professor at Heidelberg University similarly commented that articles in a recent edition of *Neue Zeitung* concerning issues such as the coal

shortage and the reopening of factories held a lot more interest for him than the IMT.
20. Konrad H. Jarausch, *After Hitler: Recivilising Germans, 1945–1995* (Oxford: Oxford University Press, 2006) 3–17.
21. Caroline Sharples, 'Holocaust on Trial: British Responses to the Nuremberg Tribunal, 1945–46', unpublished paper delivered at the Fourth Annual Aubrey Newman Lecture and Colloquium, University of Leicester, May 6, 2009. See also Bloxham, *Genocide on Trial*, 147, 153–154.
22. Gregor, *Haunted City*, 89.
23. Report No. 16, 'German Attitudes towards the Nuremberg Trials, August 7 1946', Anna J. Merritt & Richard L. Merritt eds., *Public Opinion in Occupied Germany: The OMGUS Surveys, 1945–1949* (Urbana: University of Illinois Press, 1970) 93–94.
24. Bloxham, *Genocide on Trial*, 148.
25. For a discussion on this theme, see Burchard, 'The Nuremberg Trial and Its Impact on Germany', 802–806. For an overview of Allied plans for the punishment of war criminals and an assessment of the tribunal's 'fairness', see Michael Biddis, 'Victors' Justice? The Nuremberg Tribunal', *History Today*, Vol. 45 No. 5 (1995) 40–46.
26. In addition to Hess, the other defendants that tended to be singled out as innocent included Albert Speer and the Wehrmacht personnel.
27. See, for example, Alexandra Przyrembel, 'Transfixed by an Image: Ilse Koch, the "Kommandeuse of Buchenwald"', *German History*, Vol. 19 No. 3 (2001) 369–399; Hannah Caven, 'Horror in Our Time: Images of the Concentration Camps in the British Media, 1945', *Historical Journal of Film, Radio and Television*, Vol. 21 No. 3 (2001) 230–233; Weckel & Wolfrum, *'Bestien' und 'Befehlsempfänger'*.
28. 'War Crimes Trial Dull to Germans', *New York Times*, January 2, 1946.
29. 'German Attitudes towards the Nuremberg Trials, August 7, 1946, 93–94.
30. 'Nuremberg Trial Too Slow Reich Man-in-Street Says', *Toronto Daily Star*, November 2, 1945, 7.
31. Wes Gallagher, 'Some Germans Brand War Trials As Too Slow', *Milwaukee Journal*, November 1, 1945, 62.
32. 'German Views on War Trial', *The Times*, September 30, 1946, 5.
33. Ibid.
34. Ibid.
35. Robert Kempner, 'Impact of Nuremberg on the German Mind', *New York Times*, October 6, 1946, SM5.
36. Ibid.
37. Ibid.
38. British observers also expressed concern that allowing the defendants to make final statements before they were hanged meant 'the guilty men have increased in stature among sectors of the German public'. Memorandum by George W. Houghton, Control Office for Germany and Austria, October 17, 1946, NA, FO 946/43: German Reaction to Nuremberg Sentences.
39. Kathleen McLaughlin, 'Germans Haggard Awaiting Fate; Only Göring Can Muster a Smile', *New York Times*, October 1, 1946, 11.
40. These six comprised Hermann Göring, Alfred Jödl, Wilhelm Keitel, Konstantin von Neurath, Joachim von Ribbentrop and Alfred Rosenberg.
41. 'Acquitted Nazis Should be Tried by German Court', *Manchester Guardian*, October 3, 1946, 5.
42. 'Berlin Left Urges Death for 22 Nazis', *New York Times*, October 3, 1946, 15.
43. 'Acquitted Nazis Should be Tried by German Court', 5.
44. 'German Public and the Nuremberg Penalties', *The Times*, October 3, 1946, 4.

144 Notes

45. West, *A Train of Powder*, 56.
46. 'German Reaction to Nuremberg Sentences'.
47. Survey of German Public Opinion No. 8, NA, FO 1056/166, Control Commission for Germany, Information Services Control Branch Publicity Material.
48. Ibid.
49. 'Berlin Left Urges Death for 22 Nazis', 15.
50. 'Acquitted Nazis Should be Tried in German Court', *The Times*, October 3, 1946, 5. Claims that 'most Germans' thought the IMT had been about retribution contradicts the earlier findings of the OMGUS surveys that showed the majority were convinced of the trial's fairness.
51. 'German Posters Decry War Trial', *New York Times*, November 10, 1946, 47.
52. Ibid.
53. Ibid.
54. 'Army Investigates Suicide of Göring as Mystery Grows', *New York Times*, October 17, 1946, 1.
55. 'German Posters Decry War Trial', 47.
56. Survey of German Public Opinion No. 8.
57. Survey of German Public Opinion (Period ending December 1946), National Archives, FO 1056/93, Control Commission for Germany, Information Services Control Branch.
58. Survey of German Public Opinion No. 8.
59. Ibid.
60. 'German Reaction to Nuremberg Sentences'.
61. Ibid.
62. Survey of German Public Opinion No. 8.
63. Letter to P.H. Dean, British Foreign Office by M.L.G. Balfour, Information Services Control Branch, Zonal Executive Offices, October 26 1946, NA, FO 946/43: German Reaction to Nuremberg Sentences.
64. Ibid.
65. Cohen *et al.* eds., *The Holocaust and the Press*, 25–26.
66. Burchard, 'The Nuremberg Trial and its Impact on Germany', 811–813.
67. Survey of German Public Opinion No. 10 (Period ending 14 January 1947), NA, FO 1056/93: Control Commission for Germany, Information Services Control Branch.
68. 'Nuremberg Law', *Die Zeit*, January 22, 1948, German History in Documents and Images, http://germanhistorydocs.ghi-dc.org/sub_document.cfm?document_id=2309
69. Ibid.
70. Barbara Marshall, 'German Attitudes to British Military Government, 1945–7', *Journal of Contemporary History*, Vol. 15 No. 4 (1980) 672. For further details of the denazification process, see Lutz Niethammer, *Die Mitläuferfabrik: Die Entnazifizierung am Beispiel Bayerns* (Berlin & Bonn: J.H.W. Dietz, 1982); Clemens Vollnhals ed., *Entnazifizierung, politische Säuberung und Rehabilitierung in dem vier Besatzungszonen, 1945–1949* (Munich: Deutscher Taschenbuch Verlag, 1991); Constantine Fitzgibbon, *Denazification* (London: Joseph, 1969); John H. Herz, 'The Fiasco of Denazification in Germany', *Political Science Quarterly*, Vol. 63 No. 4 (1948) 569–594; John Gimbel, 'Denazification and German Local Politics, 1945–1949: A Case Study in Marburg', *American Political Science Review*, Vol. 54 No. 1 (1960) 83–105.
71. Donald Bloxham, '"The Trial That Never Was": Why There Was No Second International Trial of Major War Criminals at Nuremberg', *History*, Vol. 87 (2002) 41–60.

Notes 145

72. Donald Bloxham, 'British War Crimes Trial Policy in Germany 1945–1957: Implementation and Collapse', *Journal of British Studies*, Vol. 42 (2003) 91–118.
73. Control Council Law No. 10, reprinted in Beate Ruhm von Oppen, *Documents on Germany under Occupation, 1945–1954* (Oxford: Oxford University Press, 1955) 97–101. See also Henry Friedlander, 'Trials of the Nazi Criminals: Law, Justice and History', *Dimensions: A Journal of Holocaust Studies*, Vol. 2 No. 1 (1986) 7 and 'The Judiciary and Nazi Crimes in Postwar Germany', *Simon Wiesenthal Center Annual*, Vol. 1 (1984) 32; Bernd Hey, 'Die NS-Prozesse—Versuch einer juristischen Vergangenheitsbewältigung', *Geschichte in Wissenschaft und Unterricht*, Vol. 6 (1981) 347.
74. Hermann Langbein, *Im Namen des deutschen Volkes: Zwischenbilanz der Prozesse wegen nationalsozialistischer Verbrechen* (Vienna: Europa Verlags-AG, 1963) 27–28.
75. Statistics taken from C.M. Clark, 'West Germany Confronts the Nazi Past: Some Recent Debates on the Early Postwar Era, 1945–1960', *The European Legacy*, Vol. 4 No. 1 (1999) 122.
76. Christiaan F. Rüter & Dick W. de Mildt eds., *Justiz und NS-Verbrechen: Sammlung deutscher Strafurteile wegen nationalsozialistischer Tötungsverbrechen 1945–1966. Register zu den Bänden I–XXII* (Amsterdam: Holland University Press, 1998).
77. Ibid.
78. Alaric Searle, 'Revising the "Myth" of a "Clean Wehrmacht": Generals' Trials, Public Opinion and the Dynamics of Vergangenheitsbewältigung in West Germany, 1948–60', *German Historical Institute London Bulletin*, Vol. 25 No. 2 (2003) 17–48 and 'The Tolsdorff Trials in Traunstein: Public and Judicial Attitudes to the Wehrmacht in the Federal Republic, 1954–60', *German History*, Vol. 23 No. 1 (2005) 50–78.Searle, 'Revising the "Myth" of a "Clean Wehrmacht"', 40, 44–45.
79. Elizabeth Noelle-Neumann ed., *The Germans: Public Opinion Polls, 1947–1966* (Westport, Connecticut: Greenwood, 1967) 202. Opinions were more mixed with regards to Party figures; 43 percent felt Rudolf Hess had been unfairly treated and 38 percent responded similarly with regards to Baldur von Schirach.
80. David Clay Large, 'Reckoning Without the Past: The HIAG of the Waffen-SS and the Politics of Rehabilitation in the Bonn Republic, 1950–1961', *Journal of Modern History*, Vol. 59 (March 1987) 79–113.
81. Donald Bloxham, 'Punishing German Soldiers during the Cold War: The Case of Erich von Manstein', *Patterns of Prejudice*, Vol. 33 No. 4 (1999) 25–45. For examples of earlier British debate on this issue, see 'War Crimes: Case of German Generals in British Custody', Emanual Shinwell, June 17, 1948, and Hartley W. Shawcross, June 22, 1948, NA, CAB/129/28. German attempts to downplay or ignore some of the military's involvement in the atrocities persisted right up until the 1990s when the travelling exhibition *Crimes of the Wehrmacht* began to challenge some of these assumptions—and provoked much controversy as a result.
82. For a detailed overview of this, see Norbert Frei, *Adenauer's Germany and the Nazi Past: The Politics of Amnesty and Integration*, translated by Joel Golb (New York: Columbia University Press, 2002), 67–91.
83. National Council of the National Front of Democratic Germany, *The Brown Book: War and Nazi Criminals in West Germany—State, Economy, Administration, Army, Justice, Science* (Dresden: Zeit im Bild, 1965).
84. Frei, *Adenauer's Germany*, 217, 218.
85. Ibid., 177.

86. Elizabeth Noelle-Neumann & Erich Peter Neumann, *Jahrbuch der öffentlichen Meinung, 1947–1955* (Allensbach: Verlag für Demoskopie, 1955) 202. The English version of the 1947–66 opinion polls uses the phrase 'best known war criminals' instead.
87. Wolfgang Koppel ed., *Ungesühnte Nazijustiz: Hundert Urteile klagen ihre Richter an* (Karlsruhe: Organisationskomitees der Dokumentenausstellung 'Ungesühnte Nazijustiz' in Karlsruhe, 1960). The exhibition is fleetingly referred to in Klaus Bästlein, 'Nazi-Blutrich als stützen des Adenauers Regimes: Die DDR-Kampagne gegen NS-Richter', Helge Grabitz, Klaus Bästlein & Johannes Tuchel eds., *Die Normalität des Verbrechens. Bilanz und Perspektiven der Forschung zu den nationalsozialismus Gewaltverbrechen* (Berlin: Edition Hentrich, 1994) 415, and Gerd Knischewski & Ulla Spittler, 'Memories of the Second World War and National Identity in Germany', Martin Evans & Kenneth Lunn eds., *War and Memory in the Twentieth Century* (Oxford: Berg, 1997) 243.

NOTES TO CHAPTER 2

1. For more on Staudtke's work, see Ulrike Weckel, 'The *Mitläufer* in Two German Post-war Films', *History and Memory*, Vol. 15 No. 2 (2003) 64–93.
2. For details on Fischer-Schweder's arrest and the investigations leading up to the Ulm trial, see Adalbert Rückerl, *The Investigation of Nazi Crimes, 1945–1978: A Documentation*, translated by D. Rutter (Karlsruhe: C.F. Müller, 1979) 48.
3. Such narratives are typified by Jean-Paul Bier, 'The Holocaust, West Germany and Strategies of Oblivion, 1947–1979', Anson Rabinbach & Jack Zipes eds., *Germans and Jews Since the Holocaust: The Ongoing Situation in West Germany* (New York: Holmes & Meier, 1986) 189; Jörg Friedrich, *Die Kalte Amnestie: NS Täter in der Bundesrepublik* (Frankfurt am Main: Fischer Taschenbuch, 1984) 324–330; Helge Grabitz, 'Die Verfolgung von NS-Gewaltverbrechen in Hamburg in der Zeit von 1945 bis heute', Helge Grabitz, Klaus Bästlein & Johannes Tuchel eds., *Die Normalität des Verbrechens: Bilanz und Perspektiven der Forschung zu den nationalsozialistischen Gewaltverbrechen* (Berlin: Edition Hentrich, 1994) 305; Erich Haberer, 'History and Justice: Paradigms of the Prosecution of Nazi Crimes', *Holocaust and Genocide Studies*, Vol. 19 No. 3, 495; Christa Hoffmann, *Stunden Null? Vergangenheitsbewältigung in Deutschland 1945 und 1989* (Bonn: Bouvier Verlag, 1992) 121–123, 141; Marcuse, *Legacies of Dachau*, 207; Peter Steinbach, 'Nationalsozialistische Gewaltverbrechen in der deutschen Öffentlichkeit nach 1945', Jürgen Weber & Peter Steinbach eds., *Vergangenheitsbewältigung durch Strafverfahren? NS-Prozesse in der Bundesrepublik Deutschland* (Munich: Günther Olzog, 1984) 15–24.
4. For details on these trials, see Irene Sagel-Grande, Christiaan Rüter & H.H. Fuchs eds., *Justiz und NS-Verbrechen, Band XIV* (Amsterdam: University Press Amsterdam, 1976).
5. For details on the Einsatzgruppen, and the Einsatzkommando Tilsit in particular, see Christoph Dieckmann, 'The War and the Killing of the Lithuanian Jews', Ulrich Herbert ed., *National Socialist Extermination Policies: Contemporary German Perspectives and Controversies* (New York & Oxford: Berghahn Books, 2000) 240–275 and Konrad Kwiet, 'Rehearsing for Murder: The Beginning of the Final Solution in Lithuania in June 1941', *Holocaust and Genocide Studies*, Vol. 12 No. 1 (1998) 3–26.

6. The charges against the ten Ulm defendants are reproduced in Irene Sagel-Grande, H.H. Fuchs & Christiaan F. Rüter eds., *Justiz und NS-Verbrechen, Band XV* (Amsterdam: University Press Amsterdam, 1976) Case No. 465.
7. 'The Einsatzgruppen Case', Military Tribunal II, Case No. 9: The United States of America v. Otto Ohlendorf et al., Trials of War Criminals before the Nuernberg Military Tribunals under Control Council Law No. 10. Vol. IV: Nuernberg October 1946–April 1949 (Washington, DC: U.S. Government Printing Office). The former *SS-Sturmbannführer* and officer in Einsatzkommando 12 attached to Einsatzgruppe D, Emil Haussmann, committed suicide in his cell before the arraignment.
8. 'Späte Scham', *Hannoversche Presse*, August 19, 1958.
9. Trials of War Criminals before the Nuernberg Military Tribunals under Control Council Law No. 10. Vol. IV, 13–14.
10. 'Lieber Leser', *Neue Presse*, June 13, 1958. Gorzkowska and Zakowska likewise argued that 'Ulm was the first major indictment by German prosecution authorities in a German court on German soil. Thus there could be no challenge to the authenticity of the facts revealed'. See Jadwiga Gorzkowska & Elzbieta Zakowska, *Nazi Criminals before West German Courts* (Warsaw: Western Press Agency, 1965) 21.
11. For details on West German reconstruction, see Robert G. Moeller ed., *West Germany under Construction: Politics, Society and Culture in the Adenauer Era* (Ann Arbor: University of Michigan Press, 1997); Rebecca Boehling, *A Question of Priorities: Democratic Reforms and Economic Recovery in Postwar Germany: Frankfurt, Munich, and Stuttgart under U.S. Occupation 1945–1949* (Providence, Rhode Island: Berghahn Books, 1996).
12. Rückerl, *The Investigation of Nazi Crimes*, 48.
13. Langbein, *Im Namen des deutschen Volkes*, 36.
14. Bier, 'The Holocaust, West Germany and Strategies of Oblivion', 189.
15. Brochhagen, *Nach Nürnberg*, 292.
16. Langbein, *Im Namen des deutschen Volkes*, 36. For a similar claim, see Marcuse, *Legacies of Dachau*, 207. Christa Hoffmann has reflected on how, before this, most war crimes proceedings seemed to have been set in motion more or less by chance, often the result—as in the case of Ulm—of some surprising revelations about the true identity of members of the local community. In the wake of the Einsatzkommando proceedings, though, there emerged a far more co-ordinated system for the investigation of Nazi crimes—*Stunden Null?* 121–123; 141.
17. Gorzkowska & Zakowska, *Nazi Criminals before West German Courts*, 21.
18. Compare, for example, the following reports on the first day of proceedings: 'Der SD war kämpfer gegen die Korruption', *Schwäbische Donau-Zeitung*, and 'Deutschland und die Welt', *Frankfurter Allgemeine Zeitung*, both April 30, 1958—and the extensive coverage of the final sentencing in 'Sühne für tausendfachen Mord', *Schwäbische Donau-Zeitung*; 'Das dunkelste Kapitel', *Düsseldorfer Nachrichten*; 'Zuchthausstrafen im Ulmer Einsatzkommando-Prozeß' and 'Gespenstische Vergangenheit vor Gericht zitiert', *Süddeutsche Zeitung*; 'Hohe Zuchthausstrafen im Ulmer-Prozeß', *Frankfurter Rundschau*; 'Das Bild des Kalten Henkers', *Frankfurter Allgemeine Zeitung*; 'Wirklich Sühne?' and 'Die Gerechtigkeit darf nicht länger vom Zufall abhängen', *Stuttgarter Zeitung*; 'Zuchthaus für alle im Ulmer-Prozeß' and 'Mord verjährt nicht', *Kölnische Rundschau*; 'Macht ohne Moral', *Weser-Kurier*; 'Verhängnis Voller Gehorsam', *Trierischer Volksfreund*—all August 30, 1958.
19. 'Wirklich Sühne?', *Stuttgarter Nachrichten*, August 30, 1958—original emphasis.

20. 'Ein Mord—fünf Tage Haft', *Bild-Zeitung am Abend*, September 4, 1958. See also 'Gespenstische Vergangenheit vor Gericht zitiert', *Süddeutsche Zeitung*; 'Mord verjährt nicht', *Kölnische Rundschau*; 'Die Gerechtigkeit darf nicht länger vom Zufall abhängen', *Stuttgarter Zeitung*, August 30, 1958; 'Die Ulmer Urteile', *Christ und Welt*, September 4, 1958.
21. 'Betrunken aus dem "Einsatz" zurück', *Frankfurter Rundschau*, June 19, 1958.
22. 'Himmlers Henker hören den Staatsanwalt', *Süddeutsche Zeitung*, August 4, 1958.
23. 'Porträt eines Herrenmenschen', *Die Welt*, July 25, 1958.
24. 'Lieber Leser', *Neue Presse*, June 13, 1958.
25. 'Wirklich Sühne?', *Stuttgarter Nachricten*, August 30, 1958. See also 'Die Gehilfen', *Die Gegenwart*, September 6, 1958.
26. 'Das dunkelste kapital', *Düsseldorfer Nachrichten*, August 30, 1958.
27. 'Grim Reminders', *Jewish Chronicle*, September 5, 1958, 20.
28. Report by R.G. Dundas, British Consulate General, Stuttgart, September 29, 1958, NA, FO371/137596: War Crimes 1958; WG1661/20.
29. Reports on the Trial at Ulm—Dispatch from the British Embassy, Bonn, to the Western Department of the Foreign Office, September 5, 1958, NA, FO371/137596: War Crimes 1958; WG1661/16.
30. 'Sühne für tausendfachen Mord im Urteil des Volkes', *Schwäbische Donau-Zeitung*, September 1, 1958.
31. Ibid.
32. Ibid.
33. Ibid.
34. Ibid.
35. Ibid.
36. Such apologetic views were encouraged throughout the Ulm trial by the defendants themselves, who testified how the orders for the mass execution of Lithuanian Jews and Communists had come from Reinhard Heydrich in the RSHA and, ultimately, from Hitler himself. Recent historiography, though, has been able to draw upon material now made available from the former Soviet archives which indicates how such decisions had actually originated on the ground from Stahlecker and Ulm defendant Böhme. See: Kwiet, 'Rehearsing for Murder', 4*ff* and Dieckmann, 'The War and the Killing of the Lithuanian Jews', *passim*.
37. 'Sühne für tausendfachen Mord im Urteil des Volkes', *Schwäbische Donau-Zeitung*, September 1, 1958.
38. Ibid.
39. Ibid.
40. Reports on the Trial at Ulm—Dispatch from the British Embassy, Bonn, to the Western Department of the Foreign Office, September 5, 1958.
41. 'Sühne für tausendfachen Mord im Urteil des Volkes', *Schwäbische Donau-Zeitung*, September 1, 1958.
42. Ibid.
43. Report by R.G. Dundas, British Consulate General, Stuttgart, September 29, 1958.
44. 'Sühne für tausendfachen Mord im Urteil des Volkes', *Schwäbische Donau-Zeitung*, September 1, 1958.
45. Ibid.
46. Ibid.
47. Ibid.
48. Ibid.
49. Ibid.

50. Ibid.
51. Ibid.
52. Ibid.
53. Report by R.G. Dundas, British Consulate General, Stuttgart, September 29, 1958.
54. Dispatch from British Embassy, Bonn, to the Western Department of the Foreign Office, October 16, 1958, NA, FO371/137597: War Crimes 1958; WG1661/22.
55. Peter Steinbach, 'Zur Auseinandersetzung mit nationalsozialistichen Gewaltverbrechen in der Bundesrepublik Deutschland', *Geschichte in Wissenschaft und Unterricht*, No. 2 (1984) 68. Concerns over the 'murderers among us' were expressed at the time in 'In gerechter Weise beenden', *Schwäbische Donau-Zeitung*, July 30, 1958 and 'Aufräumen', *Frankfurter Allgemeine Zeitung*, October 6, 1958.
56. Dick de Mildt, *In the Name of the People: Perpetrators of Genocide in the Reflection of Their Post-war Prosecution in West Germany: The 'Euthanasia' and 'Aktion Reinhard' Trial Cases* (The Hague: Martinus Nijhoff Publishers, 1996) 27.
57. Steinbach, 'Zur Auseinandersetzung mit nationalsozialistichen Gewaltverbrechen', 68.
58. 'Zentrale Ermittlungsbehörde?', *Trierischer Volksfreund*, September 15, 1958. See also 'Nicht zögern', *Freie Presse*, September 12, 1958; 'Zentrale Ermittlungsbehörde muß klarheit über NS-Verbrechen schaffen', *Stuttgarter Zeitung*, September 3, 1958; 'Justiz und Konkursmasse', *Frankfurter Neue Press*, October 3, 1958; 'Aufräumen', October 6, 1958 and 'Die Vergangenheit laßte', *Frankfurter Allgemeine Zeitung*, October 13, 1958.
59. Rückerl, *The Investigation of Nazi Crimes*, 50.
60. Ibid. For more on the history of the Zentralstelle, see Rüdiger Fleiter, 'Die Ludwigsburg Zentrale Stelle und ihr politisches und gesellschaftliches Umfeld', *Geschichte in Wissenschaft und Unterricht*, Vol. 53 No. 1 (2002) 32–50.
61. Heinz Keil ed., *Dokumentation über die Verfolgungen der Jüdischen Bürger von Ulm/Donau* (Hergestellt im Auftrage der Stadt Ulm) i.
62. Ibid., 20. For details of the Nazi rise to power and life in Ulm during the Third Reich and Allied occupation see Silvester Lechner, *Ulm im Nationalsozialismus: Stadtführer auf den Spuren des Regimes, der Verfolgten des Widerstands* (Ulm: Dokumentationszentrum Oberer Kuhberg Ulm, 1997).
63. 'Causerie', *Common Ground*, Vol. 26 No. 3 (1962) 23–24.
64. Keil, *Dokumentation über die Verfolgungen der Jüdischen Bürger von Ulm/Donau*, 303.
65. Ibid.

NOTES TO CHAPTER 3

1. 'In gerechter Weise beenden', *Schwäbische Donau-Zeitung*, July 30, 1958.
2. Langbein, *Im Namen des deutschen Volkes*, 35–36. The Sommer trial is also referred to briefly in Brochhaagen, *Nach Nürnberg*, 292; Marc von Miquel, *Ahnden oder Amnestieren? Westdeutsche Justiz und Vergangenheitspolitik in den sechziger Jahre* (Göttingen: Wallstein Verlag, 2004) 146–148; John P. Teschke, *Hitler's Legacy: West Germany Confronts the Aftermath of the Third Reich* (New York: Peter Lang, 1999) 282.
3. Helmut Paulus, 'Der Bayreuther 'KZ-Prozess Martin Sommer': Der Henker von Buchenwald hatte sich vor dem Bayreuther Schwurgericht zu verantworten' (Unpublished paper, 2002).

150 Notes

4. Jeremy Noakes & Geoffrey Pridham eds., *Nazism: A Documentary Reader, 1919–1945*, Vol. 1: *The Rise to Power, 1919–1934* (Exeter: University of Exeter Press, 1983) Source 60.
5. For further details on the relationship between the Wagner family and the Nazi regime see Frederick Spotts, *Bayreuth: A History of the Wagner Festival* (New Haven, Connecticut: Yale University Press, 1994); Nike Wagner, *The Wagners: The Dramas of a Musical Dynasty*, translated by E. Oseis & M. Downes (London: Phoenix, 2001); Berndt W. Wessling ed., *Bayreuth im Dritten Reich: Richard Wagners politische Erben. Eine Dokumentation* (Weinheim & Basel: Beltz Verlag, 1983).
6. Spotts, *Bayreuth*, 171, 193.
7. Details on Sommer's personal life can be found in his indictment, the original files of which are held in the archives of the Landgericht Bayreuth, Rep. K105. The information is also reproduced in Sagel-Grande *et al.* eds., *Justiz und NS-Verbrechen, Band XV*, Case No. 464; and Hendrik Georg van Dam & Ralph Giordano eds., *KZ-Verbrechen vor Deutschen Gerichten: Dokumente aus den Prozessen gegen Sommer (KZ Buchenwald), Sorge, Schubert (KZ Sachsenhausen), Unkelbach (Ghetto in Czenstochau)* (Frankfurt am Main: Europäische Verlagsanstalt, 1962).
8. Reported in '"Totschläger von Buchenwald" steht vor dem Richter', *Bayreuther Tagblatt*, June 12, 1958.
9. Ibid.
10. David A. Hackett ed., *The Buchenwald Report* (Boulder, Colorado: Westview Press, 1995) 203–204.
11. Ibid. Further details on atrocities perpetrated by Sommer can be found pp. 196–204.
12. Eugen Kogon, *Der SS-Staat: Das System der deutschen Konzentrationslager* (Frankfurt am Main: Europäische Verlagsanstalt, 1946) 202. Sommer's name appears thirty times over the course of Kogon's description of the Buchenwald cell block, 199–207. For an overview of the Buchenwald concentration camp and its liberation see *Buchenwald Camp: The Report of a Parliamentary Delegation Presented by the Prime Minister, First Lord of the Treasury and Minister of Defence to Parliament by Command of His Majesty* (London: H.M. Stationary Office, 1945); Victor Gollancz, *What Buchenwald Really Means* (London: Victor Gollancz, 1945); Robert H. Abzug, *Inside the Vicious Heart: Americans and the Liberation of Nazi Concentration Camps* (New York & Oxford: Oxford University Press, 1985); Jon Bridgmann, *The End of the Holocaust: The Liberation of the Camps* (London: B.T. Batsford, 1990); Annadora Miethe ed., *Buchenwald* (Buchenwald Concentration Camp Musuems and National Memorial Guidebook); Jens Schley, *Nachbar Buchenwald: Die Stadt Weimar und ihr Konzentrationslager, 1937–1945* (Cologne, Weimar & Vienna: Böhlau Verlag, 1999).
13. Katharina von Kellenbach, 'Vanishing Acts: Perpetrators in Postwar Germany', *Holocaust and Genocide Studies*, Vol. 17 No. 2 (2003) 310.
14. Debates on whether Sommer was fit to stand trial were published in 'Amtsarzt fälschlich der Begünstigung verdächtigt', *Bayreuther Tagblatt*, November 8, 1956; 'Sommer soll entlassen werden', *Münchner Merkur* and 'Wird "Totschläger" Sommer nun verhaftet', *Erlanger Tageblatt*, both December 8, 1956. West German press interest in the Sommer case was also revived during this period amid revelations that Sommer was able to furnish his comfortable lifestyle through his receipt of a state pension; see 'Sommer hofft auf 10,000 DM Renten Nahzahlung', *Fränkische Presse*, June 22, 1956; and 'Bemerkungen', *Stuttgarter Zeitung*, October 8, 1956. Pressure from the German Democratic Republic may have also been a factor in finally bringing the case to

court, with 'KZ-Mörder als Staatspensionär?', *Frankfurter Rundschau* and 'Der Rentenfall des SS-Führers Martin Sommer', *Süddeutsche Zeitung*, both June 23, 1956, acknowledging how the 'Eastern' press was criticising West Germany's treatment of Martin Sommer.
15. See, for instance, the following items which were published after the first day of proceedings on June 12, 1958: '"Totschläger von Buchenwald" steht vor dem Richter', *Bayreuther Tagblatt*; 'So wurden die Häftlinge geprügelt', *Süddeutsche Zeitung*; 'Er prügelte sich die Hände wund', *Hamburger Echo*; 'Haftlinge mit Evipan-Spritzen ermordet', *Frankfurter Rundschau*; '"Bestie von Buchenwald" vor Gericht', *Hannoversche Presse*; 'Wenn Sie mich fragen', *Wiesbadener Kurier*.
16. Reported in 'Schlechte Aussichten für Gipfeltreffen', *Bayreuther Tagblatt*, June 19, 1958.
17. 'Neue Zeugen—neue schwere Belastungen für Sommer', *Bayreuther Tagblatt*, June 20, 1958.
18. See, for example, '"Totschläger von Buchenwald" steht vor dem Richter', June 12, 1958 and 'Begründete Verbote im Sommer-Prozeß', June 14–15, 1958, both *Bayreuther Tagblatt*; 'Zum Tage', *Wetzlauer Neue Zeitung*, June 14, 1958; 'Späte Gerechtigkeit und keine Reue', *Fränkische Presse*, July 5, 1958.
19. See, for example, 'KZ-Sommer bald wieder vor den Richtern', *Die Abendpost*, April 18, 1959; 'Das Urteil', *Hannoversche Presse*, July 4, 1958; 'Prozeß gegen Martin Sommer', *Frankfurter Rundschau*, June 10, 1958.
20. Report from Sir Christopher Steel, British Embassy in Bonn to the Right Honourable Selwyn Lloyd MP in the Foreign Office, July 9, 1958, 2, NA, FO 371/137596: War Crimes Trials 1958; WG1661/5.
21. See for instance 'Ein Mensch ohne Empfinden', *Frankfurter Rundschau*, Parts 1 & 2, June 30 & July 1, 1958.
22. Cited in David Clay Large, 'Reckoning Without the Past: The HIAG of the Waffen-SS and the Politics of Rehabilitation in the Bonn Republic, 1950–1961', *Journal of Modern History*, Vol. 59 (1987) 94; and Eleonore Sterling, 'Scapegoatisms', *World Jewry*, Vol. 1 No. 7 (1958) 5.
23. 'Ehe mit dem Satan', *Der Stern*, June 28, 1958. A recurring image of the Sommer trial was the sight of Barbara Sommer helping her husband into the courtroom, a photograph reproduced in 'Die Bestie vom Lager Buchenwald', *Süddeutsche Zeitung*, June 23, 1958; '"Sie rauben mir auch den Schlaf!"', *Stuttgarter Nachrichten*, June 24, 1958; 'Das Grauen went durch den Gerichtssaal', *Nürnberger Nachrichten*, June 25, 1958; 'Bärbel Sommer: "Ich bleib ihm treu"', *Main-Post*, June 26, 1958; 'Sommers Frau hält zu ihren Mann', *Frankenpost*, June 28, 1958, among others. Further outrage over Frau Sommer's demeanour throughout the proceedings was expressed in 'Die Macht der Peitsche', *Bild-Zeitung*, June 22, 1958; 'Notizbuch der Woche', *Fränkische Presse*, June 28, 1958; *Frankfurter Rundschau*, '"Ein Mensch ohne Empfinden"', Part 2 (July 1, 1958); 'Frau Sommer muß kündigen', *Frankfurter Allgemeine Zeitung*, July 2, 1958; '"Meine Liebe ist stärker als die Kerkermauern"', *8-Uhr Blatt*, July 5, 1958.
24. See 'Die Mörder leben unter uns', *Freie Presse*, June 20, 1958; 'Die Mörder sind unter uns', *Hamburger Echo*, July 1, 1958; 'Lieber Leser', *Neue Presse*, July 2, 1958; as well as the observations in 'Die unbewältigte Vergangenheit', *AJR Information*, Vol. 13 No. 8 (1958) 1. Evidence of public debate on the subject can be found among the readers' letters printed in 'Mörder leben unter uns', *Süddeutsche Zeitung*, July 12, 1958.
25. 'Zweierlei Reaktion', *Frankfurter Rundschau*, July 4, 1958.
26. 'Redaktion', *Rhein-Zeitung*, July 18, 1958.

27. 'Briefe', *Frankfurter Allgemeine Zeitung*, July 11, 1958.
28. 'Mörder leben unter uns', *Süddeutsche Zeitung*, July 12, 1958.
29. 'Der Sommer-Prozeß', *Deutsche Woche*, July 9, 1958.
30. 'Die unbewältigte Vergangenheit', *AJR Information*, 1.
31. 'Die Mörder sind unter uns', *Hamburger Echo*, July 1, 1958.
32. Ibid.
33. 'Gerichtet', *Rhein-Zeitung*, July 5, 1958.
34. 'Gottes Mühlen', *Kasseler Post*, July 4, 1958.
35. 'Lieber Leser', *Neue Presse*, July 2, 1958.
36. Ibid.
37. Ibid.
38. 'Die Stimmung im Bundesgebiet: Die KZ Prozesse', Institut für Demoskopie Allensbach am Bodensee, October 27, 1958.
39. Ibid.
40. Ibid.
41. Ibid.
42. Ibid.
43. Ibid.
44. Ibid.
45. For details on the post-war history of the Wagner family see Spotts, *Bayreuth: A History of the Wagner Festival*, 203–211.
46. Ibid., 205. See also Ceilia Applegate, 'Saving Music: Enduring Experiences of Culture', *History and Memory*, Vol. 17 No. 1–2 (2005) 217–237.
47. Spotts, *Bayreuth: A History of the Wagner Festival*, 206.
48. Ibid., 211.
49. Ibid. Similarly, during the 1958 festival, the press confined themselves to writing solely about the music, despite the recent war crimes trial staged in the town. In an article entitled 'Bayreuth Then and Now', *The Times* compared that year's performance of *Parsifal* with its last rendering in the pre-Nazi Germany of 1927, noting 'the town has changed but the *Festspielhaus* remains the unique, acoustically incomparable theatre it always was', August 11, 1958, 2.
50. Spotts, *Bayreuth: A History of the Wagner Festival*, 211.
51. Ibid.
52. Typical was the *Bayreuther Tagblatt*'s juxtaposition of 'Dichtung und Wahrheit tendenziös gemixt' next to '"Sieglinde" nach sieben Jahren wiedergekehrt', June 27, 1958; and 'Lebenslänglich Zuchthaus für Sommer' alongside 'Neue Gesichter auf dem "Hügel"', July 4, 1958.
53. 'Späte Gerechtigkeit und keine Reue', *Fränkische Presse*, July 5, 1958.
54. 'Dichtung und Wahrheit tendenziös gemixt', *Bayreuther Tagblatt*, June 27, 1958.
55. 'Massenandrang vor dem Schwurgericht', *Bayreuther Tagblatt*, June 25, 1958.
56. 'Der Sommer-Prozeß', *Deutsche Woche*, July 9, 1958.
57. 'The German Reaction to the Trial of "The Raving Beast of Buchenwald"', *World Jewry*, 16.
58. For examples of such reports on concentration camps, see Robert Gellately, *Backing Hitler: Consent and Coercion in Nazi Germany* (New York & Oxford: Oxford University Press, 2001) 51–69; Sybil Milton, 'Die Konzentrationslager der dreißiger Jahre im Bild der in- und ausländischen Presse', Ulrich Herbert, Karin Orth & Christoph Dieckmann eds., *Die nationalsozialistischer Konzentrationslager: Entwicklung und Struktur Band I* (Göttingen: Wallstein Verlag 1998) 135–147; Schley, *Nachbar Buchenwald*, 117–122.

59. For an overview of the VVN, see: Peter Monteath, 'Organising Antifascism: The Obscure History of the VVN', *European History Quarterly*, Vol. 29 No. 2 (1999) 289–303.
60. Sterling, 'Scapegoatisms', 5.
61. Archives of the Landgericht Bayreuth, Ks3/1957, Letter to the Landgericht Bayreuth No. 40, June 11, 1958.
62. Ibid., No. 113, June 24, 1958.
63. Ibid., No. 136, June 22, 1958.
64. John P. Teschke also argues that much of the interest in Sommer can be explained by the fact the trial was dealing with crimes perpetrated in Buchenwald; see *Hitler's Legacy*, 282.
65. Archives of the Landgericht Bayreuth, Ks3/1957, Letter to the Landgericht Bayreuth No. 150, June 24, 1958.
66. Ibid., No. 44, June 16, 1958.
67. Ibid., No. 150, June 24, 1958. For similar concerns see too No. 113, June 24, 1958.
68. Ibid., No. 150, June 24, 1958.
69. Ibid., No. 11 (undated).
70. Sterling, 'Scapegoatisms', 5.
71. 'Aug in Auge mit unserer Geschiche', *Frankfurter Allgemeine Zeitung*, December 3, 1958. The comparison made to Bonn refers to the prosecution of two former Sachsenhausen guards, Wilhelm Schubert and Gustav Sorge, which took place between October 1958 and February 1959. Both defendants received life imprisonment for murdering prisoners. Details on this case can be found in Irene Sagel-Grande *et al.* eds., *Justiz und NS-Verbrechen, Band XV*, Case No. 473.

NOTES TO CHAPTER 4

1. For details on the circumstances leading up to Eichmann's discovery, see Cesarani, *Eichmann*, 221–236; and Simon Wiesenthal, *The Murderers Are among Us* (London: Pan Books, 1968).
2. Cesarani, *Eichmann*, 1.
3. For further details of the trial itself, see *The Trial of Adolf Eichmann: Record of Proceedings in the District Court of Jerusalem* (Jerusalem: Trust for the Publication of the Proceedings of the Eichmann Trial, 1992–1995); Haim Gouri, *Facing the Glass Booth: The Jerusalem Trial of Adolf Eichmann* (Detroit, Michigan: Wayne State University Press, 2004); Bernd Nellessen, *Der Prozess von Jerusalem: ein Dokument* (Düsseldorf: Econ, 1964).
4. See, for instance, Irving Crespi, 'Public Reaction to the Eichmann Trial', *Public Opinion Quarterly*, Vol. 28 No. 1 (1964) 91–103; Charles Y. Glock, Gertrude J. Selznick & Joe L. Spaeth, *The Apathetic Majority: A Study Based on Public Responses to the Eichmann Trial* (London: Harper & Row, 1966); Peter Novick, *The Holocaust and Collective Memory: The American Experience* (London: Bloomsbury, 1999); George Salomon, 'The End of Eichmann: America's Response', *American Jewish Yearbook*, Vol. 64 (1963) 247–259; Jeffrey Shandler, 'The Man in the Glass Box', *While America Watches: Televising the Holocaust* (Oxford: Oxford University Press, 1999) 83–132; Yechiam Weitz, 'The Holocaust on Trial: The Impact of the Kasztner and Eichmann Trials on Israeli Society', *Israel Studies*, Vol. 1 No. 2 (1996) 1–26; Hanna Yablonka, 'The Development of Holocaust Consciousness in Israel: The Nuremberg, Kapos, Kasztner and Eichmann Trials', *Israel Studies*, Vol. 8 No. 3 (2003) 1–24. A rare, more detailed insight into German

responses to the Eichmann case can be found in Ulrich Brochhagen, 'Auch das noch! Der Eichmann-Prozess in Jerusalem', *Nach Nürnberg: Vergangenheitsbewältigung und Westintegration in der Ära Adenauer* (Berlin: Ullstein, 1999) 389–408.
5. Douglas, *The Memory of Judgement*, 6.
6. On the legacy of this trial, see David Cesarani ed., *After Eichmann: Collective Memory and the Holocaust since 1961* (London: Routledge, 2005).
7. Hannah Arendt, *Eichmann in Jerusalem: A Report on the Banality of Evil* (London: Faber, 1963) 12.
8. Ibid., 11. Arendt's remarks have been challenged by other scholars; see, for example, Jacob Robinson, *And the Crooked Shall Be Made Straight: The Eichmann Trial, the Jewish Catastrophe and Hannah Arendt's Narrative* (New York: MacMillan, 1965); and Rebecca Wittmann, 'The Wheels of Justice Turn Slowly: The Pre-trial Investigations of the Frankfurt Auschwitz Trial 1963–65', Central European History, Vol. 35, No. 3 (2002) 345–378.
9. 'Bonn and Eichmann', *New York Times* April 5, 1961, 15.
10. Rudy Koshar, *From Monuments to Traces: Artefacts of German Memory, 1870–1990* (Berkeley: University of California Press, 2000) 235.
11. Arendt, *Eichmann in Jerusalem*, 6.
12. Jean-Paul Bier, 'The Holocaust, West Germany and Strategies of Oblivion, 1947–1979', Anson Rabinbach & Jack Zipes eds., *Germans and Jews since the Holocaust: The Ongoing Situation in West Germany* (New York: Holmes & Meier, 1986) 190. Newspapers, though, remained people's primary source of information on the trial. Data gleaned by the Allensbach Institut für Demoskopie in June 1961 found 56 percent of West Germans were following the trial through the press reports, compared with 36 percent who relied on television coverage and 25 percent on radio broadcasts; 15 percent admitted they had not been following the case at all. See 'Prozessberichte', Elizabeth Noelle & Erich Peter Neumann eds., *Jahrbuch der öffentlichen Meinung, 1958–1964* (Allensbach & Bonn: Institut für Demoskopie, 1964) 226.
13. 'Trial Impact Assessed', *New York Times*, May 27, 1961, 6. Meyers was speaking at the Overseas Press Club amid a three week tour of the United States.
14. Statistics gleaned from Joel Carmichael, 'Reactions in Germany', *Midstream*, Vol. 7 No. 3 (1961) 14.
15. Rolf Hochhuth, *The Representative*, translated by R.D. MacDonald (London: Methuen & Co., 1963). On the controversy surrounding this play, see Eric Bentley, *The Storm over 'The Deputy'* (New York: Grove, 1964); Jan Berg, *Hochhuth's 'Stellvertreter' und die 'Stellvertreter'-Debatte: Vergangenheitsbewältigung in Theater und Presse der sechziger Jahre* (Kronberg im Taunus: Scriptor, 1977); Michael Patterson, '"Bewältigung der Vergangenheit" or "überwältigung der Befangenheit": Nazism and the War in Post-war German Theatre', *Modern Drama*, Vol. 33 No. 1 (1990) 125–126.
16. 'Germans Admit Role', *New York Times*, April 10, 1961, 12.
17. Seeliger had taken a keen interest in raising awareness of the Nazi past and produced a number of works on this theme throughout the 1960s. See, for instance, his *Braune Universität: Deutsche Hochschullehrer gestern und heute. Dokumentation mit Stellungnahmen III* (Munich: Rolf Seeliger, 1965). For an example of the VVN's work during this period, see *Die unbewältigte Gegenwart: Eine Dokumentation über Rolle und Einfluss ehemals führender Nationalsozialisten in der Bundesrepublik Deutschland* (Frankfurt am Main: Vereinigung der Verfolgten des Naziregimes, 1962).
18. Quoted in 'Blick in eine düstere Vergangenheit', *Süddeutsche Zeitung*, February 20, 1961.

19. For details on the Globke scandal, see: *Globke: Adenauer's State Secretary and the Extermination of the Jews. On the Criminal Past of Dr. Hans Globke, State Secretary in the Office of Federal Chancellor Adenauer* (East Berlin: Committee for German Unity, 1960); *Globke: Der Burokrat des Todes. Eine Dokumentation über die Blutschuld des höchsten Bonner Staatsbeamten bei der Ausrottung der Juden* (East Berlin: Anschluss für Deutsche Einheit, 1963); Klaus Gotto ed., *Der Staatssekretär Adenauers: Persönlichkeit und politisches Wirken Hans Globkes* (Stuttgart: Klett-Cotta, 1980); Jan Zaborowski, *Dr. Hans Globke: The Good Clerk* (Poznan: Zachodnia Agencja Prasowa, 1962); Jean Boulier ed., *Der Prozess gegen Dr. Hans Globke* (Dresden: Verlag Zeit im Bild, 1963).
20. 'Blick in eine düstere Vergangenheit', *Süddeutsche Zeitung*, February 20, 1961. See also: 'Protest gegen Beschlagnahme', *Abendzeitung*, February 21, 1961. The Globke connection also became the focus for Anglo-Jewish reporting on the exhibition; see 'Globke Exhibits Seized', *Jewish Chronicle*, February 24, 1961.
21. For details on newspaper coverage of the trial, see Akiba Cohen *et al*, *The Holocaust and the Press*; and Hans Lamm, *Der Eichmann Prozeß in der deutschen öffentlichen Meinung* (Frankfurt am Main: Ner-Tamid-Verlag, 1961).
22. Reported in 'Adenauer is Worried', *Jewish Chronicle*, March 17, 1961, 19. See also reports in *The Times*: 'Dr. Adenauer's Misgivings over Eichmann Trial', March 11, 1961, 7; and 'Eichmann Reviving a Past Still Hard to Face', April 7, 1961, 11.
23. 'Nazi Trial Issues Worry Adenauer', *New York Times*, March 11, 1961, 1.
24. 'Berlin Mayor Appeals to World Jewry', *Jewish Chronicle*, March 24, 1961, 20.
25. Tim Grady '"They Died for Germany": Jewish Soldiers, the German Army and Conservative Debates about the Nazi Past in the 1960s', *European History Quarterly*, Vol. 39 No. 1 (2009) 27–46.
26. 'Der Prozeß', *Frankfurter Illustrierte*, April 9, 1961.
27. Cited in 'German Reputation', *Jewish Chronicle*, April 7, 1961, 36.
28. Ibid. For details on how veterans of the Waffen-SS sought to portray their past after 1945, see David Clay Large, 'Reckoning without the Past: The HIAG of the Waffen-SS and the Politics of Rehabilitation in the Bonn Republic, 1950–1961', *Journal of Modern History*, Vol. 59 (1987) 79–113.
29. *Rhein-Zeitung*, April 12, 1961, cited in Carmichael, 'Reactions in Germany', 20.
30. Sydney Gruson, 'Bonn and Eichmann', *New York Times*, April 5, 1961, 15.
31. 'Eichmann soll leben—bis er sterben muss', *Quick*, March 12, 1961.
32. 'Noch sind Mörder unter uns', *Revue*, April 16, 1961.
33. Cited in 'German Reputation', *Jewish Chronicle*, April 7, 1961, 36.
34. *Frankfurter Rundschau*, May 1, 1961, cited in Carmichael, 'Reactions in Germany', 17.
35. *Bonner General-Anzeiger*, May 17, 1961, cited in Carmichael, 'Reactions in Germany',18.
36. *Frau und Politk*, April 1961, cited in Carmichael, 'Reactions in Germany', 20.
37. Carmichael, 'Reactions in Germany', 15. The *New York Times* also reported incidents of swastika daubing in the run up to and during the course of the trial. In Duisburg, the slogan 'long life Eichmann' appeared on a wall. See 'Ruhr Vandals Hail Eichmann', March 12, 1961, 9; and 'Nazi Signs Daubed in a German Town', April 13, 1961, 5.
38. Letter to *Die Welt*, March 1961, cited in Carmichael, 'Reactions in Germany', 23.

39. Die Zeit, March 17, 1961, cited in Carmichael, 'Reactions in Germany', 22.
40. Letter to Die Zeit, March 31, 1961, cited in Carmichael, 'Reactions in Germany', 24. Original emphasis.
41. Letter to Suddeutsche Zeitung, May 27, 1961, cited in Carmichael, 'Reactions in Germany', 24.
42. Letter to Die Welt, May 17, 1961, cited in Carmichael, 'Reactions in Germany', 25.
43. On the issue of knowledge about the Nazi crimes, see Norbert Frei, 'Auschwitz and the Germans: History, Knowledge and Memory', Neil Gregor ed., *Nazism, War and Genocide: Essays in Honour of Jeremy Noakes* (Exeter: University of Exeter Press, 2005) 147–165.
44. 'BILD-Leser zum Eichmann-Prozeß', *Bild-Zeitung*, June 1, 1961. This continues to be the biggest-selling German newspaper and is part of the Springer press, which is renowned not only for its conservatism, but also for its philosemitism.
45. Ibid.
46. Ibid.
47. Ibid.
48. Ibid.
49. Ibid.
50. Ibid.
51. Ibid.
52. Ibid.
53. Ibid.
54. Ibid.
55. Ibid.
56. Ibid.
57. Ibid.
58. 'Eichmann Image Repels Germans', *New York Times*, July 16, 1961, 27.
59. 'Eichmann: Impact on Germany', *New York Times*, April 16, 1961, E4.
60. Ibid.
61. Elizabeth Noelle & Erich Peter Neumann eds., *Jahrbuch der Öffentlichen Meinung, 1958–1964* (Alllensbach & Bonn: Institut für Demoskopie, 1964).
62. Ibid.
63. The results of this survey can be found in Noelle & Neumann eds., *Jahrbuch der Öffentlichen Meinung*.
64. Ibid.
65. Ibid.
66. Ibid.
67. Ibid. Note that 31 percent of respondents in this survey felt things were being exaggerated for propaganda and retaliation purposes, while 48 percent argued that, if Germany had won the war, there would have been no need for the moral degradation of seeing such things continually on the television and in the newspaper.
68. Ibid.
69. Ibid.
70. Ibid.
71. 'German Government Moves to Cut Ex-Nazis' Pensions', *Calgary Herald*, April 7, 1961, 36.

NOTES TO CHAPTER 5

1. For details on the swastika outbreak, see *Papers of the Institute of Jewish Affairs*, University of Southampton Special Collections, Folder 1: Neo-

Notes 157

Nazism—General (IJA N (SUB) MS241/3/28) and Folder 1: Swastika Epidemic (IJA S (SUB) MS241/3/44); Brochhagen, *Nach Nürnberg*, 319–344; Helmut Dubiel, *Niemand ist frei von der Geschichte: Die nationalsozialistische Herrschaft in den Debatten des Deutschen Bundestages* (Munich: Carl Hanser Verlag, 1999) 81–82. Schleswig-Holstein, the subject of this chapter, continued to experience a number of such incidents even as the 'epidemic' began to decline in the rest of the country.
2. Timothy A. Tilton, *Nazism, Neo-Nazism and the Peasantry* (Bloomington: Indiana University Press, 1975) 39–45.
3. Statistics taken from Jeremy Noakes & Geoffrey Pridham eds., *Nazism: A Documentary Reader, 1919–1945*, Vol. 1: *The Rise to Power, 1919–1934* (Exeter: University of Exeter Press, 1983) 81–83. See also Edgar J. Feuchtwanger, *From Weimar to Hitler: Germany 1918–33* (London: MacMillan, 1993) 202.
4. 'Schalten der Gewaltzeit', *Schleswig-Holsteinische Volkszeitung*, January 7, 1961.
5. 'Who Helped Nazi Doctor?', *Jewish Chronicle*, November 27, 1959. For further information on the Heyde/Sawade scandal, see Klaus-Detlev Godau-Schüttkeaz, *Die Heyde-Sawade Affäre: Wie Juristen und Mediziner den NS-Euthanasieprofessor Heyde nach 1945 decken und straflos blieben* (Baden-Baden: Nomos Verlagsgesellschaft, 1998); Teschke, *Hitler's Legacy*, 295–308. Heyde, though, was not an isolated case but representative of an endemic problem for the Federal Republic during this period. See also, for example, the case of Hans Schwerte/Schneider in Helmut König, Wolfgang Kuhlmann & Klaus Schwahe, *Vertuschte Vergangenheit: Der Fall Schwerte und die NS-Vergangenheit der deutscher Hochschulen* (Munich: C.H. Beck, 1997).
6. 'Schalten der Gewaltzeit', *Schleswig-Holsteinische Volkszeitung*, January 7, 1961.
7. 'Ex-Nazis' Hunting Ground Seen In Schleswig-Holstein', *New York Herald Tribune*, December 23, 1960.
8. Ibid.
9. 'Victims of Denazification', *Wiener Library Bulletin*, Vol. 9 No. 3–4 (1955) 26.
10. For details on Katzmann's career, see Dieter Pohl, *Einsatzgruppen C and D in the Invasion of the Soviet Union* (London: Holocaust Educational Trust, 2000).
11. Biographical details for Martin Fellenz reproduced in Christiaan F. Rüter & Dick W. de Mildt eds., *Justiz und NS-Vebrechen: Sammlung deutscher Strafurteile wegen nationalsozialistischer Tötungsverbrechen 1945–1966, Band XXIII* (Amsterdam: APA—Holland University Press, 1998) Case No. 619.
12. References to Fellenz's role in these actions can be found in Reinhard Henkys, Kurt Scharf, Jürgen Baumann & Dieter Goldschmidt, *Die nationalsozialistischen Gewaltverbrechen: Geschichte und Gericht* (Stuttgart: Kreuz-Verlag, 1965) 101; Seev Goshen, 'Albert Battels Widerstand gegen die Judenvernichtung in Przemysl', *Vierteljahreshefte für Zeitgeschichte*, Vol. 33 No. 3 (1985) 478–488; Heiner Lichtenstein, *Himmlers grüne Helfer: Die Schutz- und Ordnungspolizei im Dritten Reich* (Cologne: Bund-Verlag, 1990) 130–131; Israel Gutman & Bella Gutterman, 'Aktion Reinhard', 'Erntefest' and 'Scherner, Julian', *Enzyklopädie des Holocaust: Die Verfolgung und Ermordung der europäischen Juden, Band I* (Berlin: Argon, 2002) 14–18, 418–419, 1281–1282.
13. Figure stated in Jeremy Noakes & Geoffrey Pridham eds., *Nazism 1919–1945: A Documentary Reader*, Vol. 3: *Foreign Policy, War and Racial Extermination* (Exeter: University of Exeter Press, 1988) 1153.

14. The website for the Männerchor Schaalby acknowledges Fellenz's activities during this period, listing him as their choir leader between August 16, 1956 and April 30, 1987. His absence from the day to day running of the choir during much of the 1960s while attending to the war crimes charges, however, is not mentioned. See www.schleswig-holstein.de/Maennerchor-Schaalby/index/MCS_Geschichte.htm
15. 'Chorleitermangel und wirksame Abhilfe', *Schleswiger Nachrichten*, June 1, 1960.
16. 'Kandidaten stellen sich vor', *Schleswiger Nachrichten*, April 19, 1955.
17. Hayes and Harlington Urban District Council, *Town Twinning Celebrations with Schleswig and Mantes-La-Jolie* (1960). Held by the Heritage Service, Uxbridge Central Library. London Borough of Hillingdon Films: F9. No. 013 654 063.
18. 'FDP Fellenz besaß großes Vertrauen', *Flensburger Tageblatt*, June 27, 1960. Similarly, the *Südschleswigische Heimatzeitung* described news of Fellenz's arrest as going down 'like a bomb' in England in its article 'Erregung in England über den Fall Fellenz', June 27, 1960.
19. 'The Gentle Butcher', *Daily Express*, June 22, 1960.
20. Ibid.
21. 'Schleswiger Ratsherr unter Verdacht der Judenvernichtung', *Schleswig-Holsteinische Volkszeitung*; 'Schleswiger Ratsherr der Judenvernichtung verdächtigt', *Südschleswigische Heimatzeitung*, June 21, 1960; 'Schleswiger Ratsherr wurde verhaftet', *Flensburger Presse*, June 23, 1960; 'FDP Fellenz besaß großes Vertrauen', *Flensburger Tageblatt*, June 27, 1960.
22. 'FDP Fellenz besaß großes Vertrauen', *Flensburger Tageblatt* and 'Erregung in England über den Fall Fellenz', *Südschleswigische Heimatzeitung*, June 27, 1960. For further evidence of local newspapers imposing a sense of distance between Fellenz and the rest of the community, see 'Ehemaliger Schleswiger Ratsherr wegen Judenaussiedlung angeklagt', *Südschleswigische Heimatzeitung*, July 20, 1960; and 'Angeklagte des 40,000 fachen Mordes', *Schleswig-Holsteinische Volkszeitung*, October 19, 1962.
23. See, for example, 'Mordanklage gegen frühen SS-Führer in Schleswig', *Südschleswigische Heimatzeitung*, April 20, 1962; 'Ehemaliger Ratsherr des Mordes angeklagt', *Schleswig-Holsteinische Volkszeitung*, April 21, 1962; 'Gestern begann der Prozeß gegen Fellenz', *Flensburger Tageblatt*, November 15, 1962.
24. 'Jahrelang bekannt—aber niemand zeigte ihn an', *Frankfurter Rundschau*, July 13, 1960.
25. 'Martin Fellenz war ein angesehener Bürger', *Die Zeit*, November 23, 1962.
26. 'Erster Nachtragshaushalt genehmigt', *Schleswiger Nachrichten*, June 29, 1960.
27. Landesarchiv Schleswig, 'Schleswig-Holsteinische Korrespondenz der Freien Demokratischen Partei, Kiel', June 25, 1960, Abt. 354 No. 11419.
28. Ibid., 'Letter from Herr N. to the Amtsgericht Flensburg', August 6, 1960.
29. Ibid., 'Letter from Herr T. to the Amtsgericht Flensburg', August 6, 1960.
30. Ibid., 'Letter from Herr D. to Martin Fellenz', August 9, 1960.
31. See, for instance, coverage of the first day of proceedings in 'Fellenz bestreitet jede Schuld', *Schleswig-Holsteinische Volkszeitung*; 'Fellenz muß sich verantworten', *Flensburger Presse*; 'Gestern begann der Prozeß gegen Fellenz', *Flensburger Tageblatt*; 'Der Prozeß gegen Fellenz eröffnet', *Frankfurter Allgemeine Zeitung*; 'Judenmörder Fellenz vor Gericht', *Frankfurter Rundschau*—all November 15, 1962. The Fellenz trial received only an occasional mention in the national West German press with the slight exception of *Die Zeit*, although this was based in Hamburg. Even this publication waited until

November 23, 1962, before producing its first report on the trial, 'Martin Fellenz war ein angesehener Bürger'.
32. Trials conducted in 1962 are summarised in Rüter & De Mildt eds., *Justiz und NS-Verbrechen, Register zu den Bänden I-XXII*. For details on the Eccarius and Waltke proceedings see Case Nos. 545 and 544, respectively, in Vol. XVIII.
33. 'Martin Fellenz war ein angesehener Bürger', *Die Zeit*, November 23, 1962.
34. 'Sicherheitspolizei unterstand nicht dem SS-Gericht', *Flensburger Tageblatt*, December 1, 1962.
35. Ibid.
36. 'Keine Klarheit über die Zuständigkeiten', *Flensburger Tageblatt*, November 21, 1962.
37. 'Die Zeugen konnten sich nicht mehr erinnern', *Flensburger Tageblatt*, November 27, 1962.
38. 'Zeugen sagen Auschwitz im Fellenz-Prozeß', *Flensburger Tageblatt*, November 20, 1962.
39. 'Die Zeugen konnten sich nicht mehr erinnern', *Flensburger Tageblatt*, November 27, 1962.
40. 'Meine Verwandten sind nicht wiedergekommen', *Flensburger Tageblatt*, November 28, 1962; 'Ich sah nur Blut und Leichen', *Frankfurter Rundschau*, December 20, 1962; 'Abgeschossen—wie Hasen', *Die Zeit*, January 11, 1963.
41. 'Totales Vergessen?', *Rheinische Merkur*, January 18, 1963.
42. 'Jüdische Kritik am Fellenz-Urteil', *Frankfurter Allgemeine Zeitung*, January 17, 1963.
43. Wiener Library Press Summary, Wiener Library, London. G5b1: Fellenz.
44. 'Was heißt da Bewahrung?', *Die Zeit*, January 18, 1963.
45. Ibid.
46. 'Das kalte Grauen beim Fellenz-Urteil', *Südschleswigische Heimatzeitung*, January 14, 1963.
47. 'Werden die vielen Gleichgültigen leider recht behalten?', *Die Welt*, January 18, 1963.
48. 'Abgeschossen—wie Hasen', *Die Zeit*, January 11, 1963. For further references to the lack of spectators in the Flensburg court, see 'Jüdischer Zeuge: "Sie lügen"', *Schleswig-Holsteinische Volkszeitung*, January 3, 1963; and 'Ist Martin Fellenz schuldig?', *Flensburger Presse*, November 22, 1962.
49. Hannah Arendt, *Eichmann in Jerusalem*, 13.
50. 'Councillor Imprisoned for Part in Killing Jews', *The Guardian*, January 12, 1963.
51. 'Wurst und Schnapps am Todesgraben', *Schleswig-Holsteinische Volkszeitung*, December 12, 1962.
52. '100 Zeugen haben gesprochen', *Schleswig-Holsteinische Volkszeitung*, December 13, 1962. 'Burned at the Stake', *Jewish Chronicle*, December 21, 1962, also acknowledged the presence of school classes at the trial, but added 'local interest remains small'.
53. For details on Holocaust education during this period, see Randolph L. Braham, *The Treatment of the Holocaust in Textbooks: The Federal Republic of Germany, Israel and the United States of America* (Boulder, Colorado: Social Science Monographs, 1987).
54. Fellenz's retrial in Kiel saw him receiving a seven year prison sentence for crimes committed in Poland. Details of this case can be found in Rüter & de Mildt eds., *Justiz und NS-Verbrechen, Band XXIII*, Case No. 619.
55. Letter to the author from Dr. Hans-Jörg Herold, November 15, 2004.
56. Ibid.

57. 'Dönitz Addresses High School', *AJR Information*, Vol. 18 No. 3 (1963) 2.
58. Letter from Manfred Lichtenthal, Langen, 'Das Urteil von Flensburg', *Die Zeit*, February 8, 1963.
59. 'Mindeststrafmaß im SS-Polizeiführer-Prozeß', *Südschleswiger Heimatzeitung*, January 12, 1963.
60. Landesarchiv Schleswig, 'Letter from Herr C to the Flensburg Schwurgericht', January 14, 1963, Abt. 354 No. 11419.
61. Ibid., 'Letter to the Flensburg Schwurgericht by Herr B.', January 15, 1963.
62. Ibid., 'Letter to the Flensburg Schwurgericht by Herr W.', January 15, 1963. Willi Dusenschön was the head of the Fuhlsbüttel concentration camp near Hamburg during the war. In 1962, he was acquitted of the murder of camp prisoner and Lübeck SPD representative Fritz Solmitz.
63. Ibid., 'Letter to the Flensburg Schwurgericht by Herr C.', January 14, 1963.
64. Ibid.
65. Ibid., 'Letter to the Flensburg Schwurgericht by Herr P.' December 28, 1962.
66. Landesarchiv Schleswig, 'Letter to the Flensburg Schwurgericht by Herr Br.', January 5, 1963, Abt. 354 No. 11524.
67. Landesarchiv Schleswig, 'Letter to the Flensburg Schwurgericht by Herr S.', January 6, 1963, Abt. 354 No. 11419.

NOTES TO CHAPTER 6

1. For details on the Auschwitz trial, see Friedrich-Martin Balzer & Werner Renz, *Das Urteil im Frankfurter Auschwitz Prozess 1963–1965: erste selbständige Veröffentlichung* (Bonn: Pahl-Rugenstein, 2004); Fritz Bauer Institut ed., *Auschwitz: Geschichte, Rezeption und Wirkung: Jahrbuch zur Geschichte und Wirkung des Holocaust* (Frankfurt am Main: Campus, 1996); Fritz Bauer Institut ed., *'Gerichtstag haben über uns selbst . . . ' Geschichte und Wirkungsgeschichte des ersten Frankfurter Auschwitz-Prozesses: Jahrbuch zur Geschichte und Wirkung des Holocaust* (Frankfurt am Main: Campus, 2001); Rudolf Hirsch, *Um die Endlösung: Prozessberichte über den Lischka-Prozess in Köln und den Auschwitz-Prozess in Frankfurt/Main* (Rudolstadt: Greifenverlag, 1984); Hermann Langbein, *Der Auschwitz-Prozess: Eine Dokumentation* (Vienna: Europa Verlag, 1965); Bernd Naumann, *Auschwitz: A Report on the Proceedings against Robert Karl Ludwig Mulka and Others before the Court at Frankfurt*, translated by J. Steinberg (London: Pall Mall Press, 1966); Sybille Steinbacher, "Auschwitz before the Courts", *Auschwitz: A History*, translated by Shaun Whiteside (Munich: C.H. Beck, 2004) 137–152; Gerhard Werle & Thomas Wandres, *Auschwitz vor Gericht: Völkermord und bundesdeutsche Justiz: mit einer Dokumentation des Auschwitz-Urteiles* (Munich: Beck, 1995); Wittmann, *Beyond Justice*.
2. Eleonore Sterling, 'Letter from Frankfurt: Twenty Years From Auschwitz', *Jewish Chronicle*, December 27, 1963, 6.
3. Eleonore Sterling, 'Letter from Frankfurt: Auschwitz Trial Nears Its End after Eighteen Months', *Jewish Chronicle*, June 18, 1965, 22; and 'Letter from Frankfurt: In The Name of the People', *Jewish Chronicle*, August 27, 1965, 8. A courtroom guard informed Sterling that the few adults who had decided to watch the proceedings firsthand 'were always the same people'.
4. Emmi Bonhoeffer, *Auschwitz Trials: Letters from an Eyewitness*, translated by U. Stechow (Richmond, Virginia: John Knox Press, 1967) 15, 20.

5. Cesarani, *Eichmann*, 222–225. For further details on Bauer and the preparations for the Auschwitz trial, see Wittmann, 'The Wheels of Justice Turn Slowly', 361.
6. Irene Sagel-Grande, Christiaan F. Rüter, H.H. Fuchs & Adelheid L. Rüter-Ehlermann eds., *Justiz und NS-Verbrechen, Sammlung deutscher Strafurteile wegen nationalsozialistischer Tötungsverbrechen, 1945–1999, Band XXII* (Amsterdam: University Press Amsterdam, 1981) Case No. 596.
7. Irene Sagel-Grande, Christiaan F. Rüter & H.H. Fuchs eds., *Justiz und NS-Verbrechen, Sammlung deutscher Strafurteile wegen nationalsozialistischer Tötungsverbrechen, 1945–1999, Band XXI* (Amsterdam: University Press Amsterdam, 1979) Case No. 591.
8. Anthony Kauders, *German Politics and the Jews: Düsseldorf and Nuremberg 1910–1933* (Oxford: Clarendon Press, 1996) 193. See also Mary Nolan, *Social Democracy and Society: Working Class Radicalism in Düsseldorf 1890–1920* (Cambridge: Cambridge University Press, 1981); and Beatrix Herlemann, *Kommunalpolitik der KPD im Ruhrgebiet, 1924–1933* (Wüppertal: Peter Hammer, 1977).
9. 'Stripping Away Layers of Wistful Anti-Nazi Myth', *New York Times*, August 14, 1997.
10. Ibid.
11. Ibid. See also Karola Fings, 'Kriegsenden, Kriegslegenden: Bewältigungsstrategien in einer deutschen Großstadt', Bernd-A. Rusinek ed., *Kriegsende 1945. Verbrechen, Katastrophen, Befreiungen in nationaler und internationaler Perspektive* (Dachau: Wallstein, 2004) 219–238.
12. Kauders, *German Politics and the Jews*, 2–19.
13. See, for example, Zimmermann, *NS Täter vor Gericht*; Gitta Sereny, *The German Trauma: Experiences and Reflections, 1938–2001* (London: Penguin, 2001); Ulrike Weckel & Edgar Wolfrum eds., *'Bestien' und 'Befehlsempfänger'*.
14. Buruma, *The Wages of Guilt*, 149.
15. 'Bald Sachsenhausen-Prozeß', *Kölnische Rundschau*, September 25, 1964. The newspaper issued a further reminder the day before the trial started: 'Massenmordprozeß beginnt Morgen in Köln', October 14, 1964.
16. 'In Treblinka genau nach Reichsbahn-Fahrplan gemordet', *Kölnische Rundschau*, October 27, 1964.
17. 'Ein Berg von Kinderleichen', March 7, 1964 and '25000 Ermordete in 24 Stunden', *Frankfurter Allgemeine Zeitung*, October 9, 1964.
18. Wittmann, *Beyond Justice*, 176.
19. Ibid.
20. 'Der Zeuge stürzte weinend aus dem Gerichtssaal', *Frankfurter Rundschau*, December 22, 1964.
21. See, for example, 'Kinder in der Luft erschossen', April 13, 1965 and 'Ich sah es: er hat ihn erschossen', February 23, 1965 in *Frankfurter Allgemeiner Zeitung*. Jörg Friedrich has also highlighted this tendency, comparing the media treatment of Kurt Franz—'the classic Nazi criminal'—who would set Barry the dog onto the prisoners with the dramatic headlines that greeted Wilhelm Boger's 'swing' during the Auschwitz trial. See *Die Kalte Amnestie: NS-Täter in der Bundesrepublik* (Frankfurt am Main: Fischer Taschenbuch, 1984) 333–343.
22. 'Mordlust, Heimtücke, Grausamkeit', *Frankfurter Allgemeine Zeitung*, August 6, 1965. For a further discussion on Franz's photograph album and perpetrator mentality, see Ernst Klee, Willi Dressen & Volker Riess, *Those Were the Days: The Holocaust as Seen by the Perpetrators and Bystanders*,

translated by D. Burnstone (London: Hamish Hamilton, 1991). Much was also made of the fact Franz had been nicknamed 'Lalka' or 'The Doll' by Polish camp prisoners, a description that seemed incongruous with the horrific details of his crimes. Likewise, during the Cologne Sachsenhausen proceedings, newspapers emphasised chief defendant Otto Kaiser's predilection for using ice cold water to torture prisoners. See 'Schnallplattenmusik übertönte Schüsse von Sachsenhausen', *Kölnische Rundschau*, October 16, 1964; 'Späte Sühne für Ströme von Blut', *Frankfurter Allgemeine Zeitung*, May 6, 1965.
23. 'Willi Wöhne ließ sich an die Front versetzen', *Kölnische Rundschau*, October 21, 1964.
24. 'Schallplattenmusik übertönte Schüsse von Sachsenhausen', *Kölnische Rundschau*, October 16, 1964. The *Frankfurter Rundschau* offered similar musings during the Treblinka trial—'Nach dem Massenmord wurden sie brave Bürger', August 31, 1965.
25. 'Beweisstücke im Treblinka-Prozeß', *Stuttgarter Zeitung*, April 1, 1965; 'Sie nannten ihn "Puppe"', *Der Mittag*, Hauptstaatsarchiv Düsseldorf Press Cuttings Collection, Rep. 388 No. 884.
26. See, for example, 'Globke als Zeuge', *Hamburger Abendblatt*; 'Globke soll als Zeuge aussagen', *Braunschweiger Zeitung*; 'Globke im Zeugenstand', *Wetzlarer Neue Zeitung*; 'Globke wird als Zeuge gehört', *Kölner Stadtanzelger*; 'Globke als Zeuge im Treblinka-Prozeß', *Kölnische Rundschau*; 'Globke als Zeuge', *Darmstädter Echo*—all from January 15, 1965.
27. 'Lebheftes Pressecho auf das Auschwitz-Urteil', *Stuttgarter Zeitung*, August 21, 1965; and 'Gegen Mulka und andere', *Frankfurter Rundschau*, August 21, 1965.
28. 'Sie nannten ihn "Puppe"', *Der Mittag*, Hauptstaatsarchiv Düsseldorf Press Cuttings Collection, Rep. 388 No. 884.
29. 'Sie nannten ihm "Lalka"', *Rheinische Post*, November 14, 1964.
30. 'Moral Stocktaking', *AJR Information*, Vol. 20 No. 10 (1965) 1.
31. Sereny, *The German Trauma*, 79.
32. Ibid.
33. 'Die Sühne für die Verbrechen von Treblinka', *Stuttgarter Zeitung*, September 4, 1965.
34. 'Schallplattenmusik übertönte Schüsse von Sachsenhausen', *Kölnische Rundschau*, October 16, 1964.
35. 'BBC Examines German Views on Auschwitz', *Jewish Chronicle*, March 20, 1964, 14.
36. Reported in 'What Germans Know About Nazi Crimes', *Jewish Chronicle*, November 13, 1964, 9.
37. Sterling, 'Letter from Frankfurt: In The Name of the People', 8.
38. 'The Treblinka Trial', *World Jewry*, Vol. 8 No. 1 (1965) 9.
39. 'Kennen Sie Wilhelm Boger?', *Die Zeit*, April 23, 1965.
40. Ibid.
41. Ibid. Original emphasis.
42. Wittmann, *Beyond Justice*, 261–267.
43. 'Überlebende gingen in die Schule', *Westdeutsche Allgemeine Zeitung*, February 12, 1965.
44. A. Wolfman ed., *The Eichmann Trial* (Düsseldorf: German Trade Union Movement, 1963)—reviewed in 'Book Notes', *Common Ground*, Vol. 17 No. 1 (1963) 33.
45. Peter Weiss, *The Investigation: Oratorio in Eleven Cantos*, translated by A. Gross (London: Calder & Boyous, 1966). See too Robert Cohen, 'The Political Aesthetics of Holocaust Literature: Peter Weiss's "The Investigation" and Its Critics', *History and Memory*, Vol. 10 (1998) 43–67; Christoph Weiss,

Auschwitz in der geteilten Welt: Peter Weiss und 'Die Ermittlung' im kalten Krieg (St. Ingbert: Röhrig, 2000); 'Weiss: Gesang vor der Schaukel', *Der Spiegel*, Vol. 43 (1965); Michael Patterson, '"Bewältigung der Vergangenheit" or "Uberwaltigung der Befangenheit": Nazism and the War in Postwar German Theatre', *Modern Drama*, Vol. 33 No. 1 (1990) 120–128.
46. Classen, *Bilder der Vergangenheit*, 62. Between the 1960s and early 1970s, ZDF (Zweites Deutsches Fernsehen) screened 1600 prime-time minutes of historical programmes per year—see also Wulf Kansteiner, 'Nazis, Viewers and Statistics: Television History, Television Audience Research and Collective Memory in West Germany', *Journal of Contemporary History*, Vol. 39 No. 4 (2004) 577, 581.
47. Helmut Krausnick & Martin Broszat eds., *Anatomy of the SS State* (London: Collins, 1968). For details on its reception see Norbert Frei, 'Der Frankfurter Auschwitz-Prozeß und die deutsche Zeitgeschichtsforschung', Fritz Bauer Institut ed., *Auschwitz, Geschichte, Rezeption und Wirken* (Frankfurt: Campus Verlag, Jahrbuch 1996) 130–131.
48. Cornelia Brink, *'Auschwitz in der Paulskirche': Erinnerungspolitik in Fotoausstellungen der sechziger Jahre* (Marburg: Jonas-Verlag, 2000) 25. An exhibition entitled 'Life, Struggle and Death in the Warsaw Ghetto, 1940–1943' had already travelled through West Berlin, Munich and Krefeld at the start of the decade, organised by trade unionists, youth groups and victims' organisations. See 'Warsaw Ghetto Exhibition', *Jewish Chronicle*, November 15, 1963.
49. Konrad Schilling ed., *Monumenta Judaica: 2,000 Jahre Geschichte und Kultur der Juden am Rhein. Handbuch & Katalog* (Cologne: J. Melzer-Verlag, 1963).
50. 'Monumenta Judaica in Cologne', *AJR Information*, Vol. 19 No. 3 (1964) 5.
51. Ibid.
52. Ibid.
53. Ibid. Not everyone agreed with the sentiments being expressed in the West German media and in December 1963, posters advertising *Monumenta Judaica* were defaced with swastikas: 'Swastika Devils in Cologne', *Jewish Chronicle*, December 6, 1963.
54. See, for example, the account on Bishop August von Galen who publicly denounced the Nazi 'euthanasia' programme from his pulpit in 1941 in Beth Griech-Polelle, 'Image of a Churchmann-resistor: Bishop von Galen, The Euthanasia Project and the Sermons of Summer 1941', *Journal of Contemporary History*, Vol. 36 No. 1 (2001) 41–57.
55. John S. Conway, 'Coming to Terms with the Past: Interpreting the German Church Struggles 1933–1990', *German History*, Vol. 16 No. 3 (1998) 378–381. See too Michael Phayer, 'The German Catholic Church after the Holocaust', *Holocaust and Genocide* Studies, Vol. 10 No. 2 (1996) 151–167; Richard Gutteridge, *Open Thy Mouth for the Dumb: The German Evangelical Church and the Jews, 1879–1950* (Oxford: Blackwell, 1976); Matthew D. Hockenos, *A Church Divided: German Protestants Confront the Nazi Past* (Bloomington: Indiana University Press, 2004).
56. On the CCJ, see Marcus Braybrooke, *Children of One God: A History of the Council of Christians and Jews* (London: Vallentine Mitchell, 1991); William W. Simpson & Ruth Weyl, *The International Council of Christians and Jews: A Brief History* (Heppenheim: International Council of Christians and Jews, 1988); Geoffrey Wigoder, *Jewish-Christian Relations since the Second World War* (Manchester: Manchester University Press, 1988).
57. 'Causerie', *Common Ground*, Vol. 16 No. 1 (1962) 25.
58. 'The Thorn in the Flesh', *Wiener Library Bulletin*, Vol. 10 No. 5–6 (1956) 38.

59. 'Silent Witness', *Jewish Chronicle*, November 13, 1959, 48.
60. 'Commemorating "Crystal Night"', *Jewish Chronicle*, November 17, 1961, 17.
61. Ibid.
62. Statement by the Kirchentag: Conference of German Evangelical Churches held in Berlin July 19–23, 1961. Cited in *Common Ground*, Vol. 16 No. 1 (1962) 19–20.
63. Ibid.
64. 'Church Leader on Guilt', *AJR Information*, Vol. 17 No. 12 (1962) 2.
65. See Bestand Schlingensiepen, Archiv der Evangelischen Kirche im Rheinland, Düsseldorf.
66. For contemporary accounts of the Statute of Limitations, see Jürgen Baumann, *Der Aufstand des schlechten Gewissens: ein Diskussionsbeitrag zur Verjährung der NS-Gewaltverbrechen* (Bielefeld: Ernst & Werner Giseking, 1965); Rolf Vogel, *Ein Weg aus der Vergangenheit: Eine Dokumentation zur Verjährungsfrage und zu den NS-Prozessen* (Frankfurt am Main: Ullstein, 1969); Karl Jaspers, *Die Schuldfrage: Für Völkermord gibt es keine Verjährung* (Munich: Piper, 1979).
67. 'Das Wort des Rates der EKD zu den NS-Verbrecher-Prozessen', *Kirchliches Jahrbuch*, (Gütersloh: C. Bertelsmann Verlag,1963) 75–79.
68. Ibid.
69. Ibid.
70. Ibid.,199.
71. 'Fragen um die Verjährung', *Rheinischer Merkur*, November 27, 1964.
72. 'NS-Verbrechen straflos?', *Rheinischer Merkur*, December 4, 1964.
73. 'Die Verjährungsfrist muß fallen', *Rheinischer Merkur*, October 23, 1964.
74. Report from A.W. Rhodes, British Embassy Bonn, to D.N. Beevor, March, 4, 1964, NA, FO1042/254: Nazi Trials in FRG.
75. Ibid.
76. 'Germans Against Trials of Nazis', *Jewish Chronicle*, January 17, 1964, 1.
77. See, for example, 'Bekanntheitsgrad des Auschwitz-Prozesses und Einstellung der Bundesbürger zu seiner Durchführung zwanzig Jahre danach', *DIVO-Pressedienst*, July I-II (1964); 'Verjährung von NS-Verbrechen, Institut für Demoskopie, May 5, 1965; 'Verjährung für NS-Verbrechen', *EMNID-Informationen*, No. 11 (1978) and No. 2 (1979); 'Sollen NS-Verbrechen verjähren?', *Umfrage*, November 1978; 'Verjährung von NS-Verbrechen: Nach Holocaust ist jeder zweite dagegen', *Umfrage*, February 1979.

NOTES TO THE CONCLUSION

1. Resolution adopted by the General Assembly of the United Nations on Holocaust Remembrance (A/RES/60/7), November 1, 2005.
2. See, for example, David Cesarani & Mark Levene eds., *'Bystanders' to the Holocaust: A Re-evaluation* (London: Frank Cass, 2002); Martin Gilbert, *Auschwitz and the Allies* (London: Arrow, 1984); Tom Boyer, *Blind Eye to Murder: Britain, America and the Purging of Nazi Germany: A Pledge Betrayed* (London: Andre Deutsch, 1981).
3. David Gaunt ed., *Collaboration and Resistance during the Holocaust: Belarus, Estonia, Latvia, Lithuania* (New York: Peter Lang, 2004); Tadeusz Piotrowski, *Poland's Holocaust: Ethnic Strife, Collaboration with Occupying Forces and Genocide in the Second Republic, 1918–1947* (Jefferson, North Carolina: McFarland, 1998); Radu Ioanid, *The Holocaust*

Notes 165

in Romania: The destruction of Jews and Gypsies under the Antonescu Regime, 1940–1944 (Chicago: Ivan R. Dee, 2008).
4. See, for example, Dick de Mildt, *In the Name of the People: Perpetrators of Genocide in the Reflection of Their Post-war Prosecution in West Germany: The 'Euthanasia' and 'Aktion Reinhard' Trial Cases* (The Hague: Martinus Nijhoff Publishers, 1996) 30.
5. Bloxham, *Genocide on Trial*, 223.
6. Wittmann, *Beyond Justice*, 247.
7. The case also inspired Aaron Freiwald, *The Last Nazi: Josef Schwammberger and the Nazi Past* (New York: W.W. Norton, 1994).
8. Details on all of these cases can be found in Christiaan F. Rüter & Dick W. de Mildt eds., *Justiz und NS-Verbrechen, Band XLVI* (in preparation). See Cases 919, 922 and 923, http://www1.jur.uva.nl/junsv/JuNSVEng/Casenrsfr.htm
9. 'Das Gespenst von Bad Feilnbach', *Der Spiegel*, June 17, 2011.

Bibliography

ARCHIVAL SOURCES

Hauptstaatsarchiv Düsseldorf: Gerichte Rep. 299 No. 767, 783, 794, 797
Gerichte Rep. 388 No. 878, 884
Heritage Service, Uxbridge Central Library, London Borough of Hillingdon Films: F9 No. 013 654 063: Hayes and Harlington Urban District Council, 'Town Twinning Celebrations with Schleswig and Mantes-La-Jolie' (1960)
Landesarchiv Schleswig: Abt. 354 Nos.11419, 11523–11528
Landgericht Bayreuth: Ks3/1957
National Archives, London, Foreign Office Papers:
FO 371   137596–137597, 146061–146062, 154294–154295, 161120, 169317, 57563
FO 946   43
FO 953   2022–2023
FO 1042   106, 128, 253–255
FO 1056   93, 166
University of Southampton Archive, Papers of the Institute of Jewish Affairs:
MS 237 Seq. 2: *Legal Issues, 1939–1991*
MS 237 Seq. 6: *Holocaust and War Crimes, 1946–1988*
MS 237/T2/33: *Germany (correspondence)*
MS 237/T3: *War Crimes/Criminals*
MS 241 Seq. 2: *Germany*
MS 241 Seq. 3: *Antisemitism, War Crimes, National Socialism, Neo-Nazism*
Wiener Library, London Press Cuttings Collection:
G4b (9): *Political Reports: Schleswig-Holstein*
G5b (1): *War Crimes Trials by Defendant*
G5b (5): *Zentralstelle, Ludwigsburg*

OPINION POLL DATA

Institut für Demoskopie Allensbach am Bodensee, *Die Stimmung im Bundesgebiet*:
Chancen für führende Männer des Dritten Reiches (November 19, 1953)
Die KZ-Prozesse (October 27, 1958)
Der Fall Eichmann (August 12, 1960)
Verjährung von NS-Vebrechen (May 5, 1965)
Verjährung der Nazi-Verbrechen? (February 13, 1969)
Anna J. & Richard L. Merritt eds., *Public Opinion in Occupied Germany: The OMGUS Surveys, 1945–1949* (Urbana: University of Illinois Press, 1970).

168 Bibliography

E. Noelle & E.P. Neumann eds., *Jahrbuch der öffentlichen Meinung, 1947–1955, 1958–1964, 1965–1967* (Allensbach & Bonn: Institut fur Demoskopie Allensbach).
———, *The Germans: Public Opinion Polls, 1947–1966* (Allensbach & Bonn: Verlag für Demoskopie, 1967).
———, *The Germans: Public Opinion Polls, 1967–1980, Instit für Demoskopie, Allensbach* (Westport, Connecticut: Greenwood Press, 1981).

NEWSPAPERS AND PERIODICALS

AJR Information (Association of Jewish Refugees in Great Britain)
Bayreuther Tagblatt
Common Ground
Flensburger Tageblatt,
Jewish Chronicle
Kieler Nachrichten
Milwaukee Journal
New York Times
Rheinische Merkur
Schleswig-Holstein Volks-Zeitung
Der Spiegel
Südschleswig Heimat Zeitung
Toronto Daily Star
Die Welt
Wiener Library Bulletin
World Jewry
Yad Vashem Bulletin
Die Zeit

PUBLISHED PRIMARY SOURCES

Astor, David, *The Meaning of Eichmann* (Royston, Hertfordshire: Parkes Library, 1961).
Ausschuss für Deutsche Einheit, *Neue Beweise für Globkes Verbrechen gegen die Juden* (East Berlin: Ausschuss für Deutsche Einheit, 1960).
———, *Globke und die Ausrottung der Juden: über der verbrecherische Vergangenheit des Staatssekretärs im Amt des Bundeskanzlers Adenauer* (East Berlin: Ausschuss für Deutsche Einheit, 1960).
———, *Globke: Der Burokrat des Todes. Eine Dokumentation über die Blutschuld des höchsten Bonner Staatsbeamten bei der Ausrottung der Juden* (East Berlin: Ausschuss für Deutsche Einheit, 1963).
———, *The Truth About Theodor Oberländer: Brown Book on the Criminal Fascist Past of Adenauer's Minister* (East Berlin: Ausschuss für Deutsche Einheit, 1960).
Bonhoeffer, Emmi, *Auschwitz Trials: Letters from an Eyewitness*, translated by Ursula Stechow (Richmond, Virginia: John Knox Press, 1967).
Boulier, Jean ed., *Der Prozess gegen Dr. Hans Globke* (Dresden: Verlag Zeit im Bild, 1963).
Buchenwald Camp: The Report of a Parliamentary Delegation Presented by the Prime Minister, First Lord of the Treasury and Minister of Defence to Parliament by Command of His Majesty (London: H.M. Stationary Office, April 1945).

Carmichael, Joel, 'The Eichmann Case: Reactions in West Germany', *Midstream*, Vol. 7 No. 3 (1961) 13–27.
Crespi, Irving, 'Public Reaction to the Eichmann Trial', *Public Opinion Quarterly*, Vol. 28 No. 1 (1964) 91–103.
van Dam, Hendrik George & Ralph Giordano eds., *KZ-Verbrechen vor Deutschen Gerichten: Dokumente aus den Prozessen gegen Sommer (KZ-Buchenwald), Sorge, Schubert (KZ-Sachsenhausen), Unkelbach (Ghetto in Czenstochau)* (Frankfurt am Main: Europäische Verlagsanstalt, 1962).
Federal Ministry of Justice, *The Prosecution Since 1945 of National Socialist Crimes by Public Prosecutors and Courts in the Territory of the Federal Republic of Germany* (Düsseldorf: Oskar Leiner-Druck KG, 1962).
Glock, Charles Y., Gertrude J. Selznick & Joe L. Spaeth, *The Apathetic Majority: A Study Based on Public Responses to the Eichmann Trial* (London: Harper & Row, 1966).
Gollancz, Victor, *What Buchenwald Really Means* (London: Victor Gollancz, 1945).
Hochhuth, Rolf, *The Representative*, translated by R.D. MacDonald (London: Methuen & Co., 1963).
Institute of Jewish Affairs, *Statute of Limitations and the Prosecution of the Nazi Crimes in the Federal German Republic*, Background Paper No. 14 (London: Institute of Jewish Affairs, 1969).
Keil, Heinz ed., *Dokumentation über die Verfolgungen der Jüdischen Bürger von Ulm/Donau* (Hergestellt im Auftrage der Stadt Ulm, 1960).
Kirchliches Jahrbuch, 'Das Wort des Rates der EKD zu den NS-Verbrecher-Prozessen' (1963) 75–89.
Kogon, Eugen, *Der SS-Staat: Das System der deutschen Konzentrationslager* (Frankfurt am Main: Europäische Verlagsanstalt, 1946).
Koppel, Wolfgang, *Ungesühnte Nazijustiz: Hundert Urteile Klagen ihre Richter an* (Karlsruhe: Organisationskomitees der Dokumentenausstellung 'Ungesühnte Nazijustiz', August 1960).
Lamm, Hans, *Der Eichmann Prozeß in der deutschen öffentlichen Meinung* (Frankfurt am Main: Ner-Tamid-Verlag, 1961).
Langbein, Hermann, *Der Auschwitz-Prozess: Eine Dokumentation* (Vienna: Europa Verlag, 1965).
Mendelsohn, John ed., *The Holocaust. Selected Documents*, Vol. 10: *The Einsatzgruppen or Murder Commandos*; Vol. 17: *Punishing the Perpetrators of the Holocaust: The Brandt, Pohl and Ohlendorf Cases;* Vol. 18: *Punishing the Perpetrators of the Holocaust: The Ohlendorf and von Weizsaecker Cases* (New York & London: Garland, 1982).
Miethe, Annadorra ed., *Buchenwald* (Buchenwald Concentration Camp Museums and National Memorial Guidebook).
National Council of the National Front of Democratic Germany, *The Brown Book: War and Nazi Criminals in West Germany—State, Economy, Administration, Army, Justice, Science* (Dresden: Zeit im Bild, 1965).
Naumann, Bernd, *Auschwitz: A Report on the Proceedings against Robert Karl Ludwig Mulka and Others before the Court at Frankfurt*, translated by J. Steinberg (London: Pall Mall Press, 1966).
Nellessen, Bernd, *Der Prozess von Jerusalem: ein Dokument* (Düsseldorf: Econ, 1964).
Noakes, Jeremy & Geoffrey Pridham eds., *Nazism: A Documentary Reader, 1919–1945*, Vol. 1: *The Rise to Power, 1919–1934* (Exeter: University of Exeter Press, 1983); Vol. 3: *Foreign Policy, War and Racial Extermination* (Exeter: University of Exeter Press, 1988).
Protokoll der Verhandlungen der Landessynode, 'Wort des Rates der Evangelischen Kirche in Deutschland' (1963) 21–22.

——, 'Verjährung von NS-Verbrechen' (1965) 114, 177, 199, 226–227.
Ruhm von Oppen, Beate, *Documents on Germany under Occupation, 1945–1954* (Oxford: Oxford University Press, 1955).
Rüter, Christiaan & Dick W. de Mildt eds., *Justiz und NS-Verbrechen: Sammlung deutscher Strafurteile wegen nationalsozialistischer Tötungsverbrechen 1945–1966. Register zu den Bänden I-XXII* (Amsterdam: APA—Holland University Press, 1998).
Sagel-Grande, Irene, Christiaan F. Rüter, & H.H. Fuchs eds., *Justiz und NS-Verbrechen: Sammlung deutscher Strafurteile wegen nationalsozialistischer Tötungsverbrechen 1945–1966* (Amsterdam: University of Amsterdam Press, 1976–1988).
Schilling, Konrad, *Monumenta Judaica: 2000 Jahre Geschichte und Kultur der Juden am Rhein. Handbuch und Katalog* (Cologne: J. Melzer-Verlag, 1963).
Strecker, Reinhard M., *Dr. Hans Globke: Aktenauszüge: Dokumente* (Hamburg: Rütten & Loening, 1961).
The Trial of Adolf Eichmann: Record of Proceedings in the District Court of Jerusalem (Jerusalem: Trust for the Publication of the Proceedings of the Eichmann Trial, 1992–1995).
Trials of War Criminals before the Nuernberg Military Tribunals under Control Council Law No. 10, Vol. IV: Nuernberg October 1946–April 1949: Military Tribunal II, Case No. 9: The United States of America v. Otto Ohlendorf et al.
Vereinigung Demokratischer Juristen, *Dr. Hans Maria Globke: Tatsachen und Dokumente* (Berlin: Vereinigung Demokratischer Juristen, 1963).
Weiss, Peter, *The Investigation: Oratorio in Eleven Cantos*, translated by A. Gross (London: Calder & Boyous, 1966).
Zaborowski, Jan, *Dr. Hans Globke: The Good Clerk* (Poznan: Zachodnia Agencja Prasowci, 1962).

UNPUBLISHED SECONDARY SOURCES

Helmut Paulus, 'Der Bayreuther "KZ-Prozess Martin Sommer": Der Henker von Buchenwald hatte sich vor dem Bayreuther Schwurgericht zu verantworten' (Unpublished paper, 2002).

PUBLISHED SECONDARY SOURCES

Abzug, Robert H., *Inside the Vicious Heart: Americans and the Liberation of Nazi Concentration Camps* (Oxford: Oxford University Press, 1985).
Adorno, Theodor W., 'What does Coming to Terms with the Past Mean?', Geoffrey H. Hartman ed., translated by Timothy Bahti & Geoffrey H. Hartman, *Bitburg in Moral and Political Perspective* (Bloomington: Indiana University Press, 1986) 114–129.
——, 'Opinion Research and Publicness', translated by Andrew J. Perrin & Lars Jarkko, *Sociological Theory*, Vol. 23 No. 1 (2005) 116–123.
Alderman, S.S., 'Negotiating the Nuremberg Trial Agreements, 1945', Raymond Dennett & Joseph E. Johnson eds., *Negotiating with the Russians* (Boston: World Peace Foundation, 1951) 49–100.
Applegate, Ceilia, *A Nation of Provincials: The German Idea of Heimat* (Berkeley: University of California Press, 1990).
——, 'The Mediated Nation: Regions, Readers and the German Past', J. Retallack ed., *Saxony in German History: Culture, Society and Politics, 1830–1933* (Ann Arbor: University of Michigan Press, 2000) 33–50.

Bibliography 171

———, 'Saving Music: Enduring Experiences of Culture', *History and Memory*, Vol. 17 No. 1–2 (2005) 217–237.
Arendt, Hannah, *Eichmann in Jerusalem: A Report on the Banality of Evil* (New York: Viking Press, 1963).
Aronson, Shlomo, 'Preparations for the Nuremberg Trial: The OSS, Charles Dwork and the Holocaust', *Holocaust and Genocide Studies*, Vol. 12 (1998) 257–281.
Ashplant, Timothy G., *The Politics of War Memory and Commemoration* (London: Routledge, 2000).
Balzer, Friedrich-Martin & Werner Renz, *Das Urteil im Frankfurter Auschwitz Prozess, 1963–1965: erste selbständige Veröffentlichung* (Bonn: Pahl-Rugenstein, 2004).
Bar-On, Dan, *Legacy of Silence: Encounters with Children of the Third Reich* (Cambridge, Massachusetts: Harvard University Press, 1989).
Bark, Dennis L. & David R. Gress, *Democracy and its Discontents, 1963–1988* (Oxford: Basil Blackwell, 1989).
Barnouw, Dagmar, *The War in the Empty Air: Victims, Perpetrators and Post-war Germans* (Bloomington: Indiana University Press, 2003).
Bartov, Omer, 'Defining Enemies, Making Victims: Germans, Jews and the Holocaust', *American Historical Review*, Vol. 103 No. 3 (1998) 771–816.
Baumann, Jürgen, *Der Aufstand des schlechten Gewissens: ein Diskussionsbeitrag zur Verjährung der NS-Gewaltverbrechen* (Bielefeld: Gieseking, 1965).
Bentley, Eric, *The Storm over 'The Deputy'* (New York: Grove, 1964).
Benz, Werner, 'Nachkriegsgesellschaft und Nationalsozialismus: Erinnerung, Amnesie, Abwehr', *Dachauer Hefte 6: Erinnern oder Verweigern*, (Dachau: Verlag Dachauer Hafte, 1990) 12–24.
———, 'The Persecution and Extermination of the Jews in the German Consciousness', John Milfull ed., *Why Germany? National Socialist Anti-Semitism and the European Context* (Providence, Rhode Island: Berg, 1993) 91–104.
Berg, Jan, *Hochhuth's 'Stellvertreter' und die 'Stellvertreter'-Debatte: Vergangenheitsbewältigung in Theater und Presse der sechziger Jahre* (Kronberg im Taunus: Scriptor, 1977).
Bergmann, Werner, 'Die Reaktion auf den Holocaust in Westdeutschland von 1945 bis 1989', *Geschichte in Wissenschaft und Unterricht*, Vol. 43 (1992) 327–350.
Biddis, Michael, 'Victors' Justice? The Nuremberg Tribunal', *History Today*, Vol. 45 No. 5 (1995) 40–46.
Bier, Jean-Paul, 'The Holocaust, West Germany and Strategies of Oblivion, 1947–1979', Anson Rabinbach & Jack Zipes eds., *Germans and Jews since the Holocaust: The Ongoing Situation in West Germany* (New York: Holmes & Meier, 1986) 185–207.
Bloxham, Donald, *Genocide on Trial: War Crimes Trials and the Formation of Holocaust History and Memory* (Oxford: Oxford University Press, 2001).
———, 'Punishing German Soldiers during the Cold War: The Case of Erich von Manstein', *Patterns of Prejudice*, Vol. 33 No. 4 (1999) 25–45.
———, 'British War Crimes Trial Policy in Germany, 1945–1957: Implementation and Collapse', *Journal of British Studies*, Vol. 42 (2003) 91–118.
———, '"The Trial That Never Was": Why There Was No Second International Trial of Major War Criminals at Nuremberg', *History*, Vol. 87 (2002) 41–60.
Bodemann, Y. Michal, 'Eclipse of Memory: German Representations of Auschwitz in the Early Postwar Period', *New German Critique*, Vol. 75 (Autumn 1998) 57–89.
———, 'Reconstructions of History: From Jewish Memory to Nationalised Commemoration of Kristallnacht in Germany', *Jews, Germans, Memory: Reconstructions of Jewish Life in Germany* (Ann Arbor: University of Michigan Press, 1996) 179–226.

172 Bibliography

Boehling, Rebecca, *A Question of Priorities : Democratic Reforms and Economic Recovery in Postwar Germany: Frankfurt, Munich, and Stuttgart under U.S. Occupation 1945–1949* (Providence, Rhode Island: Berghahn Books, 1996).

Braham, Randolph L., *The Treatment of the Holocaust in Textbooks: The Federal Republic of Germany, Israel and the United States of America* (Boulder, Colorado: Social Science Monographs, 1987).

Braybrooke, Marcus, *Children of One God: A History of the Council of Christians and Jews* (London: Vallentine Mitchell, 1991).

Bridgman, Jon, *The End of the Holocaust: The Liberation of the Camps* (London: B.T. Batsford, 1990).

Brink, Cornelia, *'Auschwitz in der Paulskirche': Erinnerungspolitik in Fotoausstellungen der sechziger Jahre* (Marburg: Jonas-Verlag, 2000).

Brochhagen, Ulrich, *Nach Nürnberg: Vergangenheitsbewältigung und Westintegration in der Ära Adenauer* (Berlin: Ullstein, 1999).

Broszat, Martin, 'Siegerjustiz oder Strafrechtliche 'Selbstreinigung': Aspekte der Vergangenheitsbewältigung der deutschen Justiz während der Besatzungszeit, 1945–1949', *Vierteljahreshefte für Zeitgeschichte*, Vol. 4 (1981) 477–544.

Browder, George C., 'Perpetrator Character and Motivation: An Emerging Consensus?' (Review Essay), *Holocaust and Genocide Studies*, Vol. 17 No. 3 (2003) 480–497.

Browning, Christopher R., *Ordinary Men: Reserve Police Battalion 101 and the Final Solution in Poland* (New York: Harper Collins, 1992).

Bunn, Ronald F., 'The Spiegel Affair and the West German Press: The Initial Phase', *Public Opinion Quarterly*, Vol. 30 No. 1 (1966) 54–68.

Burchard, Christoph, 'The Nuremberg Trial and Its Impact on Germany', *Journal of International Criminal Justice*, Vol. 4 (2006) 800–829.

Burns, Rob & Wilfried Van der Will eds., *Protest and Democracy in West Germany: Extra-Parliamentary Opposition and the Democratic Agenda* (Basingstoke: Macmillan, 1988).

Buruma, Ian, *Wages of Guilt: Memories of War in Germany and Japan* (London: Vintage, 1995).

Buscher, Frank M., 'Kurt Schumacher, German Social Democracy and the Punishment of Nazi Crimes', *Holocaust and Genocide Studies*, Vol. 5 No. 3 (1990) 261–273.

Carrier, Peter, *Holocaust Monuments and National Memory Cultures in France and Germany since 1989: The Origins and Political Function of the Vél d'Hiv in Paris and the Holocaust Monument in Berlin* (New York & Oxford: Berghahn Books, 2004).

Caven, Hannah, 'Horror in Our Time: Images of the Concentration Camps in the British Media, 1945', *Historical Journal of Film, Radio and Television*, Vol. 21 No. 3 (2001) 205–253.

Cesarani, David, *Eichmann: His Life and Crimes* (London: William Heinemann, 2004).

Clark, C.M., 'West Germany Confronts the Nazi Past: Some Recent Debates on the Early Postwar Era, 1945–1960', *The European Legacy*, Vol. 4 No. 1 (1999) 113–130.

Classen, Christoph, *Bilder der Vergangenheit: Die Zeit des Nationalsozialismus im Fernsehen der Bundesrepublik Deutschland, 1955–1965* (Cologne: Böhlau Verlag, 1999).

Cohen, Akiba, Tamar Zemach-Marom, Jürgen Wilke & Birgit Schenk eds., *The Holocaust and the Press: Nazi War Crimes Trials in Germany and Israel* (Cresskill, New Jersey: Hampton Press Inc., 2002).

Cohen, Robert, 'The Political Aesthetics of Holocaust Literature: Peter Weiss's *The Investigation* and Its Critics', *History and Memory*, Vol. 10 No. 2 (1998) 43–67.

Confino, Alon, 'Collective Memory and Cultural History: Problems of Method', *American Historical Review*, Vol. 102 No. 5 (1997) 1386–1403.

———, 'Edgar Reitz's Heimat and German Nationhood: Film, Memory and Understandings of the Past', *German History*, Vol. 16 No. 2 (1998) 185–208.

———, *The Nation as a Local Metaphor: Württemberg, Imperial Germany and National Memory, 1871–1918* (Chapel Hill: University of North Carolina Press, 1997).

———, 'Travelling as a Culture of Remembrance: Traces of National Socialism in West Germany, 1945–1960', *History and Memory*, Vol. 12 No. 2 (2000) 92–121.

———, *Germany as a Culture of Remembrance: Promises and Limits of Writing History* (Chapel Hill: University of North Carolina Press, 2006).

——— & Ajay Skaria, 'The Local Life of Nationhood', *National Identities*, Vol. 4 No. 1 (2002) 7–24.

Connerton, Paul, *How Societies Remember* (Cambridge: Cambridge University Press, 1987).

Conway, John S., 'Coming to Terms with the Past: Interpreting the German Church Struggles, 1933–1990', *German History*, Vol. 16 No. 3 (1998) 377–396.

Crew, David, 'Remembering German Pasts: Memory in German History, 1871–1989', *Central European History*, Vol. 33 No. 2 (2000) 217–234.

———, *Town in the Ruhr: A Social History of Bochum, 1860–1914* (New York: Columbia University Press, 1979).

Dawidowicz, Lucy, *The Holocaust and the Historians* (Cambridge, Massachusetts: Harvard University Press, 1981).

Dieckmann, Christoph, 'The War and the Killing of the Lithuanian Jews,' Ulrich Herbert ed., *National Socialist Extermination Policies: Contemporary German Perspectives and Controversies* (New York and Oxford: Berghahn Books, 2000) 240–275.

Diehl, James M., *The Thanks of the Fatherland: German Veterans after the Second World War* (Chapel Hill: University of North Carolina Press, 1993).

von Dirke, Sabine, *'All Power to the Imagination': The West German Counterculture from the Student Movement to the Greens* (Lincoln: University of Nebraska Press, 1997).

Domansky, Elisabeth, 'A Lost War: World War II in Postwar German Memory', Alvin H. Rosenfeld ed., *Thinking about the Holocaust after Half a Century* (Bloomington & Indianapolis: Indiana University Press, 1997) 233–276.

Douglas, Lawrence, *The Memory of Judgement: Making Law and History in the Trials of the Holocaust* (New Haven, Connecticut: Yale University Press, 2001).

———, 'Film as Witness: Screening Nazi Concentration Camps before the Nuremberg Tribunal', *The Yale Law Journal*, Vol. 105 No. 2 (1995) 449–481.

Dubiel, Helmut, *Niemand ist frei von der Geschichte: Die nationalsozialistische Herrschaft in den Debatten des Deutschen Bundestages* (Munich: Carl Hanser Verlag, 1999).

Eley, Geoff, 'Protest Movements in 1960s West Germany: A Social History of Dissent and Democracy', *Journal of Social History*, Vol. 38 No. 3 (2005) 776–780.

Enssle, Manfred J., 'Five Theses on German Everyday Life after World War II', *Central European History*, Vol. 26 No. 1 (1993) 1–20.

Feuchtwanger, Edgar J., *From Weimar to Hitler: Germany 1918–33* (London: MacMillan, 1993).

Fink, Carole, Philipp Gassert & Detlef Junker eds., *1968: The World Transformed* (Cambridge: Cambridge University Press, 1998).

Fitzgibbon, Constantine, *Denazification* (London: Joseph, 1969).

Fleiter, Rüdiger, 'Die Ludwigsburg Zentrale Stelle und ihr politisches und gesellschaftliches Umfeld', *Geschichte in Wissenschaft und Unterricht*, Vol. 53 No. 1 (2002) 32–50.
Fox, John, 'The Jewish Factor in British War Crimes Policy in 1942', *English Historical Review*, Vol. 92 No. 362 (1977) 82–106.
Fraser, Ronald, *1968: A Student Generation in Revolt* (London: Chatto & Windus, 1988).
Frei, Norbert, *Adenauer's Germany and the Nazi Past: The Politics of Amnesty and Integration*, translated by Joel Golb (New York: Columbia University Press, 2002).
———, Dirk van Laak & Michael Stolleis eds., *Geschichte vor Gericht: Historiker, Richter und die Suche nach Gerechtigkeit* (Munich: Beck, 2000).
Friedlander, Henry, 'The Deportation of the German Jews: Post-war German Trials of Nazi Criminals', Michael R. Marrus ed., *The Nazi Holocaust: Historical Articles on the Destruction of the European Jews*, Vol. 9: *The End of the Holocaust* (Westport, Connecticut & London: Meckler, 1989) 635–664.
———, 'The Judiciary and Nazi Crimes in Postwar Germany', *Simon Wiesenthal Center Annual*, Vol. 1 (1984) 27–44.
———, 'The Trials of the Nazi Criminals: Law, Justice and History', *Dimensions: A Journal of Holocaust Studies*, Vol. 2 No. 1 (1986) 4–10.
Friedlander, Saul, *Memory, History and the Extermination of the Jews of Europe* (Bloomington: Indiana University Press, 1993).
———, *Probing the Limits of Representation: Nazism and the Final Solution* (Cambridge, Massachusetts: Harvard University Press, 1992).
———, 'Some German Struggles with Memory', G.H. Hartman ed., *Bitburg in Moral and Political Perspective* (Bloomington: Indiana University Press, 1986)
Friedrich, Jörg, *Die kalte Amnestie. NS-Täter in der Bundesrepublik* (Frankfurt am Main: Fischer Taschenbuch, 1984).
Fritz Bauer Institut ed., 'Auschwitz: Geschichte, Rezeption und Wirkung', *Jahrbuch zur Geschichte und Wirkung des Holocaust* (Frankfurt am Main: Campus, 1996).
———, '"Gerichtstag haben über uns selbst . . ." Geschichte und Wirkungsgeschichte des ersten Frankfurter Auschwitz-Prozesses', *Jahrbuch zur Geschichte und Wirkung des Holocaust* (Frankfurt am Main: Campus, 2001).
Gedi, Noa & Yigal Elam, 'Collective Memory—What Is It?', *History and Memory*, Vol. 8 No. 1 (1996) 30–50.
Gellately, Robert, *Backing Hitler: Consent and Coercion in Nazi Germany* (Oxford: Oxford University Press, 2001).
———, *The Nuremberg Interviews* (New York: Alfred A. Knopf, 2004).
Geyer, Michael & Miriam Hansen, 'German-Jewish Memory and National Consciousness', G.H. Hartman ed., *Holocaust Remembrance: The Shapes of Memory* (Oxford: Basil Blackwell, 1994) 175–190.
Gimbel, John, 'Denazification and German Local Politics, 1945–1949: A Case Study in Marburg', *American Political Science Review*, Vol. 54 No. 1 (1960) 83–105.
Ginsburgs, George, *The Nuremberg Trial and International Law* (Dordrecht: Martinus Nijhoff Publishers, 1990).
Godau-Schüttke, Klaus-Detlev, *Die Heyde/Sawade-Affäre: Wie Juristen und Mediziner den NS-Euthanasieprofessor Heyde nach 1945 deckten und straflos blieben* (Baden-Baden: Nomos Verlagsgesellschaft, 1998).
Gorzkowska, Jadwiga & Elzbieta Zakowska, *Nazi Criminals before West German Courts* (Warsaw: Western Press Agency, 1965).
Goschler, Constantin, 'The Attitude towards Jews in Bavaria after the Second World War', *Leo Baeck Yearbook*, Vol. 36 (1991) 443–458.

———, *Wiedergutmachung: Westdeutschland und die Verfolgten des Nationalsozialismus, 1945–1954* (Munich: Oldenbourg, 1992).
Goshen, Seev, 'Albert Battels Widerstand gegen die Judenvernichtung in Przemysl', *Vierteljahreshefte für Zeitgeschichte*, Vol. 33 (1985) 478–488.
Gotto, Klaus ed., *Der Staatssekretär Adenauers: Persönlichkeit und politisches Wirken Hans Globkes* (Stuttgart: Klett-Cotta, 1980).
Gouri, Haim, *Facing the Glass Booth: The Jerusalem Trial of Adolf Eichmann* (Detroit, Michigan: Wayne State University Press, 2004).
Grabitz, Helge, 'Problems of Nazi Trials in the Federal Republic of Germany', *Holocaust and Genocide Studies*, Vol. 3 No. 2 (1988) 209–222.
———, Klaus Bästlein & Johannes Tuchel eds., *Die Normalität des Verbrechens. Bilanz und Perspektiven der Forschung zu den nationalsozialismus Gewaltverbrechen* (Berlin: Edition Hentrich, 1994).
Grady, Tim, '"They Died for Germany": Jewish Soldiers, the German Army and Conservative Debates about the Nazi Past in the 1960s', *European History Quarterly*, Vol. 39 No. 1 (2009) 27–46.
Graml, Hermann, 'Die verdrängte Auseinandersetzung mit dem Nationalsozialismus', M. Broszat ed., *Zäsuren nach 1945: Essays zur Periodisierung der deutschen Nachkriegsgeschichte* (Munich: Oldenbourg, 1990) 169–183.
Gray, Peter & Kendrick Oliver eds., *The Memory of Catastrophe* (Manchester: Manchester University Press, 2004).
Gregor, Neil, '"Is He Still Alive, or Long Since Dead?": Loss, Absence and Remembrance in Nuremberg, 1945–1956', *German History*, Vol. 21 No. 2 (2003) 183–203.
———, '"The Illusion of Remembrance": The Karl Diehl Affair and the Memory of National Socialism in Nuremberg, 1945–1999', *Journal of Modern History*, Vol. 75 No. 3 (2003) 590–633.
———, *Nazism, War and Genocide: Essays in Honour of Jeremy Noakes* (Exeter: University of Exeter Press, 2005).
———, *Haunted City: Nuremberg and the Nazi Past* (New Haven, Connecticut: Yale University Press, 2008).
Griech-Polelle, Beth, 'Image of a Churchman-resistor: Bishop von Galen, The Euthanasia Project and the Sermons of Summer 1941', *Journal of Contemporary History*, Vol. 36 No. 1 (2001) 41–57.
Gutman, Israel ed., *Enzklopädie des Holocaust: Die Verfolgung und Ermordung der europäischen Juden, Band I* (Berlin: Argon, 2002).
Gutteridge, Richard, *Open Thy Mouth for the Dumb: The German Evangelical Church and the Jews, 1879–1950* (Oxford: Blackwell, 1976).
Haas, Aaron, *The Aftermath: Living with the Holocaust* (Cambridge: Cambridge University Press, 1995).
Haberer, Erich, 'History and Justice: Paradigms of the Prosecution of Nazi Crimes', *Holocaust and Genocide Studies*, Vol. 19 No. 3 (2005) 487–519.
Hackett, David A. ed., *The Buchenwald Report* (Boulder, Colorado: Westview Press, 1995).
Hamilton, Richard F., *Who Voted for Hitler?* (Princeton, New Jersey: Princeton University Press, 1982).
Harms, Kathy, Lutz-Rainer Reuter & Volker Durr eds., *Coping with the Past: Germany and Austria after 1945* (Madison: University of Wisconsin Press, 1990).
Hasian, Marouf A., *Rhetorical Vectors of Memory in National and International Holocaust Trials* (East Lansing: Michigan State University Press, 2006).
Heineman, Elizabeth, 'The Hour of the Woman: Memories of Germany's 'Crisis Years' and West German National Identity', *American Historical Review*, Vol. 101 No. 2 (1996) 354–395.

Henkys, Reinhard, Kurt Scharf, Jürgen Baumann & Dieter Goldschmidt eds., *Die nationalsozialistischen Gewaltverbrechen: Geschichte und Gericht* (Stuttgart: Kreuz-Verlag, 1965).
Herbert, Ulrich, 'Deutsche Eliten nach Hitler', *Mittelweg*, Vol. 36 No. 8 (1999) 66–82.
Herbst, Ludolf, *Wiedergutmachung in der Bundesrepublik Deutschland* (Munich: Oldenbourg, 1989).
Herf, Jeffrey, *Divided Memory: The Nazi Past in the Two Germanys* (Cambridge, Massachusetts: Harvard University Press, 1997).
———, 'Multiple Restorations: German Political Traditions and the Interpretation of Nazism, 1945–1946', *Central European History*, Vol. 26 No. 1 (1993) 21–56.
Herlemann, Beatrix, *Kommunalpolitik der KPD im Ruhrgebiet, 1924–1933* (Wüppertal: Peter Hammer, 1977).
Herz, John H. 'The Fiasco of Denazification in Germany', *Political Science Quarterly*, Vol. 63 No. 4 (1948) 569–594.
Hey, Bernd, 'Die NS-Prozesse—Versuch einer juristischen Vergangenheitsbewältigung', *Geschichte in Wissenschaft und Unterricht*, Vol. 6 (1981) 331–362.
Hirsch, Rudolf, *Um die Endlösung: Prozessberichte über den Lischka-Prozess in Köln und den Auschwitz-Prozess in Frankfurt/Main* (Rudolstadt: Greifenverlag, 1984).
Hockenos, Matthew D., *A Church Divided: German Protestants Confront the Nazi Past* (Bloomington: Indiana University Press, 2004).
Hocketers, Hans-Günter, 'Wiedergutmachung in Deutschland: Eine historische Bilanz, 1945–2000', *Vierteljahrshefte für Zeitgeschichte*, Vol. 49 (2001) 167–214.
Hodgkin, Katharine, *Contested Pasts: The Politics of Memory* (London: Routledge, 2003).
Hoffmann, Christa, *Stunden Null? Vergangenheitsbewaltigung in Deutschland, 1945 und 1989* (Bonn: Bouvier Verlag, 1992).
Hoffmann, Detlef, *Das Gedächtnis der Dinge: KZ-Relikte und KZ-Denkmäler, 1945–1995* (Frankfurt am Main: Campus Verlag, 1998).
Hughes, Michael L., '"Through No Fault of Our Own": West Germans Remember Their War Losses', *German History*, Vol. 18 No. 2 (2000) 193–213.
Irwin-Zarecka, Iwona, *Frames of Remembrance: The Dynamics of Collective Memory* (New Brunswick, New Jersey: Transaction Publishers, 1994).
Isser, Edward R., *Stages of Annihilation: Theatrical Representations of the Holocaust* (Madison, New Jersey: Farleigh Dickinson University Press, 1997).
James, Harold, 'The Prehistory of the Federal Republic', *Journal of Modern History*, Vol. 63 (March 1991) 99–115.
Jarausch, Konrad H., *After Hitler: Recivilising Germans, 1945–1995* (Oxford: Oxford University Press, 2006).
Jaspers, Karl, *Die Schuldfrage: Für Völkermord gibt es keine Verjährung* (Munich: Piper, 1979).
Just-Dahlmann, Barbara & Helmut Just, *Die Gehilfen: NS-Verbrechen und die Justiz nach 1945* (Frankfurt am Main: Athenäum, 1988).
Kaes, Anton, *From Hitler to Heimat: The Return of History as Film* (Cambridge, Massachusetts: Harvard University Press, 1989).
Kaminsky, Annette ed., *Heimkehr 1948: Geschichte und Schicksale deutscher Kriegsgefangener* (Munich: Beck, 1998).
Kansteiner, Wulf, 'Nazis, Viewers and Statistics: Television History, Television Audience Research and Collective Memory in West Germany', *Journal of Contemporary History*, Vol. 39 No. 4 (2004) 575–598.
———, *In Pursuit of German Memory: History, Television and Politics after Auschwitz* (Athens: Ohio University Press, 2006).

Kattago, Siobhan, *Ambiguous Memory: The Nazi Past and German National Identity* (Westport, Connecticut: Praeger, 2001).
Kauders, Anthony, *German Politics and the Jews: Düsseldorf and Nuremberg, 1910–1933* (Oxford: Clarendon Press, 1996).
von Kellenbach, Katharina,'Vanishing Acts: Perpetrators in Postwar Germany', *Holocaust and Genocide Studies*, Vol. 17 No. 2 (2003) 305–329.
Keller, Sven, *Günzburg und der Fall Josef Mengele: Die Heimatstadt und die Jagd nach dem NS-Verbrecher* (Munich: Oldenbourg, 2003).
Kirsch, Jan-Holger, *'Wir haben aus der Geschichte gelernt': der 8 Mai als politischer Gedenktag in Deutschland* (Vienna: Böhlau, 1999).
Klee, Ernst, Willi Dressen & Volker Riess, *Those Were the Days: The Holocaust as Seen by the Perpetrators and Bystanders*, translated by D. Burnstone (London: Hamish Hamilton, 1991).
Klein, Kerwin L., 'On The Emergence of Memory in Historical Discourse', *Representations*, Vol. 69 (2000) 127–150.
Kleßmann, Christoph ed., *The Divided Past: Rewriting Post-war German History* (Oxford: Berg, 2001).
Klingenstein, Grete, 'Über Herrkunft und Verwendung des Wortes Vergangenheitsbewältigung', *Geschichte und Gegenwart*, Vol. 4 (1988) 301–312.
Knigge, Volkhard & Norbert Frei eds., *Verbrechen erinnern: Die Auseinandersetzung mit Holocaust und Völkermord* (Munich: Beck, 2002).
Knischewski, Gerd & Ulla Spittler, 'Memories of the Second World War and National Identity in Germany', Martin Evans & Kenneth Lunn eds., *War and Memory in the Twentieth Century* (Oxford: Berg, 1997) 239–254.
Kochavi, Arieh J., *Prelude to Nuremberg: Allied War Crimes Policy and the Question of Punishment* (Chapel Hill: University of North Carolina Press, 1998).
———, 'The British Foreign Office versus the United Nations War Crimes Commission during the Second World War', *Holocaust and Genocide Studies*, Vol. 8 No. 1 (1994) 28–49.
König, Helmut, Wolfgang Kuhlmann & Klaus Schwabe eds., *Vertuschte Vergangenheit: Der Fall Schwerte und die NS-Vergangenheit der deutscher Hochschulen* (Munich: Beck, 1997).
Koonz, Claudia, 'Between Memory and Oblivion: Concentration Camps in German Memory', John R. Gillis ed., *Commemorations: The Politics of National Identity* (Princeton, New Jersey: Princeton University Press, 1994) 258–280.
Koshar, Rudy, *From Monuments to Traces: Artifacts of German Memory, 1870–1990* (Berkeley: University of California Press, 2000).
Krause, Michael, *Flucht vor dem Bombenkrieg: 'Umquartierungen' im Zweiten Weltkrieg und die Wiedereingliederung der Evakuierten in Deutschland, 1943–1963* (Düsseldorf: Droste, 1997).
Krausnick, Helmut, *Hitlers Einsatzgruppen: Die Truppen des Weltanschauungskrieges, 1938–1942* (Frankfurt am Main: Fischer Taschenbuch Verlag, 1985).
——— & Martin Broszat, eds., *Anatomy of the SS State* (London: Collins, 1968).
Krueger, M.C., *Authors and the Opposition: West German Writers and the Social Democratic Party from 1945 to 1969* (Stuttgart: Hans-Dieter Heinz, 1982).
Kushner, Tony, *The Holocaust and the Liberal Imagination: A Social and Cultural History* (Oxford: Blackwell, 1994).
Kwiet, Konrad, 'Rehearsing for Murder: The Beginning of the Final Solution in Lithuania in June, 1941,' *Holocaust and Genocide Studies*, Vol. 12 (1998) 3–26.
Ladd, Brian, *The Ghosts of Berlin: Confronting German History in the Urban Landscape* (Chicago: University of Chicago, 1997).
Langbein, Hermann, *Im Namen des deutschen Volkes: Zwischenbilanz der Prozesse wegen nationalsozialistischer Verbrechen* (Vienna: Europa Verlags-AG, 1963).

Large, David Clay, *Germans to the Front: West German Rearmament in the Adenauer Era* (Chapel Hill: University of North Carolina Press, 1996).

——, 'Reckoning without the Past: The HIAG of the Waffen-SS and the Politics of Rehabilitation in the Bonn Republic, 1950–1961', *Journal of Modern History*, Vol. 59 (March 1987) 79–113.

——, *Contending with Hitler: Varieties of German Resistance in the Third Reich*, (Cambridge: Cambridge University Press, 1991).

Lechner, Silvester, *Ulm im Nationalsozialismus: Stadtführer auf den Spuren des Regimes, der Verfolgten des Widerstands* (Ulm: Dokumentationszentrum Oberer Kuhberg Ulm, 1997).

Lichtenstein, Heiner, *Himmlers grüne Helfer: Die Schutz- und Ordnungspolizei im Dritten Reich* (Cologne: Bund-Verlag, 1990).

Loth, Wilfried & Bernd-A Rusinek, *Verwandlungspolitik: NS-Eliten in der Westdeutschen Nachkriegsgesellschaft* (Frankfurt am Main: Campus, 1998).

Lozowick, Yaacov, 'Rollbahn Mord: The Early Activities of Einsatzgruppe C', Michael R. Marrus ed., *The 'Final Solution': The Implementation of Mass Murder, Vol II* (Westport, Connecticut & London: Meckler, 1989) 471–491.

Lübbe, Hermann, 'Der Nationalsozialismus im Deutschen Nachkriegsbewusstsein', *Historische Zeitschrift*, Vol. 236 (1983) 579–599.

Lüdtke, Alf, '"Coming to Terms With the Past": Illusions of Remembering, Ways of Forgetting Nazism in West Germany', *Journal of Modern History*, Vol. 65 (1993) 542–572.

MacDonald, Sharon, 'Words in Stone? Agency and Identity in a Nazi Landscape', *Journal of Material Culture*, Vol. 11 No. 1–2 (2006) 105–126.

——, *Difficult Heritage: Negotiating the Nazi Past in Nuremberg and Beyond* (London: Routledge, 2008).

Maier, Charles S., 'The Two Post-war Eras and the Conditions for Stability in Twentieth Century Western Europe', *American Historical Review*, Vol. 86 (1981) 327–352.

Marcuse, Harold, *Legacies of Dachau: The Uses and Abuses of a Concentration Camp, 1933–2001* (Cambridge: Cambridge University Press, 2001).

Marrus, Michael R., 'The Holocaust at Nuremberg', *Yad Vashem Studies*, Vol. 26 (1998) 5–41.

Marshall, Barbara, 'German Attitudes to British Military Government, 1945-7', *Journal of Contemporary History*, Vol. 15 No. 4 (1980) 655–684.

Matthäus, Jürgen, 'What About the 'Ordinary Men'?: The German Order Police and the Holocaust in the Occupied Soviet Union', *Holocaust and Genocide Studies*, Vol. 10 No. 2 (1996) 134–150.

May, Michael, 'Trials of Nazi War Criminals: Has Justice Been Done?', *Institute of Jewish Affairs Research Report No. 12* (London: Institute of Jewish Affairs, 1981) 1–11.

Michman, Dan ed., *Remembering the Holocaust in Germany, 1945–2000: German Strategies and Jewish Responses* (New York: Peter Lang Publishing, 2002).

de Mildt, Dick W., *In the Name of the People: Perpetrators of Genocide in the Reflection of Their Postwar Prosecution in West Germany: The 'Euthanasia' and 'Aktion Reinhard' Trial Cases* (The Hague: Martinus Nijhoff Publishers, 1996).

Miller, Judith, *One by One by One: Facing the Holocaust* (New York: Simon & Schuster, 1990).

Milton, Sybil, 'Die Konzentrationslager der dreißiger Jahre im Bild der in- und ausländischen Presse', Ulrich Herbert, Karin Orth & Christoph Dieckmann eds., *Die nationalsozialistischen Konzentrationslager—Entwicklung und Struktur. Band I* (Göttingen: Wallstein Verlag, 1998) 135–147.

——, *In Fitting Memory: The Art and Politics of Holocaust Memorials* (Detroit, Michigan: Wayne State University Press, 1991).

von Miquel, Marc, *Ahnden oder Amnestieren? Westdeutsche Justiz und Vergangenheitspolitik in den sechziger Jahre* (Göttingen: Wallstein Verlag, 2004).
Mitscherlich, Alexander & Margarete, *Die Unfähigkeit zu trauen. Grundlagen kollektiven Verhaltens* (Munich, 1977).
Moeller, Robert G. 'Geschichten aus der "Stachekdrahtuniversität": Kriegsgefangene auf Zelluoid in der Bundesrepublik Deutschland', *Amsterdamer Beiträge zur neueren Germanistik*, Vol. 50 No. 1 (2001) 57–65.
———, '"The Last Soldiers of the Great War" and Tales of Family Reunions in the Federal Republic of Germany', *Signs: Journal of Women in Culture and Society*, Vol. 24 No. 1 (1998) 129–145.
———, *West Germany under Construction: Politics, Society and Culture in the Adenauer Era* (Ann Arbor: University of Michigan Press, 1997).
———, 'War Stories: The Search for a Usable Past in the Federal Republic of Germany', *American Historical Review*, Vol. 101 No. 4 (1996) 1008–1048.
———, *War Stories: The Search for a Usable Past in the Federal Republic of Germany* (Berkeley & Los Angeles: University of California Press, 2001).
von Moltke, Johannes, *No Place Like Home: Locations of Heimat in German Cinema* (Berkeley: University of California Press, 2005).
Monteath, Peter, 'Organising Antifascism: The Obscure History of the VVN', *European History Quarterly*, Vol. 29 No. 2 (1999) 289–303.
Mosse, George L., *Fallen Soldiers: Reshaping the Memory of the World Wars* (Oxford: Oxford University Press, 1990).
Müller, Ingo, *Furchtbare Juristen. Die unbewältigte Vergangenheit unserer Justiz* (Munich: Kindler, 1987).
Murray, Bruce A. & Chris J. Wickham eds., *Framing the Past: The Historiography of German Cinema and Television* (Carbondale, Illinois: Southern Illinois University Press, 1992).
Nauman, Klaus ed., *Nachkrieg in Deutschland* (Hamburg: Hamburger Edition, 2001).
Nevermann, Knut, 'Holocaust-Mahnmal und Gedenkstätten als Kristallisationspunkte für die Erinnerungskultur in Deutschland', *Gedenkstätten Rundbrief* Vol. 96 No. 8 (2000) 3–10.
Niethammer, Lutz, *Die Mitläuferfabrik: Die Entnazifizierung am Beispiel Bayerns* (Berlin & Bonn: J.H.W. Dietz, 1982).
Noethen, Stefan, *Alter Kameraden und neue Kollegen: Polizei in Nordrhein-Westfalen, 1945–1953* (Essen: Klartext, 2003).
Nolan, Mary, *Social Democracy and Society: Working Class Radicalism in Düsseldorf, 1890–1920* (Cambridge: Cambridge University Press, 1981).
Novick, Peter, *The Holocaust and Collective Memory: The American Experience* (London: Bloomsbury, 1999).
O'Loughlin, John, Colin Flint & Luc Anselin, 'The Geography of the Nazi Vote: Context, Confession and Class in the Reichstag Elections of 1930', *Annals of the Association of American Geographers*, Vol. 84 No. 3 (1994) 351–380.
Osiel, Mark, *Mass Atrocity, Collective Memory and the Law* (New Brunswick: Transaction, 1997).
Padgett, Stephen & Tony Burkett, *Political Parties and Elections in West Germany: The Search for a New Stability* (London: C. Hurst & Co., 1986).
Patterson, Michael, '"Bewältigung der Vergangenheit" or "Uberwältigung der Befangenheit": Nazism and the War in Post-war German Theatre', *Modern Drama*, Vol. 33 No. 1 (1990) 120–128.
Pehle, Walter H. & Peter Sillem, *Wissenschaft in geteilten Deutschland: Restauration oder Neubeginn nach 1945?* (Frankfurt am Main: Fischer Taschenbuch, 1992).
Peifer, Douglas, 'Commemoration of Mutiny, Rebellion and Resistance in Post-war Germany: Public Memory, History and the Formation of "Memory Beacons"', *Journal of Military History*, Vol. 65 No. 4 (2001) 1013–1052.

180 Bibliography

Pendas, Devin O., '"Gerichtstag hatten uber uns selbst . . .": Geschichte und Wirkung des ersten Frankfurter Auschwitz-Prozesses' (Book Review), *Journal of Modern History*, Vol. 75 No. 3 (2003) 725–727.

———, '"I Didn't Know What Auschwitz Was": The Frankfurt Auschwitz Trial and the German Press, 1963–5', *Yale Journal of Law and the Humanities* (2000) 397–446.

———, *The Frankfurt Auschwitz Trial 1963–1965: Genocide, History and the Limits of the Law* (Cambridge: Cambridge University Press, 2006).

Phayer, Michael, 'The German Catholic Church after the Holocaust', *Holocaust and Genocide Studies*, Vol. 10 No. 2 (1996) 151–167.

Pohl, Dieter, *Einsatzgruppen C and D in the Invasion of the Soviet Union* (London: Holocaust Educational Trust, 2000).

Pross, Christian, *Paying for the Past: The Struggle over Reparations for Surviving Victims of the Nazi Terror* (Baltimore, Maryland: John Hopkins University Press, 1998).

Przyrembel, Alexandra, 'Transfixed by an Image: Ilse Koch, the "Kommandeuse of Buchenwald"', *German History*, Vol. 19 No. 3 (2001) 369–399.

Rabinbach, Anson, 'The Reader, the Popular Novel and the Imperative to Participate: Reflections on Public and Private Experience in the Third Reich', *History and Memory*, Vol. 3 No. 2 (1991) 5–44.

Raschhofer, Hermann, *Der Fall Oberländer: Eine vergleichende Rechtsanalyse der Verfahren in Pankow und Bonn* (Tübingen: Schlichtenmazer, 1962).

Reichel, Peter, *Das Gedächtnis der Stadt: Hamburg im Umgang mit seiner nationalsozialistischen Vergangenheit* (Hamburg: Dölling & Galitz Verlag, 1997).

Reilly, Joanne, *Belsen: The Liberation of a Concentration Camp* (London: Routledge, 1998).

Reilly, Jo, David Cesarani, Tony Kushner & Colin Richmond eds., *Belsen in History and Memory* (London: Frank Cass, 1997).

Rhodes, Richard, *Masters of Death: The SS Einsatzgruppen and the Invention of the Holocaust* (Oxford: Perseus Press, 2002).

Robinson, Jacob, *And the Crooked Shall Be Made Straight: The Eichmann Trial, the Jewish Catastrophe and Hannah Arendt's Narrative* (New York: MacMillan, 1965).

Rohe, Karl ed., *Elections, Parties and Political Traditions: Social Foundations of German Parties and Political Systems, 1867–1987* (New York, Oxford & Munich: Berg, 1990).

Roseman, Mark, *Generations in Conflict: Youth Revolt and Generation Formation in Germany, 1770–1968* (Cambridge: Cambridge University Press, 1995).

Rosenbaum, Alan S., *Prosecuting Nazi War Criminals* (Boulder, Colorado & Oxford: Westview Press, 1993).

Rosenfeld, Gavriel D., *Munich and Memory: Architecture, Monuments and the Legacy of the Third Reich* (Berkeley: University of California Press, 2000).

———, 'The Reception of William L. Shirer's *The Rise and Fall of the Third Reich* in the United States and West Germany, 1960–62', *Journal of Contemporary History*, Vol. 29 No. 1 (1994) 95–129.

Rückerl, Adalbert, 'Nazi Crime Trials', Michael R. Marrus ed., *The Nazi Holocaust: Historical Articles on the Destruction of the European Jews*, Vol. 9: *The End of the Holocaust* (Westport, Connecticut & London: Meckler, 1989) 621–634.

———, *The Investigation of Nazi Crimes, 1945–1978: A Documentation*, translated by D. Rutter (Karlsruhe: C.F. Müller, 1979).

———, *NS-Verbrechen vor Gericht. Versuch einer Vergangenheitsbewältigung* (Heidelberg: C.F. Müller, 1982).

———, *NS-Vernichtungslager im Spiegel deutscher Strafprozesse: Belzec, Sobibor, Treblinka, Chelmo* (Munich: Deutscher Taschenbuch Verlag, 1977).
Rusinek, Bernd-A. ed., *Kriegsende 1945: Verbrechen, Katastrophen, Befreiungen in nationaler und internationaler Perspektive* (Göttingen: Wallstein, 2004).
Sackett, Robert, 'Memory by Way of Anne Frank: Enlightenment and Denial among West Germans, Circa 1960', *Holocaust and Genocide Studies*, Vol. 16 No. 2 (2002) 243–265.
Salomon, George, 'The End of Eichmann: America's Response', *American Jewish Yearbook*, Vol. 64 (1963) 247–259.
Schätzle, Julius, *Stationen zur Hölle: Konzentrationslager in Baden und Württemberg, 1933–1945* (Frankfurt am Main: Röderberg-Verlag, 1974).
Schildt, Axel, Detlef Siegfried & Karl Christian Lammers eds., *Dynamische Zeiten: Die 60er Jahre in den beiden deutschen Gesellschaften* (Hamburg: Christians, 2000).
Schissler, Hanna ed., *The Miracle Years: A Cultural History of West Germany, 1949–1968* (Princeton, New Jersey: Princeton University Press, 2001).
Schlant, Ernestine, *The Language of Silence: West German Literature and the Holocaust* (New York: Routledge, 1999).
Schlemmer, Thomas, 'Grenzen der Integration: Die CSU und der Umgang mit der nationalsozialistischen Vergangenheit—der Fall Dr. Max Frauendorfer', *Vierteljahreshefte für Zeitgeschichte*, Vol. 48 (2000) 675–721.
Schley, Jens, *Nachbar Buchenwald: Die Stadt Weimar und ihr Konzentrationslager, 1937–1945* (Cologne, Weimar & Vienna: Böhlau Verlag, 1999).
Schneider, Michael, 'Fathers and Sons, Retrospectively: The Damaged Relationship between Two Generations', *New German Critique*, No. 31 (1984) 3–52.
Schönhoven, Klaus, 'Aufbruch in die sozialliberale Ära: Zur Bedeutung der 60er Jahre in der Geschichte der Bundesrepublik', *Geschichte und Gesellschaft*, Vol. 25 No. 1 (1999) 123–145.
Schütt, Siegfried, *Theodor Oberländer: Eine dokumentärische Untersuchung* (Munich: Langen Müller, 1995).
Schwartz, Thomas A., 'Die Begnadigung deutscher Kriegsverbrecher: John J. McCloy und die Häftlinge von Landsberg', *Vierteljahrshefte für Zeitgeschichte*, Vol. 38 (1990) 375–414.
Searle, Alaric, 'Revising the "Myth" of a 'Clean Wehrmacht": Generals' Trials, Public Opinion and the Dynamics of Vergangenheitsbewältigung in West Germany, 1948–60', *German Historical Institute London Bulletin*, Vol. 25 No. 2 (2003) 17–48.
———, 'The Tolsdorff Trials in Traunstein: Public and Judicial Attitudes to the Wehrmacht in the Federal Republic, 1954–60', *German History*, Vol. 23 No. 1 (2005) 50–78.
Sereny, Gitta, *The German Trauma: Experiences and Reflections, 1938–2001* (London: Penguin, 2001).
Shandler, Jeffrey, 'The Man in the Glass Box', *While America Watches: Televising the Holocaust* (Oxford: Oxford University Press, 1999) 83–132.
Shandley, Robert R., *Rubble Films: German Cinema in the Shadow of the Third Reich* (Philadelphia, Pennsylvania: Temple University Press, 2001).
Sharples, Caroline, 'Holocaust on Trial: British Responses to the Nuremberg Tribunal, 1945–46', unpublished paper delivered at the Fourth Annual Aubrey Newman Lecture and Colloquium, University of Leicester, May 6, 2009.
Sichrovsky, Peter, *Born Guilty: Children of Nazi Families*, translated by J. Steinberg (London: I.B. Tauris & Co., 1988).
Siegfried, Detlef, '"Don't Trust Anyone Older Than 30?" Voices of Conflict and Consensus between Generations in 1960s West Germany', *Journal of Contemporary History*, Vol. 40 No. 4 (2005) 727–744.

Simpson, William W. & Ruth Weyl, *The International Council of Christians and Jews: A Brief History* (Heppenheim: International Council of Christians and Jews, 1988).
Smith, Arthur L., *Heimkehr aus dem Zeiten Weltkrieg: Die Entlassung der Deutschen Kriegsgefangenen* (Stuttgart: Deutsche Verlags-Anstalt, 1985).
Smith, Bradley F., *The Road to Nuremberg* (London: A. Deutsch, 1981).
Smith, Helmut Walser, 'The Boundaries of the Local in Modern German History', James Retallack ed., *Saxony in German History: Culture, Society and Politics, 1830–1933* (Ann Arbor: University of Michigan Press, 2000) 63–76.
Spielmann, Jochen, 'Steine des Anstosses: Denkmal in der Bundesrepublik Deutschland', *Kritische Berichte*, Vol. 3 (1988) 5–16.
Spotts, Frederick, *Bayreuth: A History of the Wagner Festival* (New Haven, Connecticut: Yale University Press, 1994).
Steinbach, Peter, 'Zur Auseinandersetzung mit nationalsozialistischen Gewaltverbrechen in der Bundesrepublik Deutschland', *Geschichte in Wissenschaft und Unterricht*, Vol. 35 No. 2 (1984) 65–85.
Steinbacher, Sybille, *Auschwitz: A History*, translated by Shaun Whiteside (Munich: Beck, 2004).
Steinweis, Alan E. & Daniel E. Rogers eds., *The Impact of Nazism: New Perspectives on the Third Reich and Its Legacy* (Lincoln, Nebraska & London: University of Nebraska Press, 2003).
Stern, Frank, 'Breaking the 'Cordon Sanitaire' of Memory: The Jewish Encounter with German Society', Alvin H. Rosenfeld ed., *Thinking about the Holocaust after Half a Century* (Bloomington & Indianapolis: Indiana University Press, 1997) 213–232.
———, 'German-Jewish Relations in the Postwar Period: The Ambiguities of Antisemitic and Philosemitic Discourse', Y. Michal Bodemann ed., *Jews, Germans, Memory: Reconstructions of Jewish Life in Germany* (Ann Arbor: University of Michigan Press, 1996) 77–100.
———, *The Whitewashing of the Yellow Badge: Antisemitism and Philosemitism in Post-war Germany*, translated by W. Templer (Oxford: Pergamon Press, 1992).
Stone, Dan, 'Making Memory Work or Gedächtnis macht frei', *Patterns of Prejudice*, Vol. 37 No. 1 (2003) 87–98.
Streim, Alfred, 'The Tasks of the SS Einsatzgruppen', Michael R. Marrus ed., *The 'Final Solution': The Implementation of Mass Murder, Vol. II* (Westport, Connecticut & London: Meckler, 1989) 436–455.
Taylor, Telford, *The Anatomy of the Nuremberg Trials: A Personal Memoir* (London: Bloomsbury, 1993).
Teschke, John P., *Hitler's Legacy: West Germany Confronts the Aftermath of the Third Reich* (New York: Peter Lang, 1999).
Thomas, Nick, *Protest Movements in 1960s West Germany: A Social History of Dissent and Democracy* (Oxford: Berg, 2003).
Tilton, Timothy A., *Nazism, Neo-Nazism and the Peasantry* (Bloomington: Indiana University Press, 1975).
Twist, Susan, 'Evidence of Atrocities or Atrocious Use of Evidence: The Controversial Use of Atrocity Film at Nuremberg', *Liverpool Law Review*, Vol. 26 No. 3 (2005) 267–302.
Vogel, Rolf, *Ein Weg aus der Vergangenheit: Eine Dokumentation zur Verjährungsfrage und zu den NS-Prozessen* (Frankfurt am Main: Ullstein, 1969).
Vollnhals, Clemens & Thomas Schlemmer, *Entnazifizierung, politische Säuberung und Rehabilitierung in dem vier Besatzungszonen, 1945–1949* (Munich: Deutscher Taschenbuch Verlag, 1991).
Wachs, Philipp-Christian, *Der Fall Theodor Oberländer (1905–1998): Ein Lehrstück deutscher Geschichte* (Frankfurt am Main: Campus, 2000).

Wagner, Nike, *The Wagners: The Dramas of a Musical Dynasty*, translated by E. Oseis & M. Downes (London: Phoenix, 2001).
Weber, Jürgen & Peter Steinbach, *Vergangenheitsbewältigung durch Strafverfahren? NS-Prozesse in der Bundesrepublik Deutschland* (Munich: Günter Olzog, 1984).
Weckel, Ulrike, 'The *Mitläufer* in Two German Post-war Films', *History and Memory*, Vol. 15 No. 2 (2003) 64–93.
―― & Edgar Wolfrum eds., *'Bestien' und 'Befehlsempfänger': Frauen und Männer in NS-Prozessen nach 1945* (Göttingen: Vandenhoeck & Ruprecht, 2003).
Weil, Frederick, 'The Imperfectly Mastered Past: Antisemitism in West Germany since the Holocaust', *New German Critique*, Vol. 20 (1980) 135–153.
Weiss, Christoph, *Auschwitz in der geteilten Welt: Peter Weiss und Die Ermittlung im kalten Krieg* (St. Ingbert: Röhrig, 2000).
Weitz, Yechiam, 'The Holocaust on Trial: The Impact of the Kasztner and Eichmann Trials on Israeli Society', *Israel Studies*, Vol. 1 No. 2 (1996) 1–26.
Werle, Gerhard & Thomas Wandres, *Auschwitz vor Gericht: Völkermord und bundesdeutsche Justiz: mit einer Dokumentation des Auschwitz-Urteiles* (Munich: Beck, 1995).
Wessling, Berndt W. ed., *Bayreuth im Dritten Reich: Richard Wagners politische Erben. Eine Dokumentation* (Weinheim & Basel: Beltz Verlag, 1983).
West, Rebecca, *A Train of Powder* (London: Virago, 1984).
Wielenga, Friso, 'An Inability to Mourn? The German Federal Republic and the Nazi Past', *European Review*, Vol. 11 No. 4 (2003) 551–572.
Wierling, Dorothee, 'Generations and Generational Conflicts in East and West Germany', Christoph Klessmann ed., *The Divided Past: Rewriting Postwar German History* (Oxford: Berg, 2001) 69–89.
Wiesen, S. Jonathan, 'Overcoming Nazism: Big Business, Public Relations and the Politics of Memory, 1945–50', *Central European History*, Vol. 29 No. 2 (1996) 201–226.
Wiesenthal, Simon, *The Murderers Among Us*, J. Wechsberg ed. (London: Pan Books, 1968).
――, *Verjährung? 200 Persönlichkeiten des öffentlichen Lebens sagen nein: eine Dokumentation* (Frankfurt am Main: Europäische Verlagsanstalt, 1965).
Wigoder, Geoffrey, *Jewish-Christian Relations since the Second World War* (Manchester: Manchester University Press, 1988).
Wilhelm, Hans-Heinrich, *Die Einsatzgruppe A der Sicherheitspolizei und des SD 1941/2* (Frankfurt am Main: Lang, 1996).
Wittmann, Rebecca E., 'Holocaust on Trial? The Frankfurt Auschwitz Trial in Historical Perspective' (Unpublished PhD Thesis, University of Toronto, 2001).
――, 'Indicting Auschwitz? The Paradox of the Frankfurt Auschwitz Trial', *German History*, Vol. 21 No. 4 (2003) 505–532.
――, 'The Wheels of Justice Turn Slowly: The Pre-trial Investigations of the Frankfurt Auschwitz Trial, 1963–65', *Central European History*, Vol. 35 No. 3 (2002) 345–378.
――, *Beyond Justice: The Auschwitz Trial* (Cambridge, Massachusetts & London: Harvard University Press, 2005).
Wolfe, Robert, 'Flaws in the Nuremberg Legacy: An Impediment to International War Crimes Tribunals' Prosecution of Crimes Against Humanity', *Holocaust and Genocide Studies*, Vol. 12 No. 3 (1998) 434–453.
Wolffsohn, Michael, 'Das deutsche-israelische Wiedergutmachungsabkommen von 1952 im internationalen Zusammenhang', *Vierteljahrshefte für Zeitgeschichte* 36 (1988) 691–731.
Wurm, Clemens A., *Western Europe and Germany: The Beginning of European Integration, 1945–1960* (Oxford: Berg, 1995).

Yablonka, Hanna, 'The Development of Holocaust Consciousness in Israel: The Nuremberg, Kapos, Kasztner and Eichmann Trials', *Israel Studies*, Vol. 8 No. 3 (2003) 1–24.

Young, James E., *The Texture of Memory: Holocaust Memorials and Meaning* (New Haven, Connecticut: Yale University Press, 1993).

de Zayas, Alfred-Maurice, *The German Expellees: Victims in War and Peace* (Basingstoke: MacMillan, 1993).

Zielinski, Siegfried, 'History as Entertainment and Provocation: The TV Series "Holocaust" in West Germany', Anson Rabinbach & Jack Zipes eds., *Germans and Jews since the Holocaust: The Ongoing Situation in West Germany* (New York: Holmes & Meier, 1986) 258–283.

Zimmermann, Ludwig, *Frankreichs Ruhrpolitik von Versailles bis zum Dawesplan* (Göttingen: Musterschmidt, 1971).

Zimmermann, Volker, *NS-Täter vor Gericht: Düsseldorf und die Strafprozesse wegen nationalsozialistischer Gewaltverbrechen* (Düsseldorf: Justizministerium des Landes NRW, 2001).

Index

A
Adenauer, Konrad, 3, 28, 63, 76, 94; on effects of the Eichmann trial, 77; on Cologne, 114
allies: handling of war criminals 9, 23–24, 26, 141n1; press coverage of trials, 15, 20, 36; on the prosecution of German generals, 27; treatment of the Holocaust, 34, 74; understanding of Eichmann, 73; wartime behaviour (*see* relativisation). *See also* denazification; re-education
amnesty, calls for, 6, 28
anti-Semitism, 44, 49, 87, 115, 135
Arendt, Hannah, 36, 74, 105, 121
Association of Victims of the Nazi Regime (VVN), 66, 67, 75
Auschwitz, 1, 113, 132, 134
Auschwitz trial: 4, 8, 112, 113, 115, 127, 128, 134, 130; cultural resonance, 123–124; as educational tool, 122; legacy, 123, 124; public attendance, 112, 119; press coverage, 112, 116, 118; public interest, 118, 120, 121, 122; public opinion, 120

B
Bauer, Fritz, 113, 124
Bayreuth 7, 35, 51, 54, 134; during the Third Reich, 52–53; responses to the Sommer trial, 64–72. *See also* Sommer, Barbara; Sommer, Martin
Belzec, 95, 103
Bergen-Belsen, 2, 10, 36, 117
Behrendt, Franz, 32

blame: placed upon Nazi leadership, 6, 15, 33, 38, 41, 110, 135; assigned to a racial few, 4, 34, 49, 71, 120
Boger, Wilhelm, 112, 121
Böhme, Hans-Joachim, 31
Bonhoeffer, Emmi, 112
Bormann, Martin, 73, 79, 142n2
Brandt, Willy, 3, 77
Brown Book, 28
Buchenwald 10, 51, 58, 59, 66, 71, 134; survivors, 53–54; 55, 68. *See also* Sommer, Martin

C
Capesius, Viktor, 120
Carsten, Gerhard, 32
Christian Democratic Union (CDU), 21, 62, 63, 99
churches, 82, 131; Protestant statements on Nazism, 126–129; youth groups, 125–126
Cold War climate, 11, 29, 66, 89, 108, 132–133; and end of Allied investigations 22, 23, 28
Cologne, 92, 114, 126; and engagement with the past, 122, 124, 126. *See also* Sachsenhausen trial
Council of Christians and Jews, 125–126

D
Dachau, 10, 84
Daniell, Raymond, 12, 13
defendants: dehumanisation of, 15, 36, 39, 55–56, 67–68, 79, 116–117, 134; sense of distance from, 15, 37–38, 49, 72, 90, 116; show of

186 Index

support for, 28, 99–100, 107, 111, 114, 119, 134. *See also* perpetrators, excess
Demjanjuk, John, 136–137
Denazification, 9, 18, 47, 95, 97; limits of, 3; responses to, 22, 23, 64, 130; victims of, 63, 85, 89, 94, 98, 133
Die Mörder sind unter uns, 30
Dönitz, Karl, 20, 27, 93, 107
Düsseldorf, 20, 86, 114, 115, 134; and engagement with the past, 123, 125. *See also* Treblinka trial

E

education, ambitions for war crimes trials, 9, 11, 14, 74; and the use of Anne Frank, 2, 125; church statements upon, 126–127; debates over, 5, 92; initiatives in the wake of trials, 2, 5, 8, 34, 37, 48, 105–106, 122, 134–135; and the impact of trials, 34, 37, 59; youth criticisms of the state of, 126. *See also* re-education; youth
Eichmann, Adolf, 73, 92, 105, 108, 115, 124, 126, 127; and the banality of evil, 36, 101; cultural resonance of trial, 75–76, 123; demonization of, 79; and the Globke scandal, 76, 118; in historiography, 4, 7, 73–74; impact on German reputation, 77–78, 84–85, 88–89; and Israeli interest, 74; opinion surveys, 86–90; press coverage, 75, 76–80; public interest, 80–87, 121; use of survivor testimony, 74
Einsatzgruppen, 31–32, trial at Nuremberg, 32
Einsatzkommando Tilsit, 31, 34, 35, 36, 38, 44, 70, 100. *See also* Ulm Einsatzkommando Trial
Eisele, Hans, 58, 69, 70
exhibitions, 5, 10, 29, 90, 131; on Auschwitz, 124; on Eichmann, 118, 75–76; *Monumenta Judaica*, 124; on the Warsaw Ghetto, 124

F

Federal Republic of Germany, rearmament, 26, 28; rehabilitation, 28; concern for reputation, 7, 45, 59, 77, 81, 84, 87–89, 103–104, 130, 133
Fellenz, Martin, 8, 92–93, 95–97, 119, 131, 134; and educational impact, 105–106; impact on German reputation, 103–104; press coverage, 100–104; public interest, 104–105, 107–110; responses to arrest, 97–100; and supporters, 99–100, 107, 111
Fischer-Schweder, Bernhard, 30–31, 32, 34, 36, 46, 134
Frank, Anne, 2, 93, 122, 125
Frankfurt, 2, 75, 112, 113, 134; and engagement with the past, 121, 122, 123–124; and the Nuremberg International Military Tribunal 12, 19. *See also* Auschwitz trial
Franz, Kurt, 113, 116–117
Free Democratic Party (FDP), 63, 96, 99, 100
Fritzsche, Hans, 17, 18, 21

G

generations: conflict between, 11, 29, 41–42, 78, 90, 106, 107–108, 111; warning for, 49, 90, 123. *See also* youth
German Democratic Republic: agitation by, 28, 76, 133; western repudiation of criticisms, 107, 118
Globke, Hans, 76, 118
Göring, Hermann, 12, 13, 17, 19, 20, 86
Grusen, Sydney, 87

H

Hamburg, 20, 21, 106, 108
Harms, Hans Willms, 32
Harster, Wilhelm, 1, 2, 5
Heimat, 5–6
Herold, Dr. Hans-Jörg, 106
Hersmann, Werner, 32
Hess, Rudolf, 14, 18
Heyde, Dr. Werner, 93, 94
Hitler, Adolf, 17, 19, 58, 93, 95, 124; in Bayreuth, 52, 64, 65; blamed for atrocities, 38, 44, 51, 110; German suffering under, 6, 66, 67, 68, 101; resistance against, 21, 22, 76, 85; support for, 48, 70, 114, 125

Holocaust: Allied treatment of, 10–11, 34; appropriation of symbols of, 10; discussion of, 82–83; in historiography, 1, 10, 11, 74, 75; knowledge of, 75, 80; post-war understandings of, 1, 2, 7, 11, 71, 74–75, 77, 86, 113, 115, 132; responsibility for, 85, 86 (*see also* blame); revelations, 32, 84, 135; struggle to comprehend, 79, 80; survivor testimony, 1, 36, 51, 74, 102, 112, 116; in trials, 10–11, 32, 34, 74, 103, 105, 112–113. *See also* education; Jews

Holocaust, television series, 133

I

Institut für Demoskopie, 61–64, 71, 87–89

International Military Tribunal (IMT), 6, 9, 29, 30, 73, 86; British public interest, 13; German public interest, 11–16; in historiography, 4, 10–11; press coverage, 12; responses to the executions, 21; responses to the verdict, 17–20; selective interest in, 15. *See also* Göring, Hermann

J

Jackson, Robert, 9, 15

Jews: and attitudes to West Germany, 77, 103, 104; relations with non-Jews, 48, 77, 85, 109–110, 115, 134; and Christianity, 75, 124, 125–126; German interest in the history of, 5, 47–49, 123–124; reactionary comments about, 19, 20 (*see also* anti-Semitism); in World War One, 77

Jödl, Alfred, 20, 21

K

Kaiser, Otto, 114, 119
Katzmann, Fritz, 95
Keitel, Wilhelm, 21
Kempner, Robert M.W., 16
Kesselring, Albert, 27
Koch, Ilse, 26, 36
Koch, Karl, 53, 56
Kramer, Josef, 36
Kreuzmann, Werner, 32

L

Langbein, Hermann, 26, 34, 52, 120–121, 122
London Charter, 9
Lukys, Pranas, 32, 40, 44

M

Majdanek Trial, 115
Manteuffel, Hasso von, 27
Matthes, Heinrich, 113
McClure, Robert A, 12
Memory: in historiography, 3, 11; public and private, 3–4, 39; cultures of, 7, 8, 135; and counter memories, 50, 67–68, 83, 94; older patterns of, 51, 71, 77, 89, 90, 101, 131, 135; reliability of, 133. *See also* Vergangenheitsbewältigung

Mengele, Josef, 73, 79
Mentz, Willi, 113
Miete, August, 113, 116
Military, personnel: attempts to distinguish from the SS, 37, 43, 51, 56, 96; German concerns over the treatment of, 16, 20–21, 27; prosecution of generals, 26–28

Moscow Declaration, 9
'Murderers Among Us', rhetoric, 30, 34, 46, 54, 58, 69, 79, 86, 111

N

North Rhine Westphalia, 8, 20, 21, 114, 115

Nuremberg, subsequent trials, 23. *See also* International Military Tribunal

O

observations, foreign: by Anglo-Jewish press, 58, 118, 126; by British Foreign Office, 18, 20, 21, 22, 38, 42, 43, 46, 55, 130; by British newspapers, 15, 17, 19, 105; by *New York Times* correspondents, 12, 15, 17, 19, 20, 74, 86, 87

Office of Military Government United States (OMGUS), 14, 15, 21
O'Hare McCormick, Anne, 12, 13
Ohlendorf, Otto, 32
Operation Reinhard camps, 11, 86
opinion, public, 1, 27, 131; limits of opinion sources, 6, 39, 87; on

188 *Index*

the Auschwitz trial, 120–121;
on the Eichmann trial, 86–91;
on the International Military
Tribunal, 14–16, 20–23, 27, 29;
on the Sommer trial, 61–64,
70–71; on the Ulm trial, 38–46,
49. *See also* Institut für Demoskopie; observations, foreign;
OMGUS
orders: ability to refuse, 82, 85–86;
compulsion to follow, 27, 33,
36, 41, 43, 45, 68, 83, 97, 99,
110, 111, 133; Donitz's opinion
on, 107; Sommer's exceeding
of, 68

P
Papen, Franz von, 17, 18, 20, 21
perpetrators, excess, 54, 55, 67, 71, 92, 116, 119, 120, 135
prisoners of war (German), 3, 10, 27
Przemysl Ghetto, 95, 96, 103

R
Raeder, Erich, 20, 21
Rasch, Otto, 83
re-education, 9, 10, 20, 23, 135
relativisation of Nazi Crimes, 15, 16, 41, 70, 89, 100, 108, 110, 133
're-settlement', 8, 95, 97, 102–103, 107–108
Ribbentrop, Joachim, 18, 21

S
Sachsenhausen, 100, 113, 134
Sachsenhausen Trial, 8, 114, 115, 134;
educational impact, 122–123;
press coverage, 116–117; public
interest, 119
Sakuth, Edwin, 32
Sauckel, Fritz, 18
Schacht, Hjalmar, 14, 17, 18, 21
Schirach, Baldur von, 18
Schleswig-Holstein, 8, 20; Nazi past, 92–94, 115; political scandals, 93–94, 105, 108–109. *See also* Fellenz, Martin
Schlußstrich (final line), 3, 41, 47, 59, 61–63, 78, 90, 95, 111, 113, 131, 136
Schmidt-Hammer, Werner, 32
Schüle, Erwin, 31, 47, 130
Sereny, Gitta, 119
Slottke, Gertrud, 1

Sobibor, 1, 136
Social Democratic Party (SPD), 10, 17, 18, 21, 62, 63, 77, 114, 127
soldiers, honourable images of, 16, 27, 36, 43, 78, 86; responses to Nuremberg Trial, 20; talking about the past, 82–83, 85–86. *See also* military
Sommer, Barbara, 56–58, 60, 69, 71, 135
Sommer, Martin, 7, 8, 35, 53–55, 92, 100, 101, 105, 107, 131, 134, 135; press coverage 54–60; public opinion, 61–64; public interest 52, 64, 66–71; contrast to Ulm, 51
Spiegel Affair, 76
Stangl, Franz, 115
statute of limitations, 91, 106, 113, 127–131, 133
Sterling, Eleonore, 67, 70, 120, 121
Streicher, Julius, 12
swastika daubing, 19, 80, 92

T
Tolsdorff, Theodor, 27
Treblinka, 113
Treblinka Trial, 113, 115, 127, 134; press coverage, 116–119; public attendance, 119; public interest, 118, 120
trial fatigue, 11, 26, 32, 100, 131, 133

U
Ulm Einsatzkommando Trial, 30, 31, 47, 48, 51, 70, 71, 86, 100, 101, 106, 134; legacy, 34, 47–48; press coverage, 35–37; public interest 37–38; responses to verdict, 38; resonance compared to Nuremberg, 32–33

V
Vergangenheitsbewältigung, 11, 115, 122, 132, 136
veterans, SS, 27, 56, 78; camaraderie among, 101–102, 110
victimhood, German sense of, 10, 15–16, 22, 24, 30, 43, 51, 63, 71, 89, 94, 96, 101, 114, 133, 134; victims of fascism, 11, 66
victors' justice, 6, 9, 14, 33, 38, 46, 59, 89

W

Waffen-SS. *See* veterans
war criminals, terminology, 29. *See also* defendants
war crimes trials: attendance, 1, 2, 51, 66, 105–106, 108, 112, 119, 134; apathy towards, 13, 40, 115, 120, 133 (*see also* trial fatigue); misgivings towards, 41, 44, 91; support for 1, 8, 15, 20, 39–40, 42, 45–46, 49, 61–62, 63, 119; statistics, 24–26. *See also* statute of limitations; Schlußstrich
West, Rebecca, 11, 18
Wöhne, Willi, 117

Y

youth: attendance at trials, 5, 105–106, 108, 112, 119; attitudes to trials, 18, 20 38, 41–42; challenging the past, 1, 16, 29, 38, 90, 125–126, 133. *See also* education

Z

Zentrale Stelle der Landesjustizverwaltungen zur Aufklärung nationalsozialistischer Verbrechen (Central Agency for the Prosecution of Nazi Crimes), 47, 50, 97, 100, 106, 130
Zoepf, Wilhelm, 1

9781032927817